D1569877

Financial Services without
borders

Financial Services without borders

How to Succeed in Professional Financial Services

GREENWICH ASSOCIATES

John Wiley & Sons, Inc.

New York • Chichester • Weinheim • Brisbane • Singapore • Toronto

With personal affection and professional appreciation, we
dedicate this book to the Directors of Greenwich Associates,
particularly to four who each served over 20 years:
Chris Argyris, Don Jacobs, Henry Porter, and Everett Smith.

acknowledgments

Acknowledgments by authors of books and the appreciation for help they represent have an appropriately honored place.

This book has been made possible by the senior executives who—nearly one million times—have made time over 29 years to participate in our extensive research—in 17 languages and in 30 countries.

Our friends at Greenwich Associates have made this book possible by making it possible to produce—year after year after year—the research reports that are in so many parts of the world accepted as *the* standard.

Sharon Johnson contributed her skills as a writer and her good-humored graciousness to bringing this project from first impression to fruition.

Kimberly Breed—with her truly remarkable combination of goodness in spirit and skill in word processing technology and tenacity in fulfilling high standards—was our inspiring team leader in producing the text. Kimberly was ably assisted by Ted Hios, Rich Casey, Noreen O'Dwyer, Eddie Hayden, Fritz Owens, Wilson Owens, Ryan Randolph, Lee Jekos, Ann Link, Jason Smith, Annette Carpino, Wendy Rios, Elaine Berlind, Sally Murtha, Irene Tarkov, Julie Kast, and many other members of Greenwich Associates.

contents

Financial Services without
borders

Introduction

Charles D. Ellis

Strolling up Cornhill on the opposite side of The Royal Exchange from the Bank of England, I paused at the shop window of Searle & Company. My attention was drawn to a Victorian silver drinking cup or tankard of ample size that I thought I might give to a dear friend as a symbol of affection born out of 25 years of continuing friendship. It was the spring of 1984.

Stepping inside, I immediately realized the shop had two distinguishing characteristics: It was very small (closer in space to an outsized telephone booth than to a silver store), and most all of that space was filled with the large, genial shopkeeper and his warm welcome: "Come in, come *in,* sir. And tell me, how may I help you this morning?"

Gesturing to the tankard, which he deftly fetched from its place in the window, I inquired as to cost and was pleased that the handsome piece was indeed affordable. He then asked if it was for a special occasion and seemed well pleased when I explained my plan to memorialize a long friendship.

It was left for me to say, "I'll take it. Which credit card do you prefer?"

"Oh, I'm sorry, sir, we do not take credit cards . . . but we'd be happy to take your personal check, sir."

"Sorry, but I don't carry personal checks."

Thoughtfully, Mr. Bridges (as I later learned was his name) inquired, "May I ask, sir, what brings you to London and how long you'll be staying?"

"I'm here for the fortnight, working with clients of my firm."

"And who might they be, sir?"

A sensible enough question. I gave him their names: "Baring Brothers, Hill Samuel, Kleinwort Benson—and SG Warburg and Morgan Grenfell."

"Sad, isn't it," said Mr. Bridges in a solemn, reflective way. "Those fine old firms, sir, their world is changing—just as our world has changed. Most of them won't be around in ten years' time. All of London will be different then." And then Mr. Bridges seemed to brighten up as he said, "I'll tell you what we can do—for old time's sake. We'll wrap this tankard up properly and you just take it home with you. When you get back to the States, send us your check. Here's my card with all the information you might want to have, sir."

So the bargain was sealed, both of us knowing that the sort of person-to-person trust we then were enjoying would soon be displaced by organizations designed around computer terminals and global telecommunications, and each of us wondering what aspects of the way great firms worked then would be lost forever in the wake of all the coming changes.

The changes would be greater in number, breadth, and extent than Mr. Bridges and I would have been able to hypothesize—and they have created an extraordinary environment for the development of Greenwich Associates.

Professional financial services have been going through profound transforming experiences during the past three decades. It has been our firm's challenge to document these remarkable changes in our research. And it is our privilege to consult on effective, responsive strategies—and their effective implementation—with senior management at virtually all the leading competitors in all the major markets around the world.

Our mission has been to help senior management understand past changes and anticipate future changes in their markets, in customer expectations, in competitor capabilities, and in the performance of their own organizations. With this knowledge, they can formulate effective strategies that are right for their markets and right for their organizations. Bringing their skills and resources into powerful alignment with the rigorous disciplines of free and competitive markets, enables them to achieve their wisely chosen goals and objectives.

The extent of the transformation of professional financial services markets around the world is truly remarkable. National markets have been eclipsed, as globalization has become ascendant. Regulations have been set aside or superseded. Established leaders—J.P. Morgan, SG Warburg, Robert Fleming, and Swiss Bank among them—have been taken over. New products have been launched and have grown to dominance. Familiar products have been discontinued. Prices on some products and services are up four-fold; prices on others have been quartered. Buyers of professional financial services have been as profoundly changed as the sellers. The latest electronic equipment is "in," and neckties are "out."

Professional financial services are necessarily win-win businesses. As different as one professional financial service is from another, all service consumers and all service producers know that over the long run, all their counterparties have *alternatives* and are free to switch to those alternatives at any time. So all consumers and all producers of professional financial services are *volunteers*. As Charles Darwin explained for that extraordinarily free market—the competition for mates within a species—success depends not on combative strength or the ability to defeat a competitor, but on capacity to attract and on desirability to live with a partner in productive, mutually satisfying, cooperative relationships.

So, too, in professional financial services, where markets are continuously negotiated meritocracies: The most capable producers are constantly looking for and sorting out the most capable consumers, and the most capable consumers are constantly sorting out the most capable producers. That's why free and competitive markets are aptly called "learning markets" and why the markets for professional financial services—with very smart producers and very smart consumers—are such accelerated "learning markets."

The transforming experiences documented so extensively in our annual studies of well over 100 major markets around the globe are understandably of great interest to those who devote their lives to professional financial services.

These experiences are also important to all corporations, all governments, and all financial institutions everywhere, because financial markets are the vital circulatory system of the world's economy. "No man is an island," explained John Donne, "every man is . . . a part of the main." And so it is with financial markets. All are connected through the market mechanisms discussed in this book to the rapidly evolving financial system of the world.

Internet technologies are enabling professional financial service producers and consumers to engage in a once-in-a-century hypertransformation of their markets. Not only will this New Economy transformation change the markets for professional financial services, it will change all producers and all consumers.

As intermediaries of information and understanding, we know the work of our firm will also change, as it has many times before. While assuming that some of our changes will be difficult, or at least "very interesting," we are excited about and strongly committed to change. One particular change, in which we are making our largest-ever investment of treasure and talent, is particularly exciting: the Internet.

Our commitment is to capitalize on the Internet to deliver a remarkable array of service values to our Research Partners, the expert consumers of professional financial services. Their evaluations of the products and services of all the producers have for over 28 years informed all our research and consulting services. Once again, their turn has come to benefit directly.

Nearly 30 years ago, we innovated the proposition of reporting back to those who shared their expertise and experience with our executive Interviewers; 15 years ago, we launched *Greenwich Reports;* 5 years ago, we incorporated comparative data from peer markets in other countries; last year, we began providing information about all the leading competitors—the producers of professional financial services; and in 2001, we will be delivering extensive interactive information about the producers of financial services to the consumers of professional services, so they can be even more fully informed.

We couldn't be happier with this commitment. For many years, our Research Partners have, consistently and generously, contributed their time and knowledge. In turn, we have strived to say "Thank you" by delivering more and more value. Now the Internet is enabling us to deliver a *quid pro quo* that is truly stunning.

Professional financial markets have rapidly become more effective and efficient, and both "sides" are winners:

- Consumers have experienced the real *value* of services delivered going up through more consistency of quality, more variety of choice, more convenience in use, and faster speed of delivery.
- Producers have earned record incomes and substantial growth.

Even government regulators have benefited from the powerful self-corrective cleansing process inherent in transparent, free, and competitive markets. Professional financial markets are intolerant of malpractice. And the accepted Global Standard obliges any "slow" market to catch up on ethical behavior and Best Practices.

The purpose of all our work as professional researchers and consultants has been to enable our clients to improve the value of the services they deliver, by increasing their knowledge and understanding of what our Research Partners really want from their professional financial service producers.

We have enjoyed a great adventure as professionals and as entrepreneurs. Recognized as the global leader in our chosen field of endeavor, we have developed a worldwide full-service capability to serve the needs for information and advice of all our major clients in all their major markets, and to meet the hopes and expectations of our Research Partners.

Now, in the great tradition of sharing information and experience that is so very special in professional financial services, readers will find in this unusual book an extensive, candid sharing of what we have observed in our research and come to understand in our consulting with virtually all the leading organizations in all the world's markets for professional financial services.

This book, like many aspects of Greenwich Associates, is different. Readers might well ask whether any other consulting firm has undertaken to share its most valuable knowledge—or why the partners of Greenwich Associates (who've worked so long and hard to develop their proprietary knowledge and understanding) would do so.

These great questions generate their own answers. For many years, our clients and Research Partners have been sharing with us, so it seems appropriate to give something back and share our accumulated understanding. We hope serious readers will find our offering truly helpful.

Readers will find a treasure trove of information: hitherto confidential "league tables" of the leading competitors in each market, documentation of the key success factors in each business, and the distilled wisdom of our consultants on how to be successful in each professional financial service. In addition, a perspective is provided on different markets around the world. Here is a brief Cook's tour of our world, and of this book:

- Woody Canaday reminds us that global foreign exchange trading has increased over 2,300 percent in 20 years, to a daily volume of nearly $1.5 trillion and that most participants concentrate a whopping 80 percent of their foreign exchange business with their "Top 3" dealers. The complexity and intensity of the foreign exchange market has made it a natural center of advanced developments in electronic trading and utilization of the Internet.
- Steve Glick summarizes our experience in consulting on business strategy with the leading fixed-income dealers in market after market all around the world. The central rule of thumb is a simple and profound constant: the key to success on the customer side of the business is to be a "Very Important" or Top 3 dealer to each and every one of your chosen customers. (Dealers must also be alert, says Steve, for the most profitable opportunities to take proprietary positions while avoiding outright conflicts of interest with institutional customers.) Steve focuses our attention on this essential factor for success in a continuous professional market: The best relationships are always win-win, mutually beneficial relationships.
- Jack Mahoney, in addition to leading our firmwide strategic thrust into capitalizing on the Internet, tells us that the monetary crisis in Southeast Asia is "history" as institutional investors restructure their bond portfolios away from the liquidity and safety of U.S. Governments and into regional credit investments.
- In Japan, Tim Sangston, acknowledging the strategic imperative of being a Very Important or Top 3 dealer, underlines some of the differences in the Japanese market: frequent job rotation (which disrupts

good working relationships), increasing numbers of dealers being used, and a surprising lack of interest in electronic trading.

■ Frank Feenstra leads our consulting with derivative dealers and reminds us that in less than 20 years, derivatives have completely transformed the institutional financial markets. And with innovation as the driving force behind each competitor's successful expansion, dealers compete with each other in the elusive sector of creativity, striving to develop profitable new kinds of derivatives. They know that, no matter how exciting any established derivative once was, it soon becomes just a commodity. And the better the derivative, muses Frank, the more competitive replication it will attract, and the faster it will be driven to commodity pricing.

■ "Relationship banking is not what it used to be," begins Allan Munro, and—having been an effective relationship banker at Morgan before he joined us 27 years ago to advise and consult with America's major banks (and later on, the major banks of Europe, Latin America, and Asia)—he's seen it all. "Actually," Allan explains, "the profound change has been in what the relationship manager does. A quarter century ago, he was primarily and principally responsible for allocating *credit* to corporate customers. Today, it's not capital, but *services*. And the relationship manager's principal task is to develop strong *relationships* through which the bank can deliver strong *products*."

Allan reminds us that disintermediation has occurred on a massive scale. In 25 years, money market mutual funds have gone from zero to over $1 trillion. Use of commercial paper is up over 20 times. Even more important, information technology and risk-adjusted rate pricing have enabled bank management to focus on profit rather than loan volume. Allan goes on to describe the increasingly "transitional" aspects of banking including buyout finance, high-yield bonds, and (with Section 20 affiliates), underwriting securities.

■ Don Raftery and Steve Busby document the continuing consolidation in cash management and the impressive concentration of this business with a company's most important "cash management" bank: 85 percent with the single most important bank and another 25 percent with the next. After reviewing the impressive, competitive consolidation in cash management over the past 25 years, Steve and Don suggest that a dominating "bulge bracket" is developing nationally—and could develop internationally—that promises to continue changing the competitive landscape.

■ Allan Munro and David Fox team up (as they and Pete Garrison have teamed up for more than 25 years of research and consulting) in exploring one key part of "middle market" commercial banking: soliciting new business. Bankers, they advise, should prepare themselves and their customers for each sales call by asking: What specifically differentiates our bank from others? What is our specific, persuasive, and relevant focus of each call? What new or different—and "company specific"—idea can we advance? Exactly how will we follow up after this call?

Explicit answers to these questions are important because, as Allan and David explain, the U.S. middle market is a large and highly competitive one, with 195, 000 companies that have sales ranging from $5 million to $50 million. Allan and David estimate the combined loan needs of these companies to be $218 billion and cash balances of $170 billion. And it's a profitable banking business, with 18 to 22 percent return on equity (ROE) versus a typical bank's overall return of 12 to 15 percent.

■ John Colon, Phil Kemp, and James (Jay) Bennett have for years been our lead consultants in investment banking in the United States, Canada, the United Kingdom, and Europe. They explain how ferocious a meritocracy investment banking has become and that being "important" is not enough today: Success depends on being the *number one* investment bank to a carefully selected group of client companies that all want most what a particular firm does best.

As investment banks compete with each other for the lucrative lead bank position, they have extended deeply into bond dealing and stockbrokage and have expanded all around the world, typically into strong leadership positions. Once again, Jay, Phil, and John specify the challenge: coordinating and interpreting strong product capabilities with strong relationships.

■ In Canada, Jay Bennett has seen the nation's largest banks acquire stockbrokers and bond dealers so they could compete effectively as "full-service" firms and capitalize on strong Canadian preference to protect their turf from expansion from the United States.

■ In worldwide project finance, Robert Statius-Muller, who is now heading up our London office, says project finance has been integrated into the general work of corporate banking with lower profit margins and less risky investment structures and is no longer run as a separate business by a separate unit.

■ Dev Clifford and Pete Garrison consult with the leading master trust banks—another industry where the dropout rate has been nearly one bank each year for the 20 years we've been consulting in this business in the United States and around the world.

The automation of all sorts of sophisticated financial services is illustrated by the unrelenting competition Dev and Pete see in master trust, when capital commitments required to remain competitive are driving smaller, or less committed, organizations out of the business and are helping the expansion of a powerful group of capital intensive, high-tech competitors into each of the major institutional markets around the world.

■ In institutional investment management—where Dev Clifford, Rodger Smith, John Webster, and I continue nearly 30 years of strategy consulting with the leading investment managers—several forceful changes are underway: a profound shift from Defined Benefit to Defined Contribution or 401(k) plans; increasing use of passive investing; heightened interest in private equity investing; and increasing recognition that this is the investment *services* business, and that investor services are becoming increasingly sophisticated and automated.

■ In the United Kingdom, Rodger Smith says the leadership among investment managers has shifted from traditional "balanced" management to specialist managers (including indexation). In addition, dramatic concentration of pension assets with relatively few managers (and a recent opening up toward American managers) has and will probably continue to change the structure of competition.

■ On the continent of Europe, Berndt Perl advises that most investment managers have concentrated on serving domestic clients; the integration of Europe appears to favor the British and American investment managers, partly because they've been obliged by competition in their home countries to develop considerable capability in investment management and relationship management and partly because they are accustomed to ambitious solicitations of new business. "The big challenge for the investment management industry," says Berndt, "is the high proportion of institutional assets being managed internally."

■ In Canada, Lea Hansen also finds pension funds shifting from "balanced" managers to "specialists." The growth in Defined Contribution plans is strong. Passive investing is rising as is international investing. Lea points out that investment consultants now serve 70 percent of the larger funds.

■ In Australia, Peter Lee and Glenn Wealands show that hiring and firing investment managers is very active—60 percent of the large funds hire one or more managers in an average year and 50 percent terminate.

■ In Japan, Bill Jarvis's and Dev Clifford's pioneering research documents that this long-closed market has been dominated by a cartel of traditional Japanese organizations, but is responding to the assertion of Global Standard investment management and relationship management.

■ Institutional stockbrokerage is clearly a growth business: The number of shares traded is up 30 times in 20 years. And it's a big business:

$22.5 billion in worldwide commissions, in the estimate of John Webster, Jay Bennett, and John Colon. Equally impressive, the 50 largest institutions in America execute 50 percent of all the trading on the New York Stock Exchange. As John, Jay, and John point out, only 4 of the top 20 firms in 1974 are still in business. Some change!

■ In Europe, Jay Bennett, John Colon, John Webster, and Berndt Perl consult with clients striving to deal effectively with three great external forces: the integration of Europe and the impact of investment banking on stockbrokerage, and the proliferation of information technology. In addition, as in so many professional financial service markets, the impact of competitors' actions is remarkably forceful.

■ In Canada, Lea Hansen and John Webster are consulting with stockbrokers in a concentrated market where the 30 largest institutional investors generate three-quarters of all the institutional business. As Lea points out, over the past decade most of the large stockbrokers have been acquired by commercial banks as part of their strategic moves into investment banking.

■ In Japan, the proverbial Big Four dominated the institutional stockbrokerage business when we began our annual program of research and consulting in the late 1980s, and most of the other competitors were Japanese. Since then, a veritable Tsunami has torn through the market, wreaking havoc with the old industry structure and bringing global best practices to Japan. Today four out of five market leaders are Western firms, with talented Japanese people doing business the Western way.

■ In managing corporate investor relations programs, Rodger Smith and I emphasize two major reasons for getting it right with institutional investors and the institutional brokers that serve them: First, institutions dominate the market and, therefore, set the price of shares; and second, most individual investors are customers of those institutional stockbrokers' retail divisions, because the leaders are active in both professional and consumer markets. As we sometimes put it, "You not only have no choice, you have no need to choose."

On a personal note, I have had the great privilege of serving as Managing Partner of Greenwich Associates from its beginning and to witness the development of an interesting new idea into a strong professional organization that serves the leading professional financial services organizations around the world in long-term, value-added, working relationships that are important to all of us.

It has been an even greater privilege to experience the joy of admiring and liking my Partners and successors as they move into positions of responsible leadership, endowed with a thorough understanding of the future's technology; the past's lessons about successful operations in free competitive markets; and the primacy of a firm culture that respects the capabilities and commitments of gifted individuals and the importance of being a One-Firm Firm devoted to serving the needs of our clients and Research Partners.

As President Kennedy rightly observed, "Happiness comes in exercising capabilities along lines of excellence," and so ours is indeed a happy firm.

CHAPTER 1

Foreign Exchange: One Certainty in an Ever-Changing Business

John H. (Woody) Canaday

For a commodity business, foreign exchange is now anything but straightforward. The addition of layer upon layer of complexity has turned what was once the simple business of pricing one currency in terms of another into a tricky balancing act of satisfying customers' disparate needs and expectations while still maintaining a profitable business.

Greenwich Associates first began studying the foreign exchange business in 1981. Since then, foreign exchange has experienced spectacular growth in volume and complexity. Consider these indicators of expansion and change:

- Global foreign exchange trading among all parties has grown from a daily volume of $65 billion in 1981 to nearly $1.5 trillion in the most recent BIS survey—*up 23 times.*
- Trading in outright forwards and foreign exchange swaps has grown explosively, in parallel with more active international investment (and the liquidity and currency risk management that go with it) and the increased hedging requirements of commercial firms.
- Customers are executing more and more volume outside their domestic markets. At least one third of customer business is now traded across borders, as major centers grow in a virtuous circle of "liquidity begets liquidity." London, in particular, has grown at a rate 30 to 50 percent higher than the overall market.

A few key developments have fueled this spectacular growth. They are:

- Since the full floating of currencies following the collapse of the Bretton Woods agreement, numerous major and minor political and economic events have spawned volatility—the heart of both the need to hedge and the desire to speculate.

■ SWIFT was created in 1977, replacing error-prone cable transfers and providing a stronger technological platform for rapid growth.

■ The European Monetary System, established in 1978, created bands within which member currencies were to trade, and obliged them, within limits, to support each other's currencies.

■ The terms of the Maastricht Treaty were met in 1998, and the Euro was agreed on by the 11 first-round member nations. This dampened volatility in the member currencies, and dealers cut trading staffs in response.

■ Spectacular advances in information technology fed an enormous appetite for information—on prices, trends, forecasts, and positions—and for automating trades and transaction processing. A significant share of interbank spot broking is now executed on EBS, the Electronic Brokerage Service. In another wave of development, many banks have developed Internet access to their research, analytical tools, and prices, and many are now planning to participate in multidealer platforms to serve customers.

■ Advances in processing power have also enabled the development of foreign exchange derivatives, especially OTC options. After the Black-Scholes model was adapted to foreign exchange in 1983, the foreign exchange derivatives market grew slowly at first, but now more than two in five top-tier customers use options, and this market accounts for 5 to 6 percent of the total global trading volume.

■ More and more countries have deregulated their capital markets and lifted or reduced foreign exchange controls, leading to greater cross-border international investment activity.

■ Increased investment and hedging and deregulation have attracted global speculators and hedge funds. (In recent years, two new hedge funds were formed every week!)

CHANGE BEGETS CHANGE

These developments have had quite an impact on the rankings of the top foreign exchange dealers in the United States, as Table 1.1 shows.

Only four banks that were ranked among the top 10 in 1982 remained on the list in 1999. Three trends in particular are responsible for the marked change in the makeup of today's Top 10 dealers. They are:

■ Mergers: Of the eight banks that dropped from the list, four merged into other banks and, also as a result of mergers, Banc One and Warburg Dillon Read appear among the top 10.

TABLE 1.1 Top U.S. Foreign Exchange Dealers (by number of dealing relationships with 400 large accounts)

1982	Total Trading Relationships	1999	Total Trading Relationships
Citibank	60%	Bank of America	64%
Bank of America	40	Citigroup	58
Morgan Guaranty Trust Co.	39	Chase Manhattan Bank	43
Chase Manhattan Bank	38	ABN AMRO	26
Bankers Trust	31	Deutsche Bank	24
Continental Illinois Bank	28	Goldman Sachs	21
Royal Bank of Canada	24	Banc One	21
Harris Bank	22	RBC—Dominion Securities	21
Barclays Bank International	22	Bank of Montreal	18
National Westminster Bank	20	Warburg Dillon Read	18
Lloyds Bank International	20		
First National Bank of Chicago	20		

- Globalization: Five of the top banks are foreign owned.
- The importance of financial funds flows to the foreign exchange market, illustrated by Goldman Sachs now ranking in the top 10.

The trend toward implementation of global strategies by major European banks is also apparent in the United Kingdom, where two of the top 10 banks are continental European, as Table 1.2 shows.

In Japan, two major U.S. dealers—Chase Manhattan and Citigroup—have benefited dramatically from the implementation of deregulation. Table 1.3 shows the enormity of the gains.

THE IMPORTANCE OF BEING A TOP 3 DEALER

Though foreign exchange customers often use many dealers to execute their different foreign exchange needs, in most markets they concentrate more than *two thirds* of their business with their Top 3 dealers. Companies with trading volumes of under $1 billion typically concentrate a whopping 80 percent of their business with their Top 3 dealers. And larger volume traders, which by nature use many more dealers, still parcel out well over half of their business to their Top 3 dealers, as shown in Table 1.4(a).

In our worldwide research, we annually document developments in each of the major national markets. As shown in Table 1.4(b), the concentration with a customer's Top 3 dealers is remarkably similar—69 percent ± 5 percent in *every* region but Australia.

TABLE 1.2 Top U.K. Foreign Exchange Dealers (by number of dealing relationships with 300 large accounts)

1984	Total Trading Relationships	1999	Total Trading Relationships
Barclays Bank	53%	HSBC	51%
National Westminster Bank	46	Barclays Capital	46
Citibank	34	NatWest/GFM	46
Midland Bank	34	Citigroup	45
Lloyds Bank	34	Royal Bank of Scotland	32
Chase Manhattan Bank	30	Deutsche Bank	29
Bank of America	25	Chase Manhattan Bank	28
Standard Chartered Bank	23	ABN AMRO	25
Chemical Bank	20	Lloyds Bank	18
Banque Nationale de Paris	18	Bank of America	18

There is a tremendous advantage to being a Top 3 dealer and an ever increasing disadvantage for those dealers ranked fourth, fifth, and lower. Figure 1.1 tells the story.

Dealers with Top 3 relationships not only get the lion's share of each customer's business; they also tend to retain that business. Our research shows that banks that have a close trading relationship with their customers (and provide the attendant exceptional service) are 90 percent likely to retain the relationship, while those with a merely "good" quality of service have only a 60 percent retention rate. That's why we advise our clients to give top priority to becoming a Top 3 dealer to a carefully targeted set of

TABLE 1.3 Top Japanese Foreign Exchange Dealers (by number of dealing relationships with 140 large accounts)

1988	Total Trading Relationships	1999	Total Trading Relationships
Bank of Tokyo	95%	Bank of Tokyo-Mitsubishi	71%
Industrial Bank of Japan	65	Chase Manhattan Bank	67
Dai-Ichi Kangyo Bank	56	Citigroup	52
Citibank	49	Industrial Bank of Japan	52
Mitsubishi Bank	47	Fuji Bank	43
Fuji Bank	45	Dai-Ichi Kangyo Bank	40
Sanwa Bank	40	Sakura Bank	40
Sumitomo Bank	40	Sanwa Bank	38
Long-Term Credit Bank	38	Mitsubishi Trust and Banking	37
Mitsui Bank	37	Sumitomo Bank	37

TABLE 1.4 Concentration of Business

	First Dealer	Second Dealer	Third Dealer	Top 3 Dealers
(a) By Trading Volume				
Over $10 billion	26%	17%	13%	57%
$5–$10 billion	33	21	14	67
$1–$5 billion	33	21	14	69
Under $1 billion	46	22	12	80
(b) By Geographic Area				
United States	36%	22%	14%	73%
Canada	41	20	13	74
Latin America	40	20	12	72
Japan	33	20	13	66
Asia	32	19	13	64
Australia	26	20	16	62
United Kingdom	33	19	14	66
Continental Europe	37	20	13	70
*Total**	*36%*	*20%*	*13%*	*69%*

*Our research shows that these proportions have remained relatively constant over the past five years.

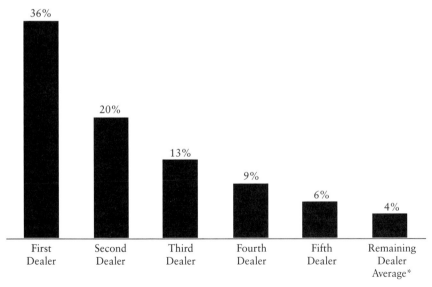

*Based on use of a total of nine dealers.

FIGURE 1.1 Concentration of business.*

customers—and to retaining this coveted position—or to have very good reasons strategically to aim for a lower-tier position.

TARGET YOUR CUSTOMERS AND ENHANCE YOUR CHANCES TO BECOME A TOP 3 DEALER

In the past few years, the number of dealers used for foreign exchange has declined overall, owing to bank mergers as well as to customers deliberately focusing their treasury activities on fewer counterparties to achieve greater efficiency. This trend will likely continue because of the underlying forces of bank consolidation, the need for efficiency in treasury operations, and the enabling power of Internet technology.

As shown in Table 1.5, the decline in dealers used occurred with all sizes of accounts and in all geographic markets. Over a two-year period, only treasury centers (which are designed to funnel the dispersed foreign exchange flows of a multinational operation and which are increasing in number) and governments added dealing relationships.

This decline makes it all the more important to be among the Top 3 dealers to your targeted accounts. Those dealers not in the Top 3 are at risk of being marginalized as customers rationalize their relationships and simplify their treasury operations.

It is neither possible nor prudent to have a Top 3 relationship with every customer, but some dealers still try to be "all things to all people." They end up with a weak, undifferentiated generalist image and fail to develop a strong and compelling capability or reputation for expertise in any particular areas. Equally damaging, some dealers become too specialized. They focus on a niche only to find that it is not large enough, important enough, or consistent enough in activity to support a good business.

We advise our clients instead to develop truly *superior* relationships with a well-defined and carefully chosen group of customers. Whether a dealer is large or small, has a global marketing approach or a niche focus, the *effective* and *profitable* use of resources is to define up front the accounts with which it most wants to conduct business. You should carefully select not only the customers with whom you not only want to do business, but those who, because of your bank's expertise, will want to do business with you.

Successful foreign exchange (FX) dealers aim for an ideal matching of customer needs with their expertise. Use the following questions to help determine which of your bank's existing and potential customers are the most likely "mutual matches." It is such a win-win scenario that holds the greatest promise for developing into a Top 3 relationship.

TABLE 1.5 Decline in Dealers Used

	1996	1997	1998
Foreign Exchange Trading Volume			
Over $10 billion	13.3	13.2	11.9
$5–$10 billion	11.2	8.7	9.2
$1–$5 billion	8.6	8.5	8.4
Under $1 billion	7.2	6.3	5.8
Type of Institution			
Corporates	9.4	8.8	8.6
Treasury Centers	11.0	10.1	11.9
Banks	18.8	13.1	14.5
Fund Managers/Pension Funds	8.6	7.8	7.4
Hedge Funds/CTAs	8.5	7.8	6.5
Insurance	8.3	7.7	8.1
Other Financials	12.3	11.0	8.6
Governments	11.1	12.0	12.0
Geographic Area			
United States	8.2	8.3	7.7
Canada	7.3	7.4	7.1
Latin America	na	7.5	8.2
Japan	12.0	9.7	10.4
Asia	14.1	11.0	11.8
Australia	11.9	8.5	8.9
United Kingdom	9.3	9.1	8.3
Continental Europe	9.9	9.1	8.9
Total Companies	9.9	9.2	9.0

Note: Based on top-tier accounts—all financials plus active corporates.

■ Do you make fully competitive markets in each of the currencies that are important to each customer in your target group of Top 3 accounts?

■ Is your FX research among the best for each of these customers?

■ Do you now have a superior sales and service relationship with each customer? What specific changes would help strengthen your position?

■ Are your policies and practices in market making "just right" for this customer's needs?

■ Do you have—or does any other dealer have—an unfair competitive advantage in becoming a Top 3 dealer?

■ Do you have a strong senior-management-to-senior-management relationship?

■ Do you offer the mix of technology tools and personal contact that is right for these clients?

When answered candidly, these questions provide a real opportunity for the dealer to assess the status of its current relationships, as well as see which relationships are no longer worth pursuing.

Once the customer dealer writes out his or her best estimates for each question, have a senior banker meet with each customer to learn first hand, and question-by-question, how the customer sees the realities. Wherever views differ and can be changed, you have an opportunity to correct a problem or capitalize on a capability. If the difference is not readily correctable, the relationship reality should be accepted and allowed to find its natural level with no further struggle to achieve Top 3 status. Concentrate your resources on your real opportunities to win.

Equally important to a well-defined group of target customers is a reasonably large and well-diversified one—with the purpose of developing a *portfolio* of clients with enough noncovariance to protect the dealer against specific risk. For example, correlated risks can occur if a bank focuses only on providing foreign exchange services to its custody accounts or to industrial companies. It is essential to capture flows from an appropriate *variety* of customers and to have diverse outlets for executing trades.

IN THE LONG RUN, SERVICE VALUE MATTERS MORE THAN PRICE

Many customers and dealers alike think of foreign exchange as purely price driven and assume that aggressive pricing is the main factor determining how much business is directed to dealers. It is not.

Our research documents that the cumulative effect of relationship and service factors outweighs the effect of competitive pricing.[1] An extensive study showed:

■ Price is a relatively short-term criterion in the selection of foreign exchange dealers.

■ The effect of "extracompetitive" pricing on the duration of relationships is insignificant.

■ Dealers achieve higher account penetration in the long run by providing superior service and advisory performance and by understanding customer needs—not by competing on price.

■ Dealers maintain relationships longer and better by being responsive to customer requests and by making the effort to visit customers at their places of business.

These conclusions are further supported by practical evidence: A large proportion of accounts, while using many dealers, do a substantial proportion of their foreign exchange on a noncompetitive bid basis, asking a single dealer to execute a trade. Table 1.6 shows to what extent this occurs.

Top 3 dealers are asked to bid more often and consequently win more deals based on the *cumulative* effect of their overall service. That is not to say pricing is unimportant. Pricing can be an effective means of getting a foot in the door, but our research has shown that price is only a short-term determinant of customer behavior. Customers most often use those dealers that combine competitive pricing within the framework of an effective, close relationship built over time through superior service and advice. Strong emphasis on relationships wins and retains big accounts that are important to both the dealers and their customers.

THE CHALLENGE OF PROVIDING GOOD SERVICE ACROSS CUSTOMERS, BORDERS, AND INDUSTRIES

In foreign exchange, the big money, as dealers are well aware, is in proprietary trading. While some customer business—such as customer trading in minor and exotic currencies, currency options, and other higher-value

TABLE 1.6 Customers Executing Noncompetitive Trades, by Geographic Area

	Customers Executing Noncompetitive Trades	Average Percentage of Volume Executed Noncompetitively
United States	64%	52%
Canada	59	63
Latin America	33	16
Japan	88	86
Asia	56	25
Australia	57	52
United Kingdom	49	44
Continental Europe	46	43

transactions—is valued for its own sake, and banks typically are able to make money on trades with smaller corporates, it is an accepted reality of the foreign exchange business that dealers do not see much profit from the day-in and day-out customer business with large accounts. But such business remains worthwhile because it provides a bank with important information and liquidity—both as a buyer and as a seller—and with this, more market knowledge and less risk of being caught out holding a position that cannot be changed as quickly as necessary. Both are crucial to a dealer's ability to maneuver in the market with its "proprietary" positions.

Whether it is to support proprietary trading or to facilitate value-added customer business, or both, a well-managed customer strategy allows a bank to:

- Maintain good order flow in all market conditions.
- Capture information about market sentiment and direction—key for its own trading and positioning as well as for drawing conclusions useful to its customers.
- Develop the close relationships that are so necessary to earning business in higher-value currency options, emerging market currencies, and other non- foreign-exchange treasury products.
- Support a "host" business with customers such as in custody or cash management.

Since service at this level matters more than price, it behooves dealers to try to improve theirs in ways other than being more price competitive. When asked how dealers can improve their service, customers stress the importance of "selling with both ears," in other words, helping the customer to be efficient and fully leveraging the overall relationship. Figure 1.2 shows other critical service factors in order of importance.

These same factors are generally the most important in every market. There are, however, differences according to the type of account, the volume of activity, the trading style, and the region. A highly tuned strategy takes into account these marginal differences and structures sales and marketing programs to capitalize on them.

The needs of financial institutions, for example, differ from those of corporations in the following ways:

- Fund managers need to move large sums rapidly and often, in conjunction with their bond and equity investments or an overlay strategy. They cite the following criteria more often than do any other accounts: "improve market knowledge," "improve quality of research," and "improve large trade execution."

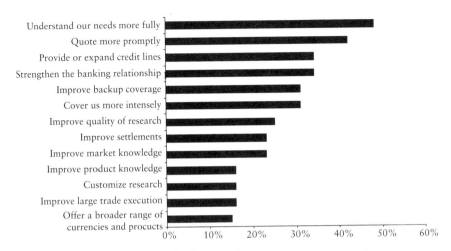

FIGURE 1.2 Ways dealers can improve customer service.

- Hedge funds, often empowered to trade in whatever markets provide the best opportunity, stress "offer a broad range of currencies and products" more than other types of accounts.
- Insurance companies, which often have a longer-term outlook and make their trades within this strategic context, cite these three criteria more than other accounts: "improve quality of research," "cover us more intensely," and "improve large trade executions."

Here are examples of how service needs differ across regions:

- Japanese accounts, given their *kairetsu* connections, less frequently cite the need for stronger banking relationships. However, Japanese accounts are surprisingly vocal about wanting more intensive coverage.
- In Southeast Asia, the currency and economic crises of 1997 and 1998 precipitated the paramount need for credit lines and basic, consistent service.
- In the United States, where 8 of the top 10 foreign exchange banks are the product of one or more mergers—with all that means for dislocation of established relationships with individual sales representatives—it is not surprising that "improve backup coverage" is the one factor that stands out more than in other markets.

These and other differences in service needs are shown in Tables 1.7 and 1.8.

TABLE 1.7   Actions Dealers Can Take to Improve Service—By Type of Institution

	Corporations	Fund Managers	Hedge Funds	Insurance Companies
Understand our needs more fully	51%	46%	40%	38%
Quote more promptly	41	42	40	38
Strengthen the banking relationship	35	29	23	20
Provide or expand credit lines	31	29	30	24
Cover us more intensely	30	36	10	38
Improve backup coverage	32	33	33	33
Improve quality of research	22	33	27	33
Improve market knowledge	20	35	30	24
Improve settlements	25	24	17	24
Offer a broader range of currencies and products	16	11	20	6
Improve large trade execution	10	24	23	24
Customize research	16	15	7	16
Improve product knowledge	16	18	13	10

TABLE 1.8   Actions Dealers Can Take to Improve Service—By Geographic Area

	United States	Canada	Japan	Asia	United Kingdom	Continental Europe
Understand our needs more fully	49%	36%	52%	54%	46%	45%
Quote more promptly	41	43	49	44	42	36
Strengthen the banking relationship	26	34	18	53	34	35
Provide or expand credit lines	26	27	38	68	32	20
Cover us more intensely	38	43	48	41	11	25
Improve backup coverage	41	32	29	26	26	31
Improve quality of research	26	32	34	32	15	20
Improve market knowledge	21	23	28	35	15	21
Improve settlements	26	18	8	19	29	27
Offer a broader range of currencies and products	13	7	16	35	8	13
Improve large trade execution	14	16	18	28	16	10
Customize research	15	18	15	29	10	12
Improve product knowledge	9	23	18	29	7	15

SERVICE RECOMMENDATIONS

Despite these differences between institutions and regions, our research with foreign exchange customers around the globe documents over and over again the following *universally* valued qualities:

- Taking a long-term partnership approach.
- Salespeople who know the markets and their products and link this with knowledge of the customer's trading requirements, with real understanding.
- Ready access to the dealer's experts on specific skills and expertise, such as specialized options, technical trading advice, or forecasting movements in exotic currencies.
- Online information sharing to save time spent faxing and telephoning.
- Strategic perspective on the outlook for emerging foreign exchange markets.

The best sales management places the greatest emphasis on fulfilling customer satisfaction on universal values of service while taking into account the important differences in various customers' needs.

It is precisely because foreign exchange is such a "commodity business" that customer service is paramount as a distinguishing characteristic, especially since the service factors now driving the business are so varied, complex, and numerous. Keeping up with it all requires significant *high-tech* investment, to be sure, but attendant with this requirement is the equally important and enduring need for effective, continuous *human* contact—to inform, advise, and sometimes simply reassure. Knowing whether the market is up or down is not nearly as helpful as knowing why it is up or down and how that movement will affect a particular customer's currency strategy and his major positions.

With this in mind, here are the recommendations we give our clients when consulting in each major area of their business: sales, research, trading product, systems and settlement, and management—all directly correlated with the factors customers most often associate with a very important or Top 3 relationship.

SALES RECOMMENDATIONS: INTENSIVE AND COMPREHENSIVE

As we consult with our foreign exchange clients, we see time and time again how effective sales begin at the very top of the organization. The most successful foreign exchange firms:

- Have global management that sets clear standards of excellence for all important relationships, develops appropriate measures of service success, and insists that regional sales management be proactive in talking with accounts to assess each customer's satisfaction with sales service, research, and market-making in various currencies.
- Are eager consumers and users of information about customers from both internal and external sources, and use this information continuously to improve their service.

Here are our sales recommendations:

- Know where you stand.
- Achieving the incremental sales edge that can advance a dealer from a fifth or sixth place ranking to Top 3 status is never a matter of making a radical shift in strategy. When, as is often the case with foreign exchange, most major dealers are playing on the same high-level field, success becomes a matter of fine-tuning an existing strategy. Often this means really paying attention to what a particular customer needs and assigning the right person to deliver the goods consistently, intelligently, and promptly.

The best relationships are covered by a top-notch salesperson who "clicks" with the account and provides the market and product information, timely research advice, and sufficiently competitive pricing that are most useful to that customer and best fit with the customer's currency strategy and the customer's work style. We advise our clients to make every effort to sustain the high quality and frequent level of coverage necessary to maintain these relationships, even though other dealers are always striving to prove they can do as well or better.

It is easy for sales managers to identify these strong relationships. It is also easy to identify weak relationships, if and when the customers care enough to complain and identify what needs to be corrected, whether it is to change a sales representative, correct a string of back-office problems, or provide more access to the dealer's product experts or senior management.

Trickier, however, is teasing out what can be done to elevate those customers who are neither "satisfied" nor "dissatisfied." In our research, we come across customers who consider it the job of the bank's sales management to figure out both the what—that they are not very happy—and *why* they are not happy. Such accounts often comprise a large percentage of a dealer's customer base, leaving the dealer vulnerable to being downtiered in overall competitive position without even knowing why.

Even though customers are beginning to be more direct when dealers ask specifically "How are we doing?" and "How can we do better?" it is still difficult for dealers to get an honest opinion about where they rank compared with the competition. Being told you're "definitely in the Top 3" is not nearly as helpful as knowing whether you are ranked number one, two, or three. And, being told you're "good" or "fine" is nothing like knowing exactly where you rank and whether you're improving position—and why.

Sales managers need to be persistently proactive in learning about the ever-changing behavior of their targeted accounts. They need a constant flow of information concerning trade volumes, win-loss ratios, frequency of calls and visits initiated by sales representatives, research coverage, and back-office issues. To stay on top of the process, it is beneficial to follow these apparently deceptively simple steps:

- *Initiate regular reviews with targeted accounts.*
- *Define mutual objectives.*
- *Measure progress toward these goals.*
- *Provide intensive sales coverage.* Frequent contact deepens knowledge of each customer's wants, objectives, process, and people—and provides opportunities to tailor ideas, solutions, and research to the customer's specific needs. We recommend dealers visit important customers up to four or five times per year, always with a substantive, action-oriented agenda. Initiating visits to accounts allows the dealer to inquire more deeply about the account's needs and sets up an environment where off-line conversations can take place and trust can be developed.
- *Pick up the phone.* Telephone calls, targeted to what clients want, provide market color and can be made as often as 15 to 20 times a day, depending on the needs of the account. Many customers complain they are "called too much," but this is a complaint about quality of calls, not quantity. Our research shows that calls and visits from sales representatives who are intent on serving well and from banks with a coherent strategy—*do matter*—provided the calls are useful and substantive. Frequent effective calls can put the dealer first in line to earn business, and the dealer will have earned that business when the content of calls demonstrates knowledge of the account's needs and the ability to meet those needs.
- *Use the computer.* E-mail and Bloomberg messaging are important elements of coverage strategy. Effective salespeople use these services, rather than the telephone, when the message to be conveyed is important but not time urgent. There is an art to this medium as well: Pungent subject headings and succinct conversational-style content encourage customer response.

■ *Use the fax.* Faxes, when welcomed by the customer, can also be a useful medium for providing intensive coverage. Given the ascendance of e-mail as a preferred medium, salespeople are wise to confirm periodically that customers still appreciate receiving a message by fax.

■ *Keep the account updated on market conditions.* Typically, keeping an account updated means providing insight into why market moves are taking place or informing an account when a market level has been reached. Such calls are best when specifically and explicitly limited to the client's current strategy and specific positions.

■ *Develop a superior understanding of each customer's needs.* Knowing an account's specific needs may sound like "Sales 101," but for many of the customers participating in our research, "lack of real understanding" is a common lament. Know your customers' objectives. Know their expected cash flows and constraints and make sure the products you try to sell them fit within those boundaries.

■ *Include the backup salesperson in roughly half of the client meetings.* This helps institutionalize the relationship while deepening the trust level. Inform the customer if the backup salesperson is replaced. In all markets, providing solid backup coverage to the primary sales representative covering an account is the sales factor that is most highly correlated with being a Top 3 dealer.

■ *Segment levels of account service.* Traditional demographic segmentation is not very effective. We urge our clients to group customers together for particular kinds of service on the basis of trading motivation or orientation rather than by industry segment. It is possible to have a corporation that acts more like a hedge fund, for example, so it would be appropriate, because of similar behavior patterns, to group such corporates with speculative investors because they will be looking for the same type of information and will provide the dealer with similar information as well.

■ *Use less experienced or less sophisticated sales representatives for covering low value-added accounts to free the senior salespeople to service priority customers.* Matching salespeople by sector, selling style, or customer requirements ultimately gives customers the right level of expertise while the dealer achieves a stronger competitive position.

■ *Organize with a global mind-set.* For those accounts with very large or complex exposures, or for those accounts with a very active, profit-oriented strategy, or for accounts physically located in a "thin" trading market, providing effective coverage from one or more foreign centers is now a key service. Examples of accounts to which such global coordination is important, and for which offering it serves the providing bank well, include hedge funds and top-tier accounts in Latin America. When organizing a team to provide such global coverage, the sales representatives outside the accounts' home trading region should be personally introduced whenever possible to the overseas accounts they serve because personal relationships go a long way to elevating a customer's comfort level and deepen the institutional relationship as well.

RESEARCH RECOMMENDATIONS: TRY A PERSONAL APPROACH

Research matters greatly to customers and is strongly correlated with being a Top 3 dealer. Greenwich Associates' research shows that almost 90 percent of customers use research and up to 50 percent reward dealers with incremental business because of research. Table 1.9 shows how the level of reward varies by region.

While the level of reward varies, what is most valued does not. Across the board, customers most value research when it is interpreted for their particular situation and helps them manage their foreign exchange exposures. Usefulness is the research factor most highly correlated with being a Top 3 dealer. Just as sales must be targeted to specific customers and adapted for regional behavior, so also must research be customized by sales representatives according to customer preferences and strategies.

What sets good research apart? Effectiveness. *Effective* research is accurate, timely, logical, concise, and easy to read. Even if the predictions are not fulfilled, clients appreciate being privy to the underlying assumptions.

When used as a strategic sales tool, research provides a specific value-added that is often the pivotal distinction for winning new accounts and, even more important, for building higher penetration with current accounts—aiming, as always, for Top 3 dealer status. To get the full benefit of

TABLE 1.9 Customers' Use of Research

	Use Dealers' Research	Increased Business Specifically Due to Research
United Kingdom	88%	30%
Continental Europe	89	35
United States	85	51
Japan	87	30
Asia	79	43

their investment in research, integrate research into the marketing effort with *all* clients, and with each client, through daily sales initiatives, seminars, access to analysts, and follow-up phone calls. The goal is always to search for ways that make the firm's research useful, important—even *necessary*—to the client's effectiveness in formulating strategy and managing his or her position.

A problem that many dealers (and many accounts) foresee, as a result of increased reliance on technology to deliver research service, is a decline in personal contact. Even though the efficiency of research distribution is increasing because of dealers' investments in their Web sites, and because of third-party aggregators of content, research can still only be fully effective when salespeople use it intensively to help accounts do their particular jobs especially well.

Here are some recommendations on how to make research more valuable to customers:

- *Sell customer dealers first.* Customer dealers should read research before the customer does, always with a view to how it can help that specific account. If customer dealers are not avid consumers of the dealer's research, they won't be proficient at merchandising that research and then customers won't become full and consistent users either.
- *If you are ever told your research is not "actionable," listen closely.* Seek to understand why it's not actionable for this particular client and what changes might convert it from "unusable" to "invaluable."
- *Use research actively in the sales process.* One-day or half-day seminars discussing research in depth can help clients both understand the full value of research and teach them how to use it most effectively. Another option is to take a few minutes to review the key points in each new research report with each client who has a "need to know." The specific manner—calls, fax, e-mail, and so on—by which the research is integrated into the dealer's sales-service strategy with each particular client, and how this "value-in-use" is linked back to the dealer, is less significant than that the connection is made—clearly and memorably.
- *Give important customers direct access to analysts.* This enables customers to test their own ideas and deepens the relationship by making it seem more like a partnership.
- *Get rid of "free riders."* Dealers often have fans who read and say they value the dealer's research, but do little or no extra trading with the bank to pay for it. Our research shows that as much as 40 percent of the enthusiastic users of research of some dealers do not trade with these firms. Actively pursue business from these free riders and— if good business is still not forthcoming—remove these deadbeat

accounts from your research distribution. While this may not lower costs appreciably in an Internet environment, it will improve the franchise value of the research for the core customers who do pay for it.

■ *Leverage information technology.* The Internet is a near-perfect tool for distributing research in a timely, low-cost, and effective way. The interactive nature of the medium also allows customers to download analytic models, upload information on positions or portfolios for assessment, and send or receive important (but not necessarily time urgent) messages about research. Most accounts globally now use dealers' Web sites to access research. While the technology and applications are evolving extremely rapidly, three key aspects of the use of the Internet for research are apparent:

1. The best Web sites are appreciated more for market commentary than for analytic tools.
2. Fresh content and ease of access to information are more important than customization or personalization. However, software applications being developed will enable subtle or invisible personalization to occur. Customers will find sophisticated Web sites to be more and more "just what I want."
3. While Web sites are rapidly being deployed by many dealers, there are significant differences on perceived quality because a Web site's immediacy of access to research and instantaneous comparisons brings into high relief each dealer's underlying quality of thinking, analysis, and recommendations.

■ This last point is key: Within the intense pace of development in the "dot.com" environment, it is essential for senior management to keep its eye on the fundamentals of quality in research because the best Web site will not overcome a poor product. Now, more than ever, management needs to stress:

Accurate projections.
Clear thinking.
Convenience for the user.
Accessibility to the experts.
Tailoring to the specific needs of each customer.

TRADING RECOMMENDATIONS: SPEED AND SERVICE FIRST; PRICING SECOND

In nearly all major currency markets, making fast, competitive quotes in major currencies—both spot and forward—are usually the trading factors most highly correlated with being a Top 3 dealer to target accounts.

We recommend dealers ask themselves whether their quotes are at the speed and price needed to support the overall effort. Sometimes, quotes can be too aggressive. We know from our research that fewer customers complain about dealers' quotes than complain about inferior service or advice. If a bank is too aggressive on price, it may be giving away profitability.

We advise our clients to ask themselves if there is a deliberate or intended difference between the dealer's forward versus spot versus options quoting. Is the quoting better in the market sectors the dealer most *wants* to focus on? Remember this: Dealers should attract customers because of their sales and service, knowledge, and counsel—and be able to compete when opportunity warrants. Superior sales and service and effective research that meets the needs of particular kinds of customers, combined with sufficiently competitive pricing, elevate accounts to the coveted Top 3 status—provided these capabilities are concentrated on serving a correctly chosen target market of customers who want most what the particular dealer is most capable of delivering.

Here are some recommendations on trading:

■ *Speed of quote is often as important as quote competitiveness.* Customers want fast quotes because they are busy, have other trades to execute, other treasury or trading functions to perform—or other dealers on the line for a competitive quote. Our analysis demonstrates that in each major market, making prompt quotes ranks second in importance to making competitive quotes in major currencies. Consistent slowpokes be warned: You will find yourselves downtiered, and it can take a lot of time and effort to rebuild or recapture your former position.

■ *Don't promise too much.* Never try to be "all things to all people," or too many things to too many customers. It's better to underpromise and overdeliver. Manage customers' expectations about where they can expect you to be especially competitive. Be sure to be judged most closely in the currencies and specialized products in which you aim to concentrate and to be expert. (Over time, if you are successful in fulfilling your declared strategy, you will earn opportunities to capture customers' noncompetitive bid business in a broader array of currencies.)

■ *Be sure that traders fully support the firm's selection of targeted or priority accounts and consistently facilitate these accounts' trades because they provide valuable information flows and the potential for more lucrative business.*

■ *Implement an internal review system that measures each trader's cooperation in developing customer business, not just the profitability of their book.*

■ *Manage trading costs efficiently, but meet local market needs.* Communications technology has made it possible to reduce the number of trading rooms in the same time zone without losing effectiveness, assuming proper management. We have seen banks reduce their trading rooms only to lose business because traders in trading centers simply do not respond to the demands of salespeople in the former office as quickly as they do to a salesperson sitting at the next desk. Management can prevent or close this gap by measuring response time and holding traders accountable for meeting performance standards.

PRODUCT RECOMMENDATIONS: AIM TO BE EXPERT

Leadership in a select range of currencies, instruments, products, or services acts as a dealer's "calling card" and can provide the reason a customer will want to trade with a particular dealer. As a rule of thumb, dealers should aim to be recognized as expert in currencies and products that span at least half of an account's needs to have a realistic chance at earning Top 3 dealer status. (A bank can have a niche strategy and aim for a lower percentage, but it must be sure it can offer a unique perspective and unrivaled expertise in its select product array.)

Ask yourself the following questions when considering your product array:

- Are the currencies and products on which you focus very important to your key customers?
- If following a niche strategy, have *all* the major users of your currencies and products been targeted?
- Are your global capabilities for passing orders or trading into other centers being fully utilized?
- If your trading in the currencies and products is competitive in the interbank market, is this expertise effectively transferred to your customer business through prompt and competitive quotes?
- Is there high "goal congruence" between the traders and the customer dealers on the importance of quoting consistently, promptly, and competitively to customers in these particular currencies?

SYSTEMS AND SETTLEMENT RECOMMENDATIONS: AIM TO ELIMINATE ERROR

Because of the size and volume of transactions flowing through dealers' back-office operations, even small errors can lead to significant losses if the dealer is continually having to make amends to its customers. The value of taking every step necessary to ensure settlement procedures are smooth is affirmed in our research, which reveals a high correlation—in every market—of superior settlement and delivery with being a Top 3 dealer. Even though much of settlement is now done electronically, there is always room for human error.

Dealer-generated errors can occur at any of several points in the settlement and delivery process and are idiosyncratic to a dealer's own systems. The first challenge is to find the source of the human error and correct it, ideally in a systematic way, so that it cannot occur again. The second challenge is to repair the damage—particularly any damage done to the client relationships and very particularly to interpersonal *feelings*—by attentive and active listening.

Dealers should keep in mind two objectives when correcting their own errors:

1. Operations personnel are responsible for tracing the error, correcting it, making amends to the customer as appropriate, and initiating systematic improvements in procedures or in technology to prevent recurrence. Even more important, they are responsible for offering the utmost professional and personal courtesy to customers who are distressed by errors.

2. Sales management should keep in close tabs with the affected customers, to assure them that the dealer considers the issue important and to inform them of improvements in process that will prevent this type of error from occurring again. Customers will decide whether the dealer "cares enough," so be "more than caring" and move "more than quickly" to correct any errors.

Straight-through processing holds great promise for further reducing dealer-generated and customer-generated errors. While a fair amount of up-front work is required to link dealer and customer systems, some customers—especially fund managers with many subaccounts involved in a single set of transactions—find this a real time-saver. For other customers, this potential for perfection of process is actually a resistance point. Since the audit trail in an electronic system where the customer clicks the "execute" button also leads right back to the account, a few firms are concerned at the prospect of not being able to "work it out" with the dealer in case of their own error. Since all Internet and electronic commerce advances are leading to greater transparency and higher expectations for accuracy, dealers need to help possible "recalcitrants" adjust to this reality by being generous during a transitional period, as well as by being informative and helpful to these customers until they are satisfied enough to trust both the new process and themselves.

MANAGEMENT RECOMMENDATIONS: ACT GLOBALLY AND LOCALLY

Becoming a leading dealer for more and more large, active, and sophisticated corporations and institutions requires a *global* approach, with a management process set up to coordinate the external and internal systems needed to support the global effort. "Antiturf" and "proteam" environments will work best to ensure congruence in global service, provided it is encouraged and rewarded fairly.

Develop an atmosphere where marketers, traders, research analysts, and clerks all work as a team across trading, sales, research, and the back office for all products—and coordinate closely with shared incentives your custody, credit, capital raising, and cash management businesses. The synergy of this type of setup can result in overall performance that is greater than the sum of the performance of the individual parts. Management sets the direction and tone of the effort and is responsible for everyone within the dealer—traders and sales representatives as well as clerks—having the resources and support they need to help the overall effort.

Here are some additional suggestions:

- Be sure each salesperson has the technical know-how to create structures applicable to customers' needs, as well as the ability to educate potential customers to the benefits of customized solutions. This will require regular, substantial investment in training and learning.
- Implement a formal process to provide a counterdiscipline to virtually all salespersons' natural human tendency to gravitate to those customers they know and like best. This should include periodic reviews of how well the bank is meeting specific objectives for business won, as well as a check that the customer dealer is able both to articulate each customer's foreign exchange needs and his or her specific plan for meeting those needs.
- Limit customer lists to ensure the service requirements of achieving and sustaining Top 3 status are fully met, or add more sales-service resources. Salespeople covering very large accounts that require significant servicing may only be able to effectively cover two or three.
- Beware free riders of research or trading. Research resources and capital should be reserved for, and concentrated on, targeted accounts.

KEY DEVELOPMENTS SHAPING THE BUSINESS

Today's foreign exchange market is anything but static. In fact, the rate of change is likely to accelerate, largely due to the following key areas of influence.

Competition

Major dealers, using capital and derivatives, have achieved substantial "throw weight" in the world's largest free market. Their sizable sales organizations and powerful proprietary research enable them to create enormous market forces that move markets, pressure governments, and speed the process by which markets clear. Informed, rational, and widely influential, the major dealers are truly "makers of markets" as well as "market makers." This is a relatively new and increasingly powerful phenomenon.

Globalization

Foreign exchange is inherently a global business, and it is becoming even more so as the overwhelming trend, even among former communist countries, is to float currencies. This allows for freer flows of capital. Large volumes are now being dealt across borders. London in particular, but also Hong Kong, New York, Singapore, and Frankfurt now figure prominently. Since customers can, they now *do,* turn to whichever market provides them with the best liquidity and the best service. Increasing acceptance of foreign dealers who operate all around the world, 24 hours a day, means there is no longer much home country advantage. Our research shows strong penetration from foreign banks in the United States and the United Kingdom, as well as increasingly significant inroads into Japan. Dealers must think of and coordinate their book of business globally while targeting customers regionally across continents and time zones, making foreign exchange global not only in nature but also in deed. Table 1.10 illustrates the point.

TABLE 1.10 Proportion of Volume Traded Domestically and Cross-Border

	Domestic Centers	Nondomestic Centers			
		London, Continental Europe	North America	Asia	Other
Customer Location					
Europe	69%	24%	5%	2%	—
North America	61	25	7	5	2
Asia	82	6	2	9	—
All Markets	67	21	5	5	1

Technology and the Use of Technical Models

Foreign exchange today has little—and less and less—to do with underlying commercial trade and almost everything to do with financial and investment interests. In the global customer business, which accounts for only 6 to 8 percent of total trading, corporations do just one fourth of the trading. (Even this figure includes speculative as well as hedging and translation requirements.) Financial organizations and investing institutions are responsible for the other three fourths. One result is that purchasing power parity theories and other forms of fundamental foreign exchange analysis, while useful for estimating where exchange rates theoretically should be, are less and less sufficient for understanding this complex and multifaceted market and for making trading decisions. In turn, use of technical models to assess past pricing behavior to project near-term future trends has grown.

Demand for technical trading models among financial institutions and treasury centers in Europe is rising. More and more foreign exchange dealers are offering technical analysis, because they and their customers believe it is more useful than fundamental analysis for predicting short-term trends.

The shift to electronic trading has taken a firm hold. Electronic Brokerage Services (EBS), the partnership of 13 major banks and Minex Corporation of Japan, was started in 1993. By 1997, EBS was executing more than one third of all interbank spot broking activity in London. The success of EBS eroded the business of voice brokers as well as the dealing that major upstream banks were executing directly with smaller regional banks, formerly a key customer group.

Electronic trading for nonbank customers has been available for at least a decade. Most such trading was directly between a single bank and a customer who needed to install software and use a dial-up service, or execute via a terminal such as Bloomberg. These and other technical (or budgetary) limitations prevented most services from being used for other than small, or "nuisance"-size trades. Both customer and bank benefited from executing these trades without sales representatives or traders' direct involvement.

The Internet enables immediate access without complex software installations or specialized equipment. Some banks, on upgrading their direct-to-customers trading service to a browser-based Internet format have expanded their reach to hundreds of additional customers in a short time span at virtually no marginal cost.

The benefits of this are obvious for those customers who are content to work with just one, or a few, single dealer-to-customer trading services. The broadened base of users and the greater convenience also make it feasible for banks to invest in creating "live" or request-based trading of larger amounts.

In this environment, electronic trading with customers will disintermediate a meaningful proportion of sales representatives' and some traders' current service to accounts.

The availability of electronic execution in market-size amounts will also create demand for multidealer trading systems, largely for the sake of convenience. Three solutions to this need are evolving:

1. Multidealer electronic trading systems have been developed by some banks and nonbank third parties. Similar to the TradeWeb service that got off to a quick start with U.S. Treasury bond investors, these services funnel quotes—whether request-based or live—through a single channel.
2. Consortiums of banks are teaming to make their individual advisory capabilities and trading more easily available through a single site, while still retaining their separate identities and their ability to link business to value-added provided services.
3. Some banks have created a benchmarking service, in which a customer can ask them to execute a price not "at best" but at the best or a fair average price at a specific time, using objectively verifiable measures. The intrigue to this solution is that it can, for some transactions, do away with the need for multiple quotes altogether regardless of whether they're given electronically or verbally.

As the need for price discovery or due diligence is diminished by the availability of online quoting, customers' criteria for selecting, evaluating, and sticking with banks will migrate toward more value-added by sales representatives, analysts, and traders, and away from basic trading prowess. Senior management should therefore encourage and develop salespeople who are creative, relationship-oriented, and technophilic. With active use of technology, the content of their dialogue with accounts can change qualitatively for the better as they spend more time listening, interpreting, advising, structuring, and executing complex or sensitive trades—and less time on making quotes for ordinary transactions.

Similarly, senior management should focus all the more on hiring and developing traders who are:

■ Skilled at and excited by the prospect of trading in a truly frictionless market.
■ Willing and able to stay close to customers (through sales representatives or directly) who have unusual needs for discreet executions and complex trades to which the bank can add value through its market knowledge and wide range of outlets for liquidity.

Electronic trading over the Internet is the latest and one of the most powerful in a string of technology improvements that have changed the foreign exchange market. This form of trading will further democratize the business, but for major corporate and institutional clients it will modify, but not overthrow, the key criteria for assessing a bank's service.

Liquidity

Overall market liquidity, as measured by trading volumes, has increased greatly. This is documented in our annual research. However, striking things have happened to the concentration of trading volumes:

- More hedge funds and institutional investment funds are using the foreign exchange markets to invest in currencies to hedge out the currency risk in their increasingly large international investments and to speculate on anticipated changes in exchange rates. Their increased involvement in the foreign exchange markets has increased available liquidity, and has concentrated trading volume with a comparatively small number of very large and active institutions. (On occasion, however, a huge trade by a hedge fund can give a false impression of liquidity in the market, when in fact it is simply creating a temporary spike in volume.)
- Business is concentrating in two ways, with opposing effects on liquidity. As a financial center, London is attracting more of the global volume as a virtuous circle causes the most liquid market to attract even more liquidity. At the same time, business is consolidating with fewer dealers—largely through international mergers, but partly through expansion by the leaders into more and more markets—into fewer, larger international organizations. In addition, the larger dealers are consolidating their dealing rooms to capitalize on communications efficiency. While each dealer ends up trading more through a single dealing room as a result, fewer counterparties clearly mean less diversity of opinion and trading behavior; and this means less market depth, resiliency, and liquidity. Nonetheless, while mergers can reduce liquidity in the short run, there remains a long list of banks with modest levels of penetration that can, in the longer term, provide additional liquidity.
- Electronic brokers, which have displaced voice brokers for a swath of interbank spot market activity, have also eaten into some of the business that major banks executed on an over-the-counter (OTC) basis with regional banks, reducing the number of counterparties that they deal with directly. By concentrating more of the most actively traded currencies through a transparent exchange, electronic brokers have

removed from the major, upstream dealers their direct access to the information content of those trades.

Volatility

Foreign exchange dealers rely on a certain amount of market volatility to be profitable. Absolute stability means no trading opportunities while extreme movements mean dealers incur high risks. Here are some factors that have driven volatility recently and will surely influence it in the future:

- Changes in the distribution of trading volumes have changed the nature of a typical transaction. The growth in volume from institutional investors, hedge funds, and other financial transactions has provided more potential for rapid price movement as funds leverage or deleverage their investments, depending on their views or changes in market sentiment.
- Creation of the euro squashed volatility in European cross-trades to zero and cut total trading volumes, but could lead to an *increase* in volatility in other areas if investors', central banks', and other large traders' views of the euro relative to the U.S. dollar become unsettled.

Currency Options

Use of OTC currency options about tripled from 1985 to 1988. Since then, dealers and customers have become increasingly sophisticated in their use of options and now OTC options account for 5 percent of total volume. With greater sophistication comes higher expectations for currency options, and now projected demand is highest for tailored, nonvanilla options and options on exotic currencies.

The introduction of currency options "upped the ante" for dealers and customers alike who had to invest in specialized knowledge and technology. Dealers have generally taken one of two approaches to providing the specialization that is required:

- Centralize options and other derivatives expertise within a single unit that markets independently of the spot and forward business and provides service to the spot and forward customer dealers. This approach can lead to earning high-value business with sophisticated accounts that value expertise. It can also lead to failure to capture all the cross-selling opportunities with a dealer's spot and forward customers, because specialists are motivated, in this structure, to focus mainly on their own targets.

■ Embed currency option expertise within the spot and forward sales force. The drawbacks to this approach are that it can be expensive to train all salespeople thoroughly, and customer dealers and spot and forward sales representatives will vary in their ability to advise on complex currency option strategies.

We advise our clients:

■ All salespeople working with active accounts need to be fully conversant in currency options as at least one half of those trading over $10 billion in total trading volume use OTC options, as Table 1.11 shows.
■ These salespeople should be closely supported by specialists with expertise in the more complex and exotic options so the firm can serve the most sophisticated clients—and keep this capability on the spot and forward marketing team or closely tied to it via management and incentives.
■ Give customers what they want, how they want it. Three in five customers prefer to meet one on one with an options specialist, while over one third prefer a call from the specialist, as Table 1.12 shows.

Costs

Increasingly large investments in technology and talented research and salespeople have "upped the ante" and naturally led banks to find ways to cut costs that would increase their competitive edge. Since it is better to provide superior service to fewer customers than to provide an average level of service to a larger number of customers, the use of technology is a good way to reduce costs as well as increase their value with select customers by doing the following:

■ Use Web site "personalization" and metrics, together with the more finely tuned in-person coverage that these tools will enable.

TABLE 1.11 Use of Currency Options

Foreign Exchange Trading Volume	
Over $10 billion	55%
$5–$10 billion	44
$1–$5 billion	46
Under $1 billion	26

TABLE 1.12   Preferred Ways to Learn about Options Strategies

Method	
One-on-one meeting with a currency option specialist	58%
Seminars held by a bank or dealer for a broad audience of corporate clients	42
Customized presentations on option strategies for your company	39
Telephone call from currency option specialist	36
Weekly written updates on currency option strategies	22
Telephone call from generalist sales rep	14
One-on-one meeting with a generalist sales rep	13

- Centralize same time-zone dealing rooms, provided there is not a loss of key local market information in doing so.
- Control costs of salespeople by making clear decisions about the type and number of customers the firm will serve and the intensity and breadth of service it will provide.

FUTURE FUNDAMENTALS

The foreign exchange market will continue to evolve in dramatic ways over the next 5 to 10 years. In addition to the key trends just listed, here are some other themes that will play out in the near future, with significant consequences:

- Emerging market currencies will continue to develop, despite the chilling effect of Russian devaluation and Southeast Asia's slump in 1998. Emerging economies themselves suffered severely, and talk of reimposing capital controls increased. Nonetheless, the aspiration to economic growth necessitates at least partial convertibility to attract investment capital. As these aspirations will not go away, trading in emerging market currencies will continue to grow and dealers willing to position the risk should be prepared to serve this need.
- Regulation of hedge funds' trading—through a transactions tax, forced transparency of investors, and limitations on leverage—could dampen or reverse volume growth that has been driven by leveraged arbitrage.
- Regulation won't end speculation (which is, after all, an essential lubricant to all markets), but it may cause a severe downdraft in volumes and profitability for dealers that are narrowly focused on this segment of the customer business and place even more of a premium on a diversified base of strong customer relationships.

▓ Further consolidation of the world's banking industry may exacerbate structural problems with market liquidity, and may help increase liquidity by having more worldwide, world-class dealers operating in all currencies and all markets worldwide.

▓ Additional advances in electronic broking and direct dealing with banks will occur—including the development of multibank pricing systems. As a result, dealers will need to adjust their trading and sales staffs accordingly, not just in quantity, but definitely also in quality.

▓ Customers will continue to obtain more and better information and decision-making tools through advances in interactive use of dealers' Web sites. Dealers' sales strategies need to evolve in parallel, and salespeople need to become "experts in expert systems" and co-workers with customers in using information to inform trading strategies.

With these themes in mind, the foreign exchange dealers on tomorrow's list of Top 10 "global" dealers will be:

▓ Flexible, and ready to respond to many different changes.

▓ Upwardly mobile in the quality of sales coverage for those accounts that continue to merit superb service.

▓ Cohesive, drawing together all their capabilities to provide all-around superior service in foreign exchange and related functions—across sales, trading, research, back office, credit, custody, and cash management.

Successful foreign exchange dealers will respond to the evolution of the market by modifying their trading, coverage, and other services appropriately. Doing so will add to the pressures imposed on their competitors and vice versa. But as much as the business of foreign exchange will continue to evolve, the primary objective will remain the same: Being a Top 3 dealer to all or almost all targeted accounts is, and will continue to be, essential for success.

CHAPTER 2

Fixed Income

Steven L. Glick, John F. Mahoney, and Timothy R. Sangston

BOND DEALING

Achieving and sustaining great importance as a dealer of choice to a carefully defined and appropriately selected, sizable group of investors is the only way to succeed in the intensely competitive business of fixed-income dealing for institutional investors.

As we consult on business strategy with the leading fixed-income dealers all around the world, our research and experience continue to demonstrate our central rule of thumb that is both simple and profound: To achieve great success, you have to be a Very Important, or Top 3, dealer to each of your chosen customers. To paraphrase the athlete's mantra, when you're not one of the Top 3 dealers for a particular institution, you are merely "playing to play." It's only when you focus on being one of that institution's Top 3 dealers that you are really "playing to *win*."

Being a major institutional dealer is too dangerous financially to do anything but play to win and that means being a Top 3 dealer for a large proportion of your selected customers. In this chapter, the decisive centrality of this simple and profound proposition will be developed with extensive evidence. But before turning to the crucial central thesis, let's be clear on two critical and apparent "tangents":

1. Dealers must be alert for profitable opportunities to take proprietary trading positions. But in a professional market with extensive transparency,

---

Steven L. Glick wrote "Bond Dealing," John F. Mahoney wrote "Asian Bond Dealing," and Timothy R. Sangston wrote "Japanese Bonds."

dealers also must stay in balance as they combine proprietary trading and customer trading. Dealers need to avoid outright conflicts of interest and stay well within the bounds of tolerance of appropriate behavior, as their institutional customers see it. Otherwise, they will put themselves "in the penalty box" and be excluded from important business.

2. The profitability of distributing new issues can be considerable. But the key to winning the mandate to underwrite new issues in the primary market is the demonstrated ability to sell or placement power in the secondary market. So the ability to distribute new issues is a function of the particular dealer's being a Top 3 dealer in the secondary market to a sizable group of institutions.

It all comes back to the essential factor for success: Be a Top 3 dealer for a sufficiently large group of institutional investors who are carefully chosen for focus because they want most in a dealer just what you do best as a dealer. The best relationships are always mutually beneficial win-win or symbiotic relationships.

This chapter focuses on the importance of being a Top 3 dealer and how to achieve this coveted position:

- Making fast and competitive *markets* in each of the instruments that are important to your chosen group of institutional customers.
- Delivering continuously effective *sales service,* by understanding customers' individual objectives and constraints, relating trade ideas to their needs, and demonstrating a long-term commitment through a range of actions.
- Providing focused *research* on the debt instruments that your chosen customers invest in most actively.
- Providing consistently superior *back-office* clearance and processing.

The objective in providing each of these "service modules" is to nurture and sustain a Very Important, or Top 3 relationship with each institution that is a natural fit with your particular capabilities and strategic commitments as a dealer.

Before developing and documenting our concepts for being successful in this very demanding, highly professional market, let's examine some of the sweeping changes that have occurred in the fixed-income markets over the past 20 years to show how we got where we are.

As everyone knows, the bond markets have expanded greatly in scale and simultaneously increased very rapidly in complexity and intensity. If you could time travel back to the typical bond trading floor of the 1970s, the most obvious difference from a contemporary one would be the poverty of information. Almost all price discovery was by phone, as only a few types of bonds' prices had become available on green brokerage screens. Sales representatives wrote out 3-ply trade tickets, trade assistants kept positions by hand, and analysts kept point-and-figure price charts by hand. Large elements of the dealing room environment that are taken for granted today would have been nonexistent.

Here are some indicators of how the markets have changed:

- U.S. Treasury securities outstanding have grown 700 percent—from $425 billion in 1977 to a high of $3.5 trillion in 1996 and $3.3 trillion at the beginning of 2000.
- The number of interest rate futures and options contracts traded at the Chicago Board of Trade grew more than 3,000 times from just 32,000 in 1977 to a high of 112 million in 1998 and 90 million in 1999.
- Mortgage- and asset-backed securities did not even exist in 1977. At the beginning of 2000, outstanding mortgage-backed securities were $2.3 trillion and asset-backed securities were $700 billion.
- The notional principal amount of outstanding interest rate swaps rose from zero in 1977, to $1.5 billion in 1989, to $58 billion in 1999—up almost 40 times in just 10 years.
- Floating-rate notes, zero-coupon bonds, and Brady bonds are all new, and there is a much wider acceptance of high yield or "junk" bonds.
- Corporate and nongovernment bonds outstanding have been growing in importance and are now approaching one half of the total outstandings around the world, up from just over one third 20 years ago.
- Megabuyers have sprung up that individually trade volumes almost unthinkable a few years ago. As a result, in most bond markets around the world, 10 percent of the active institutional investors execute nearly 50 percent of the total trading volume and 20 percent of the institutions execute 80 percent.
- The measurement of duration is new in bond research, and so is the routine use of convexity and embedded option analyses.
- Dedicated portfolios, cash matching, and immunizing portfolios are new, as is dynamic hedging.
- Bloomberg and other third-party systems terminals are now in almost all investors' offices around the world. Twenty years ago, they did not exist.

The number and power of change-forces working in concert is impressive and has transformed the bond market. Here are some of the forces for change:

- *Information.* It is now possible and even normal for a well-informed investor to know more than his or her dealers can know. Trading systems and news services have made once privileged information such as current prices, central bank actions, and credit analyses available to all investors with "just the push of a few buttons." Now the market is connected and interconnected as never before. Technology has brought the quality of information, as well as the quantity of it—and the speed at which it can be delivered—to unprecedented levels. In the relationship between investor and dealer, there has been a huge shift in who now knows what—and when they know.
- *Technology.* Online capabilities in trading and research are proliferating rapidly. As we agree with our clients, "We ain't seen nothing yet!" Until very recently, dealers and investors alike were ambivalent about the benefits of technology. Computers were used almost grudgingly and were often double-checked by hand. (Just 10 years ago, we witnessed staff at a major Tokyo dealing firm double-checking the computer with an abacus!)
- *Increasing competition.* As dealers augment their own capabilities, they put great pressure on each and all the other competitors to "meet or beat" their efforts. And their competitors do respond by getting better— to keep up or get ahead—forcing every other dealer to get better and better. That is why our clients agree with us that they not only need to know their customers, but they also need to know their competitors.

  Bond dealers are making greater and greater inroads into markets outside their home markets. And a few dealers have built a significant market presence in almost every market around the world.

  At the same time, there has been a massive rationalization of and reduction in the number of dealers used by each institutional investor. Investors are now using fewer firms to execute their transactions even though there is a larger dealer pool from which to choose. This rationalization of dealers is most dramatic in Europe where the typical investor now uses 13 dealers, down from 21 several years before the European Monetary Union (EMU). This trend will likely continue around the world as electronic trading becomes increasingly accepted; tight spreads will get even tighter, and investors will demand even more from their dealers.
- *Massive global deregulation.* The breadth and scope of deregulation— from "Big Bang" in London and "Le Petite Bang" in France to the removal of Glass-Steagall in the United States and the easing of Article 65 in Japan—has brought new dealers and new investors to the market and increased the global nature of the business. Markets are opening up in

almost every country. This has brought massive growth of the capital markets in parts of the world not previously on most investors' radar screens, particularly eastern Europe, Latin America, and Asia.

■ *Derivatives.* The development of interest rate swaps and increasing numbers of standardized derivatives and more sophisticated OTC products have allowed investors to manage their portfolios with greater rigor and precision and enabled dealers to assume larger and larger positions while reducing their risk profiles. The positions the typical dealer now carries would dwarf the positions of even the most aggressive dealers 20 years ago.

■ *Investor change of focus.* A combination of factors drove what may be the biggest and most fundamental change of all: Investors now focus on total return rather than on yield. Some of these factors include:

- The growth of pension funds and mutual funds.
- The increasing demand for investment performance relative to a benchmark.
- Regulatory changes (such as FASB statement Nos. 87, 115, and 133) that require investors to discount future benefit payments at market interest rates and to mark-to-market their positions.
- Availability of data. Naturally, with our annual research on every dealer in every market on every product, we are glad to point out the benefits of having systematic, objective data on each and every competitor on each competitive variable in each market for each product every year.

■ *Competitive dynamics.* Figure 2.1, showing U.S. government bond dealers' market penetrations in 1977 versus 2000, illustrates the massive changes in the bond-dealing community. One dozen dealers did not survive. Many dealers merged or simply went out of business, including A.G. Becker, Loeb Rhoades, Discount, Blyth Eastman Dillon, Weeden, and First Pennco; others have grown substantially.

Among the 20 largest dealers in 1977, more than half are no longer in business. Many other smaller dealers fell by the wayside, including White Weld, Bache Halsey Stuart, Continental Illinois, Pollock, Drexel, and Kidder Peabody.

Figure 2.2 shows the significant changes in Europe. Equally striking are the changes Figure 2.3 shows among investors in Japan. The same Darwinian phenomenon is evident in all the major markets around the world.

With this background perspective on the extraordinary changes in the scale and intensity in the dynamics of the bond market, let's focus now on

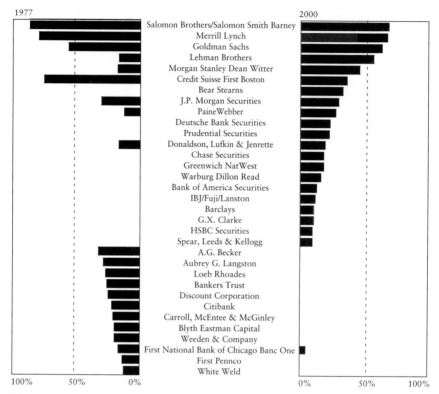

FIGURE 2.1 23 years of change. Market penetration—U.S. Government Bonds.

the salient importance for success as an institutional bond dealer of being a Top 3 dealer for your chosen customers.

TOP 3 DEALER STATUS IS KEY

The typical investor concentrates most volume with just three dealers, so those dealers on an investor's "short list" do not have to compete for every trade solely on price. They will be treated as a semipartner by the investor and will have an important competitive advantage of insight and information on the investor's main holdings and understanding of how they are being changed through shifts in portfolio strategy. Their most important

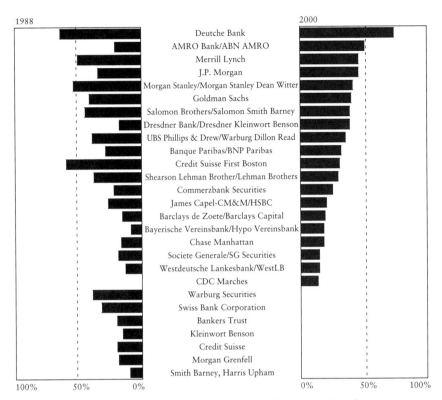

FIGURE 2.2 Change in market penetration. European Bond investors.

dealers get the first call, and have a deeper knowledge and understanding of the decisions that each institution might make to buy or to sell.

Knowing about this "almost business" and when it can be "made to happen" is the key to profitable market-making for any intermediary. That is why it is crucial for a dealer to achieve Top 3 status with each of a chosen group of institutional investor customers. Price is always important, but with Top 3 relationships, the quality of service almost always takes precedence over price.

Since the cost of service by salespeople, the cost of researchers, and the cost of market-making decline only gradually as dealers' relationships go down in importance from first to second to third, and so on, while the volume of business done declines far more rapidly, virtually all the profits made by dealers are made by those few that have achieved Top 3 status with

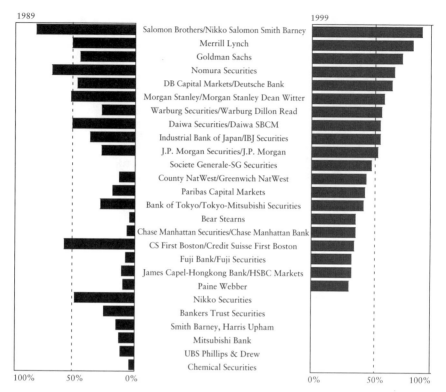

FIGURE 2.3   Changes in market penetration. International Japanese Bond investors.

each particular institutional investor. Figures 2.4 and 2.5 show volume and profitability generally decline as a dealer's status declines.

Note that the expected profitability of being a lead dealer is actually less than that of being a second dealer. This comes about because some investors try to exploit their largest dealers by obliging them to provide preferential "new issue" business as well as doing profit-free trading for them in the secondary market, as a rational trade-off for having that 30 percent of their trading volume and the repetitive opportunity for "getting the other side" by trading out those transactions to other investors. Being first can be a smart and symbiotic relationship. But it can also be a loss-maker: the victory a dealer cannot afford to win. That's why you should evaluate the profitability of each account on a "total business done" basis.

With some accounts, the best profit position for a dealer is second or third, but almost universally the key to success is to be one of the Top 3

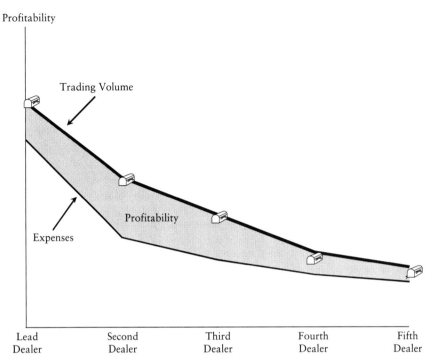

FIGURE 2.4 Profitability follows importance.

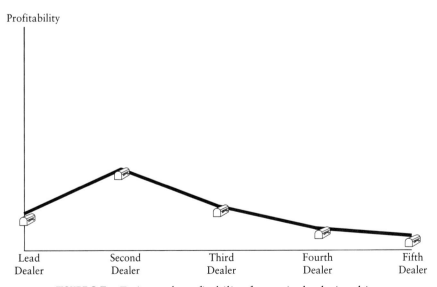

FIGURE 2.5 Estimated profitability for typical relationship.

dealers. The typical fixed-income investor executes two-thirds of its total annual volume with its three most important dealers. Said another way, each of the three leading dealers for the typical investor executes five times more volume of trading than each of the next ten dealers executes. Figure 2.6 shows this distribution graphically.

For the typical fixed-income investor, the lead dealer executes about 50 percent more volume than does the second dealer. In turn, the second dealer executes about 33 percent more volume than the third. This pattern is shown in Figure 2.7. Dealers with tier relationships are usually just breaking even, and those with lesser relationships are likely in the red.

The Top 3 phenomenon is the dominant reality in managing a profitable bond dealer business. The same Top 3 rule governs with reliable consistency in all the U.S. debt markets, where there are profoundly different types of debt instruments:

■ High-yield bonds where sophisticated credit research and new issue supply are crucial and U.S. government issues where credit is absolute and all dealers have equal access to issuance at auction.
■ Treasury bills, which are highly liquid and analytically simple, and exotic mortgage-backed issues that have complex embedded options and are often illiquid.

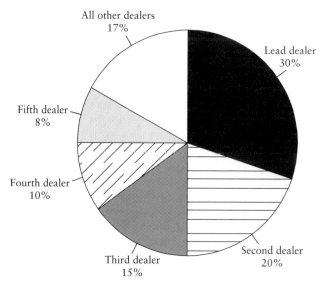

FIGURE 2.6   Percentage of total volume typically allocated to Top 3 dealers.

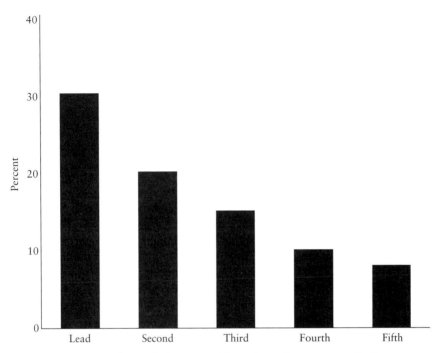

FIGURE 2.7 Volume declines significantly as importance declines.

The importance of a Top 3 dealer position also holds for various bond classes. As shown in Table 2.1, for every type of bond, investors conduct between half and three quarters of all their business with their Top 3 dealers.

The proportion of trading volume captured by the Top 3 dealers has also been stunningly consistent over many years. Figure 2.8 shows the almost constant proportion of trading volume American investors in U.S. government securities executed with their Top 3 dealers in each of the past 10 years.

While there are some year-to-year variations, Figure 2.9 shows the persistence over time of Top 3 dominance with the domestic investors in two other major markets that are very far apart in geography, culture, regulation, and time zones: Japan and the United Kingdom.

The centrality of the Rule of Top 3 persists year after year in every debt market around the world, as the typical investor uses between 8 and 15 dealers and executes between half and three quarters of his or her volume with just three dealers. Differences from around the world are shown in Table 2.2 based on our worldwide research.

TABLE 2.1   Top 3 Volume in All Types of Bonds (U.S. bond investors)

	Total Number of Dealers Used	Business Done with Top 3 Dealers
U.S. government	6.4	74%
U.S. agency securities	5.9	76
Corporate bonds	8.1	66
Mortgage-backed securities	6.7	71
Asset-backed securities	6.2	74
High-yield bonds	11.0	52
Commercial paper	8.4	74
Non-U.S. dollar bonds	8.2	68
Emerging market bonds	8.4	64

In credit bonds, there is an importance to the "seat." In other words, being at a firm with a large supply of new issues can have a significant impact on a dealer's likelihood of servicing its customers well. There is an old joke in the bond market about a firm that had a particularly large supply of new issues: Give one of their sales representatives a phone and they can

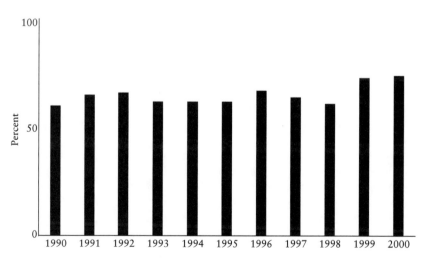

FIGURE 2.8   Top 3 volume—consistently 60 to 75 percent. U.S. Government Securities.

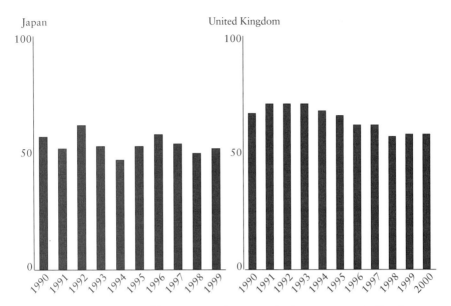

FIGURE 2.9 Percentage of business with Top 3 dealers. Domestic fixed-income investors.

make a million dollars, but give them two phones and they can make two million dollars.

The question then becomes, how important is new issue supply to achieving and obtaining overall customer satisfaction and Top 3 status in customer-dealer relationships? The answer comes from correlating dealers' new issue league table status with the Greenwich Quality Index, a measure of overall customer satisfaction derived from evaluative measures in sales coverage, market-making, research, back-office, and other issues. The answer is that the magnitude of the correlation indicates a strong relationship with a shared variance of between one quarter and one half. New issues have a strong and influential effect on the perceived quality of a dealer's franchise.

Nonetheless, competition to be on an investor's short list is obviously keen. Investors have lots of alternatives, and they know it. Any dealer that manages to become one of an investor's Top 3 dealers, can get bumped down in importance because competition is so intense and because shifting patronage from one dealer to another is remarkably easy and low cost to the investor.

Because Top 3 status is so very important to profitability, organize all your organization's resources on making sure each target account already is,

TABLE 2.2 Top 3 Volume around the World (number of dealers used and trading volume concentration)

	Total Number of Dealers Used	Business Done with Top 3 Dealers
Australia/New Zealand	13.6	59%
Austria	14.6	51
Belgium	14.6	53
Canada	9.4	63
China, Hong Kong, Macau	13.4	62
France	11.5	55
Germany	10.3	60
Ireland	11.1	53
Italy	13.7	54
Japan	15.9	52
Latin America	11.6	64
Luxembourg	14.8	51
Middle East	8.1	71
Netherlands	11.8	57
Nordics	8.5	75
Philippines	12.3	61
Singapore	11.3	67
South Korea	13.3	59
Spain, Portugal	12.4	60
Switzerland	8.3	69
Taiwan	11.3	71
United Kingdom	11.3	57
United States	11.2	74

or is well on the way to becoming, a Top 3 relationship. If your research and trading capabilities and your product strengths are in strong alignment with your account's needs and objectives, becoming a Top 3 dealer and staying there will be a natural win-win for both dealer and investor. If it's not a natural good fit, be rational and ruthless. Stop trying and move on. Rededicate your valuable and limited resources where you can and will achieve a win-win relationship and advance to a profitable Top 3 dealer position.

The surest way for a dealer to prosper in the institutional bond business is to define its target market correctly and work to become a Very Important dealer to all customers within that target group.

SELECTING CUSTOMERS

To achieve real success and the coveted Top 3 status, each dealer must select the institutions for which it intends to become a Top 3 dealer. Select very carefully those institutions for which you can realistically expect to achieve that status because your capabilities and resources as a dealer really match the wants and needs of those particular institutions; and then concentrate systematically and unrelentingly on "making it happen."

The client selection process will surely be based on trial and error, as the astute dealer probes for a good fit. The key to success is being rational and realistic, both by being selective and by trying harder and harder again with the chosen ones. Sort out your customers regularly, say once a year, into categories:

- Winners—where you already are a Top 3 dealer.
- Contenders—where you can soon expect to achieve Top 3 status.
- Losers—where the fit is, for one or more reasons, simply not right.

Next:

- Drop the Losers.
- Make certain the Winners continue to be winners.

and . . .

- Select those Contenders you can convert into Winners—if you devote the right resources—and then be certain to direct those resources so you will make and sustain the conversion.

One of the most useful exercises managers can do is to have each of their sales representatives put down in writing his business goals with each of his customers:

- With which investors does the sales representative want to be the first (or lead) dealer?
- With which is the objective to be second or third dealer?
- With which will it be okay to be a Top 5 dealer?
- With which is it okay to be just a Top 10 dealer?

And then spell out for each investor the specific actions that are needed to achieve the firm's business goal with this particular customer. We are sometimes surprised that this basic level of business planning does not happen and even more surprised by the positive reaction when we suggest it to sales managers who are not yet pursuing this approach.

This exercise is powerful and effective for two reasons. First, it forces sales representatives to recognize their own limitations. As we counsel our clients, no one, not even Superman, can be a Top 3 dealer to 10 major institutional investors. While some of the most skillful and effective senior sales representatives we know can be Top 3 dealers to five or six investors, the typical sales representative should aim to be Very Important to only two or three investors.

Second, the exercise gives management a reality check, enabling the manager to compare each sales representative's goals and expectations with what their customers think is reality and what is a realistic objective for their relationship. We recommend to our clients that this be done annually in person as part of a formal Relationship Review with each customer.

As an investor's needs and interests change, regular relationship reviews alert dealers to any important changes and give them the opportunity to develop stronger relationships. A brief, but well-planned Relationship Review can have positive impact, especially if followed up promptly and effectively.

We suggest these guidelines for a superior Relationship Review:

- Five minutes to review the major trades the investor has done over the past six months or year, looking at both the positive and negative impacts.
- Ten minutes to learn of any changes in the investor's investment situation and his portfolio strategy.
- Ten minutes to discuss what has gone well and what has *not* gone well with the relationship. This is the time for a manager to get specific information about what the investor hopes to get from doing business with his firm.
- The meeting concludes with agreement on two or three specific action steps for each side to take.
- The manager should then send a letter confirming what the dealer will do—and then make certain each and every promise is fulfilled on time.

One question we're often asked is, "How many customers is enough to build a strong business?" Since it is far more important to be better than to be bigger, we turn this question around: "How many institutions can you realistically commit to being a Top 3 dealer?" Usually, we agree with Mies Van der Rohe's famous dictum about architecture: "Less is more!"

In our consulting with dealers, we again and again recommend that their growth and development focus should be not on adding more new customers (which competitive people so often try to do), but should instead be on becoming more important to particular investors where the match is good between what the dealer does best and the investor values most. The key to success for most dealers is more better relationships, not *more* relationships.

PRODUCT MIX

It is impossible for dealers to be important in all bond products. In addition to deciding which customers to target, the key is to decide with which products to conduct significant business, and which to let alone. An essential element for success in bond dealing is recognized leadership in several products. If investors understand the two or three products that make up a dealer's "calling card," they are more likely to use the firm for these products. Visible strength in a few products that really matter to the particular investor provides the essential first step in developing Very Important relationships.

Product mix must be well thought out and consistent with the strengths for which the firm intends to be recognized. As we advise our clients, "Know yourself and how you intend to be known by your customers."

Try to carry positions or inventories in a range of products that directly match your chosen customers' needs. Dealers that are important to their customers in a full range of complementary products are most likely to be very important overall. For example, a dealer that is important in U.S. mortgage-backed securities could also develop a franchise in U.S. government securities; a dealer that is important in Brady bonds could well seek product leadership in local currency bonds in emerging markets.

RESEARCH

As credit and market analysis become increasingly complex, research becomes more important than ever to customers. Research is now accepted as a requirement of doing business. Providing relevant, useful research gives sales representatives a powerful selling tool. It shows customers that the firm understands their goals and objectives and is responsive to their needs.

Although the Internet and dealers' extra-Net sites now disseminate an avalanche of research to investors, the same tried-and-true rules apply. Here is what we recommend for making research materials highly effective:

■ Review and update the customer mailing list frequently. Comparing the mailing list with the "active customer" list and culling research free riders ensures that research goes where it has the best chance of being rewarded with business.

Using research as a door opener can be an effective tool, but sales representatives need to follow through and take advantage of the opportunity their research provides. Evergreen free samples demean a dealer's researchers and depreciate the perceived value of the research in the view of investors. (As we talk to investors, the second most frequent complaint we hear is that the bulk of the research they receive is not relevant to their particular needs. Literally, most research is not used or read by investors; it's simply thrown away or deleted from the investor's PC screen.) To put it bluntly: The value of research is never more than its value in use by the investor.

- Communicate and coordinate with individual sales representatives. Keep them "in the loop," so they know what research is going to which customers. That way, they can actively use the research throughout the sales and service process. When researchers and sales managers work closely with sales representatives to show them how to use research and track its use—and when communication with accounts is coordinated—it strengthens both research and sales. Only then will firms earn sufficient business to pay for the expensive research they provide. By the same token, dealers need to monitor use of the research they offer electronically. While some privacy issues surround the use of metrics, it is essential for a dealer to know which investors use its research so they can both better customize it for the customers and leverage the significant investment they make in the research.

- Buttress written research with direct client access to the economists and credit analysts who produce the written product. A trend over the past few years has been for investors not to want to know *where* a dealer thinks the market is going—for they are too often wrong—but *why* they think the market is going to go up or down. It is not surprising that direct and frequent access to market researchers closely correlates in most markets with being a Top 3 dealer.

- Convey the main message quickly with eye-catching graphics and a prominent summary. Good writing and careful editing help ensure that the research is read. Similarly, always have native speakers translate research into other language to avoid simple, but annoying errors.

- Focus on the types of research that are on the "leading edge" and develop recognized expertise in them. We urge our clients to keep improving research for targeted customers because in competitive markets, the bar is constantly rising.

- Monitor competitors' research. We encourage our clients to regularly ask their best customers for examples of other dealers' best research. (Sam Walton of Wal-Mart did this best by "scouring the competition," shopping at competitors' stores and then using their best display and product ideas at his own store.)

When we look at the importance of research we often see a chart that looks like Figure 2.10. The value of research, however, is its value in use. Ask always: How does this research significantly help important customers achieve their objectives in their investment process?

Much as we admire the intellectual value of the best research now being produced, such "old-time" factors as prompt response to inquiries, making good use of customers' time (always their most precious and most limited resource), and effective follow-up on past recommendations are often decisive in determining how investors value research—and what they pay for it.

TRADING

When we ask investors in our worldwide research what is the most important reason they trade with a specific dealer, their answer is often "Price!" As any trader can tell you, this is no surprise: You do win business one trade

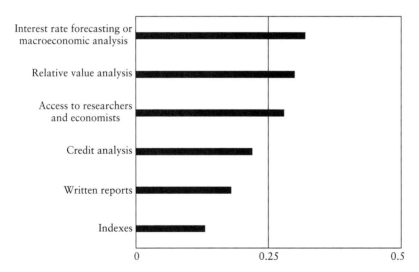

FIGURE 2.10 Importance of research factors—correlation with Top 3 dealer status.

at a time and price does matter. However, prices for most types of bonds are "in the market" and all dealers know they must be competitive on price, so quotes on almost all types of instruments are very similar.

Finding the right balance of wins and losses is an integral part of the art of trading. We advise our clients: "You don't ever want to win *all* the business" because any dealer that wins every bid and offer is simply buying the business and cannot be doing "good business." The key is to find the right balance between being not competitive enough and being too competitive. Here's a simple check to see if you have got the mix about right. If your customers generally ask three dealers for a quote, winning as much as two thirds of the trades means you are probably being too aggressive on price. If you are winning only one sixth of the trades, you are probably not quoting aggressively enough.

In the long, long string of trades done every day, each dealer needs to choose where to be competitive and where to be aggressive. Just as a dealer's trading strategy adjusts with customers and markets, so should pricing adjust to how much you want the specific piece of business. Focus on your product strengths and on your targeted, most important customers.

In determining a dealer's importance to a particular investor, the speed of quoting is usually more important than the sharpness of the quotes. This result should not be surprising as most investors find dealers' market-making abilities to be almost interchangeable. Because major dealers will all be competitive on price, the speed of responding to quotes—a measure of traders' skill as well as the coordination between sales representatives and traders—is generally more closely correlated with being a Top 3 dealer than is price. Speed of quoting is also a key determinant in electronic trading, as firms with the fastest responses to bids and offers so often win trades at the expense of slower firms.

Figure 2.10 shows how the various measures of dealers' market-making correlate with being a Top 3 dealer. Again, note that speed of response is more important than competitive pricing.

Based on our research into how investors rate dealers on market making, here are some useful guidelines:

- Respond quickly to requests for bids and offers. With widely traded instruments, one firm's price quote will usually not be much different from another's. In these instances, speed in making the quote becomes more important than price, so "getting there first" can make the difference.
- Be perceived as slightly "above average" on price competitiveness by customers that are already important and others that are chosen to become important. A dealer's most important customers and those targeted for a major upgrade in relationship should get better quotes.

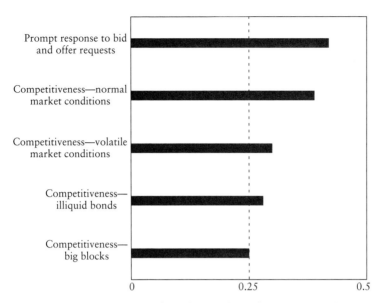

FIGURE 2.11 Importance of market making factors—correlation with Top 3 dealer status.

- Hold positions of sufficient size in your chosen product lineup to compete aggressively for the business of targeted investors.

Allocation of new issues is another part of the art of trading. With new issues often oversubscribed several times over, dealers need to use their supply to maximum advantage by distributing the new issues first to priority customers. The goal is to be fair in the distribution to priority customers without being too democratic. A recommendation we have given to many dealers is to simply coordinate which investors should receive how much of their new issue requests between the sales and capital market desks. As noted, we are occasionally surprised when this is not happening and equally surprised by the positive reception to the idea by dealers who are not doing so.

In the secondary market, because investors remember which dealers they purchased newly issued bonds from and because investors feel dealers too often do not stand ready to make bids for bonds they have previously sold, it is especially important for dealers to show continuing trading support for their own issues. We therefore measure investors' perceptions of dealers who do not.

SELLING BY LISTENING

Listening is something almost everyone thinks he or she knows how to do. But as we meet with investors, the complaint we hear most frequently is that dealers do not fully understand each investor's real needs. The perception from the investors' viewpoint is that most dealers apparently do not care about them as individuals and consider them just an interchangeable means to the dealer's own end. It is not surprising, then, that investors often respond by treating dealers as interchangeable, too.

Good listening means approaching every conversation with customers with genuine interest in learning and understanding their needs, and taking the appropriate constructive action promptly. Really good listening *begins* after the conversation has *ended*. Only then can dealers demonstrate they have really heard what the investor has said as they respond with research and trade ideas targeted to the investor's specific needs.

Listening to investors is as much a culling process as it is a selling process. Having a thorough understanding of an investor's needs helps a dealer:

- Learn whether the investor has the potential to be part of a mutually beneficial Top 3 relationship. Do the investor's interests align with the products the dealer most wants to trade? Will the investor provide the dealer with unusually valuable liquidity or market information?
- Learn if there is a realistic opportunity for a win-win relationship. Can we meet this particular investor's needs enough to earn Top 3 dealer status? How?

If the natural match is good, we advise dealers to invest the time to determine creative ways to show each investor what they will do to win that business.

We recommend sales managers have each salesperson write down each investor's investment objective and portfolio strategy and then send the write-ups to the customers for a critique. This simple practice may make your salespeople somewhat nervous, but it forces effective listening and it illustrates your desire to fully understand each investor's objectives. In addition, it can significantly help you become more important to customers because you can evaluate effectively and directly whether you are on target, and if not, how to get on target.

Our research on tens of thousands of relationships between dealers and investors, shows that a superior sales representative can make up for an average trader, but that a superior trader cannot make up for an average sales representative. All else being equal in the overall context of a relationship, selling service is more important than market-making.

Superior sales representatives possess the magical combination of raw smarts; genuine interest in understanding each customer's real needs; ability to harness a firm's research and market-making resources to serve each customer; high intensity and desire to succeed; excellent person-to-person relationship skills; and a sense of humor. When we examine what is most important in sales coverage, we see a chart that looks like the following Figure 2.12.

We give our clients the following advice to enable them to increase their effectiveness in sales and service:

- Concentrate on finding specific, practical ways to do more business with your current customers. The common and natural inclination of most salespeople is to try to do business with *new* customers. However, this extensive sales effort is almost always in conflict with the intensive sales effort that is so productive of Top 3 relationships.
- Focus on your strengths. Dealers will have the most success when they do more and better what they already do well.

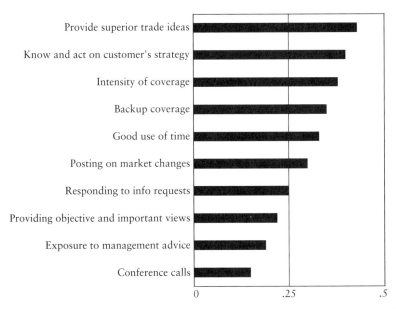

FIGURE 2.12 Importance of sales factors—correlation with Top 3 dealer status.

- In soliciting new business, remember that investors are already busy and feel well served by the dealers they have already chosen and know. To displace one of these already chosen dealers, you will need to give the investor strong reasons.
- Investors feel overwhelmed by "macho" sales representatives who approach them. Investors often have specific reasons for not trading with individual dealers. (Many investors' memories of bad experiences are understandably long.) Therefore, before the first contact, learn as much as you can about each prospect's particular ways of doing business, as well as any history they may have had with your firm.
- Leverage successes. Every great relationship was built one step at a time. A dealer who is successful with a "starter" business based on one special product should then focus *with* the investor on the next best thing to do together.
- Given the importance indicated in Figure 2.12, be sure customers know and are comfortable with their backup sales representative. High-quality backup sales coverage is vital, and in most markets it is one of the most highly correlated factors to being a Top 3 dealer.
- Sell to multiple levels. Another important way to institutionalize relationships is to develop them not only with portfolio managers, but also with traders and the institution's most senior executives.
- Entertain important customers regularly. Dealers sometimes forget that their salespeople usually earn a multiple of what their customers earn. Something as simple as theater tickets or ringside seats to a sold-out sporting event can reap benefits far beyond their cost. Small gestures like this go far to build the person-to-person relationship that in turn enhances the professional business relationship.
- Know where you stand in relation to the competition. An outside, objective evaluation shows what you do best; the areas where there has been real improvement; and any areas where you need to improve.

Finally, as every investor recognizes and every successful dealer knows, the salesperson is the frontline "make-it-happen" manager of each relationship and the orchestrator-entrepreneur who pulls it all together to build mutually profitable Top 3 relationships.

Even as we move into an environment with more and more trading online, the simple and best predictor of how much money a dealer will make remains how often it is a Very Important, or Top 3, dealer to its customers. In fact, the more commoditized the bond business becomes, the more important it will be to be a Very Important dealer to a carefully selected group of customers because service elements—not price—will more and more differentiate a dealer.

Asian Bond Dealing

During the past 5 years—which includes an extraordinary currency crisis that wreaked havoc throughout Southeast Asia—the international bond dealing business in that region of the world has gone through impressive change.

The research and consulting we do with our clients in Southeast Asia is concentrated on the dealers' business with investors like central banks, governments, domestic and foreign commercial bank portfolios, and large corporations and institutions that invest substantially in international bonds. In 1994, 60 percent of their portfolios were invested in U.S. government bonds and 40 percent in bonds issued within the Southeast Asian region. In just 5 years, that ratio has been completely reversed: 40 percent in U.S. Governments and 60 percent in regional bonds, as more accounts seek liquidity and credit in their local debt markets.

The impact on the dealers used has been substantial with particularly strong gains achieved by Deutsche Bank, HSBC Markets, and ABN AMRO (strong commercial banks with deep coverage in the local markets), as shown in Table 2.3.

The average number of dealers used has increased modestly—from 10.5 to 12.0—but the concentration of business with the typical institutional investor's most important dealers continues to be substantial and stable, as shown in Table 2.4.

Here's how the number of dealers used varies by size of portfolio and by country:

Portfolio Size

Over $1.0 billion	15.1
$250 million–$1.0 billion	12.5
Under $250 million	10.2

Geographic Area

Taiwan	11.3
South Korea	13.3
China, Hong Kong, Macau	13.4
Singapore	11.3
Philippines	12.3
Australia, New Zealand	13.6

The promise of explosive growth in the Asian bond markets has not been fulfilled. Since 1994, the *volume* of trading is up only 10 percent. Our

TABLE 2.3   Dealers in International Bonds

1994 Dealers	Used for International Bonds	Among Top 10 Dealers	1999 Dealers	Used for International Bonds	Among Top 10 Dealers
Merrill Lynch	48%	37%	Deutsche Bank	67%	48%
Goldman Sachs	42	32	HSBC Markets	66	52
Lehman Brothers	34	29	Salomon Smith Barney/		
			Citibank	65	47
CS First Boston	39	29	Merrill Lynch	64	48
Salomon Brothers	36	27	ABN AMRO	56	35
J.P. Morgan Securities	38	26	Morgan Stanley Dean		
			Witter	45	32
Nomura Securities	36	21	Goldman Sachs	43	35
Morgan Stanley	24	17	Credit Suisse First Boston	42	26
Deutsche Bank	30	16	Chase Manhattan Bank	41	25
Chemical Securities	22	16	J.P. Morgan	40	28
Swiss Bank Corporation	21	15	Warburg Dillon Read	39	31
Citibank	18	13	Societe General/SG		
			Securities	35	21
UBS Limited	20	12	Lehman Brothers	32	18
Barclays de Zoete Wedd	20	12	Barclays	30	15
Bankers Trust	18	11	Nomura	28	15
Warburg Securities	18	11	ING Barings	27	17
Daiwa Securities	23	10	Bear Stearns	24	10
Chase Manhattan	14	10	Paribas Capital Markets	23	14
Kidder, Peabody	15	10	Bank of America/BA		
			Securities	20	10
Paribas Capital Markets	17	10	Tokyo-Mitsubishi	18	3
Yamaichi Securities	21	10	Daiwa SBCM	16	8
HSBC Group	18	9	BNP Oakreed	16	8
Hambros Bank	14	9	PaineWebber	15	9
IBJ Securities	14	9	WestLB	14	5
NatWest Capital Markets	17	9	ANZ Bank	14	5
Mitsubishi Bank	12	8	Jardine Fleming	13	2
Prudential Securities	11	8	Commonwealth Bank of		
			Australia	12	6
Dresdner Bank	13	7	National Australia Bank	12	5
Long-Term Credit Bank	12	7	RBC Dominion	11	5
Bain	9	6	WestPac	11	7

TABLE 2.4   Concentration of Business

	1994	1999
First dealer	34%	32%
Second dealer	17	18
Third dealer	11	13
Total—Top 3 Dealers	61%	63%

research shows average trading volume for these accounts (excluding central banks) is up from $3.2 billion to $3.5 billion. (The composition of this volume is dominated by Australian issues—followed, at a distance, by Hong Kong and Japanese issues.) Most of the market volume is still being driven by a relatively small proportion of accounts. The central banks and local commercial bank portfolios continue to be the most active traders.

The rapid development of larger, deeper, stronger local debt capital markets—particularly in Hong Kong, Singapore, and Korea, but also in Thailand—has been driven not by government intervention, but by the institutional investors and the dealers developing the vital tools of liquidity: repo markets and swap markets. Governments have contributed with supportive changes in taxation and accounting.

The change dynamics—changes initiated by dealers, changes driven by institutional investors, and changes made by governments—are forceful, interactive, and continuing.

Japanese Bonds

The Japanese fixed-income market is similar to fixed-income markets elsewhere in the world in two important ways: the competitive landscape has changed dramatically over the past 10 years, and the key to dealer profitability is becoming a Very Important Top 3 dealer to a carefully chosen group of customers. The Japanese market, however, is intriguing because of its many profound *differences*—three of which are described in this chapter.

COMPETITIVE SITUATION

Before discussing the unique aspects of the Japanese fixed-income market, we need to point out one similarity: the significant change in the competitive environment. As Table 2.5 illustrates, in 1990 just one foreign dealer (Salomon Brothers) was among the Top 15 in Greenwich Associates' research. By 1999, seven foreign dealers had cracked the Top 15 and four of these were in the Top 10.

While Table 2.5 shows the changing competitive situation in all types of Japanese bonds taken together, a similar seismic shift has taken place in Japanese government bonds—a market traditionally owned by large domestic firms.

This dramatic change was driven by Japanese dealers' inability to react to two key market developments: declining interest rates and deregulation.

TABLE 2.5 Market Penetration in Japanese Bonds: Japanese Domestic Fixed-Income Investors

Dealer	1990	Dealer	1999
Daiwa Securities	72%	Daiwa SBCM	93%
Nomura Securities	72	Nomura Securities	86
Nikko Securities	68	IBJ Securities	75
Yamaichi Securities	61	**Nikko Salomon Smith Barney**	74
Industrial Bank of Japan	47	Tokyo-Mitsubishi Securities	60
Sumitomo Bank	43	Fuji Securities	49
Mitsubishi Bank	43	Dai-Ichi Kangyo Securities	48
Sanwa Bank	35	Sakura Securities	46
Kokusai Securities	31	**Goldman Sachs**	40
Long-Term Credit Bank	29	**Merrill Lynch**	39
New Japan Securities	28	Sanwa Securities	33
Dai-Ichi Kangyo Bank	23	**Morgan Stanley Dean Witter**	30
Salomon Brothers	23	**Deutsche Bank**	30
Sanyo Securities	22	**J.P. Morgan**	30
Fuji Bank	20	**Paribas Capital Markets**	30

As interest rates declined steadily in the 1990s to less than 1 percent by the end of the decade, Japanese institutional investors began to feel the pressure of international competition brought on by deregulation. For the first time, they were forced to compete on performance and to seek yield in non-government bond instruments, products in which they had little knowledge and experience.

At the same time, Japanese dealers were focusing on *distribution* (much of it at the *retail* level) and not on developing and delivering value-added service to their *institutional* clients. Japanese dealers—who had become comfortable in their control over the fixed-income market and in the strength and stability of their historical relationships with clients—had not developed the skills of their foreign competitors in credit research, derivatives, and product structuring.

As institutional investors began to shift assets away from Japanese government bonds and into "spread" products, they began to rely on foreign dealers to provide the product knowledge, research, and advice they needed on these instruments. Japanese dealers still had relationships with the most investors, but the *quality* or strength of these relationships and their relative importance to clients declined as investors shifted more and more of their assets into credit products.

This is not to suggest that foreign dealers in Japan employed foreign people. In fact, the people working at foreign institutions on credit analysis, product structuring, and derivatives were almost entirely *Japanese* people. Foreign institutions could attract unusual skill in this area because they reward individual contributions in value-added servicing and were therefore better equipped to serve the changing needs of institutional investors.

JOB ROTATION

One unique attribute of the Japanese fixed-income market—indeed of Japanese society as a whole—is mandatory job rotation. In theory, it makes sense: Every employee of a firm should develop generalist expertise by learning several jobs. In practice, however, it is devastating, particularly when your competitors are not following the same strategy.

For Japanese fixed-income dealers, self-imposed turnover among sales representatives virtually guaranteed that they would not be able to develop the understanding and mutual trust with their clients that are the hallmark of Top 3 relationships. Job rotation is particularly destructive in a business such as fixed-income, where clients rely heavily on their dealers for advice and information. Foreign dealers, who generally do not practice job rotation, clearly benefit as they can develop a keen understanding of their clients' needs and provide service to meet these needs.

Accordingly, we advise our fixed-income clients in Japan to abandon this tradition with respect to their salespeople. Several domestic dealers have taken our advice and have experienced substantially improved evaluations of their overall service quality.

NUMBER OF DEALERS USED

Another distinctive feature of the Japanese fixed-income market is the trend in the number of dealers used. As Table 2.6 shows, the average number of dealers used in Japan *increased* steadily from 1990 to 1999, while in the rest of the world the number *declined* or remained stable.

Outside Japan, the decline in the number of dealers used was driven in part by consolidation (there are simply fewer, but larger dealers now than in 1990) and by institutional investors' desire to be more efficient in their

TABLE 2.6 Average Number of Fixed-Income Dealers Used

	1990	1995	1999	Change
Japan	11.0	13.8	16.0	+5.0
Asia, excluding Japan	na	13.4	12.0	na
United States				
U.S. Treasury investors	7.5	6.4	6.5	−1.0
Corporate bond investors	7.8	8.0	8.1	+0.3
Mortgage-backed securities investors	7.1	6.7	6.7	−0.4
United Kingdom and continental Europe	17.3	15.2	12.6	−4.7

management of relationships. Having fewer dealers that can each provide a full range of services is much easier to manage than having many specialized relationships.

In Japan, however, the need for advice and information has become so important that investors feel obligated to establish more and more relationships to get necessary research and advice.

Also, since historical relationships play such an important role in Japanese business, investors are reluctant to sever a historical dealer relationship even if that dealer no longer provides the type of service they desire. The net effect is that Japanese investors continue to *expand* their dealers lists while investors in other parts of the world *rationalize* their lists. (This trend may not continue, however, as megamergers have begun among Japanese banks and securities firms. The merger between IBJ, Fuji Bank, and Dai-Ichi Kangyo Bank is the most highly publicized of the mergers, but several others have been announced.)

The implication for dealers is that it is comparatively easy to get onto a Japanese investor's dealing list, but increasingly difficult to break into their important short list. Accordingly, in our consulting with dealers, we advise our clients in Japan to develop and actively merchandise unique strengths in areas that will differentiate them from "the pack." Increasingly, these areas include credit bond underwriting, credit analysis and research, and product structuring.

DEMAND FOR ELECTRONIC TRADING

A final difference between the Japanese fixed-income market and the rest of the world is the lack of interest in electronic trading. As Table 2.7 illustrates,

TABLE 2.7 Demand for Electronic Trading:
Fixed-Income Investors

Country	Use of E-Trading Systems
Japan	5%
Asia, excluding Japan	20
United States (Treasury investors)	48
United Kingdom and continental Europe	25

Japanese investors have been slow to embrace fixed-income e-trading technology compared with their counterparts in the rest of the world, a surprising fact given that Japanese investors have been trading futures electronically for many years.

Japanese investors cite three primary reasons for not adopting e-trading of cash bonds:

1. *Concern over losing touch with their sales representatives.* As explained, Japanese investors are more dependent on their sales representatives than other investors because of their need for information and advice about products in which they have little experience. Accordingly, they are reluctant to use e-trading systems for fear that they will cut off their information supply. Investors in the United States and Europe, however, report that their relationships with sales representatives have *improved* with e-trading because it frees them up from "nuisance trades" and allows them to focus on value-added services.
2. *Accountability for errors.* When a trade is made over the phone and an error occurs, the dealer and the investor can fix the error through negotiation. (It isn't important who made the mistake, just that it gets resolved.) When a trade is made electronically, any error that occurs is the investor's fault, since he or she is the only party involved in the actual trade (prices are usually fed into the electronic trading system automatically). Japanese investors are not comfortable with this transparency and prefer to trade person-to-person, should a problem arise.
3. *Security concerns.* Japanese investors are rightly concerned that Internet security has not kept pace with the development of trading systems leaving a risk that sensitive information will get into the public domain. Experience in the United States suggests that these concerns have been

addressed, since no major breach of security has been reported despite the large number of trades being done over the Internet.

To overcome these obstacles, we advise fixed-income dealers to actively educate their customers about the benefits of trading online while convincing them that security concerns have been addressed. The experience in the United States and in several European countries suggests that once investors catch on, demand will grow rapidly.

CHAPTER 3

Derivatives

Frank H. Feenstra

Derivatives as we know them today are just shy of 20 years old, yet despite their tender age they have taken the financial world by storm and transformed it completely. Since their beginnings in the early 1980s, derivative products have increased geometrically in both number and complexity, and not surprisingly the business of selling them has changed as well. The ante has been raised in terms of the creativity needed to develop competitive products and the technical capabilities needed to structure them. But, while the evolution of the derivatives business has been remarkable, one thing has remained constant throughout: Innovation, the driving force behind modern-day derivatives applications, continues to be its lifeblood.

The phenomenal success of derivatives was made possible by several key economic events:

- Deregulation of the currency markets in the early to mid-1970s caused wide fluctuations in exchange rates.
- U.S. monetary policy changed in the late 1970s from managing interest rates (which led to comparatively stable interest rates) to managing the money supply (which drove interest rates up or down, thus making them unstable).
- A huge, inflation-driven runup in U.S. dollar interest rates in the early 1980s awoke companies and investors to the fact that interest rate fluctuations could have a big impact on their bottom line.

These economic and monetary policy changes created a new volatility, and with it the demand for a means to hedge against it.

Here is a brief history of the development of financial derivatives:

- In 1973, Fischer Black and Myron Scholes published their seminal paper on option pricing. It quickly became the cornerstone for the options markets and is still one of the most widely used financial models.
- Soon after publication of the Black-Scholes paper, financial futures were introduced on the Chicago Board of Trade. The first contract on Ginnie Maes was ahead of its time when it started trading in October 1975. However, Treasury futures, which were created in August 1977, became a huge success due to the jump in inflation and the explosion in federal government debt when the United States turned into a debtor nation. In 1978, the annual volume of Treasury futures was 552,649 contracts; in 1996, 84,725,128 contracts were traded.
- The World Bank and IBM legitimized the concept of swaps when they executed a $290 million swap in August 1981. This marked the beginning of a huge new market. Since then, derivatives have beget derivatives and there is now a smorgasbord of products from which to choose.
- Early swap transactions were linked to new debt issues and were used to take advantage of the comparative advantages that borrowers typically enjoy in their domestic market. They were back-to-back transactions that matched up two borrowers with matching, but opposite, requirements. The market was illiquid; and legal, accounting, and tax issues were not fully resolved.
- Trading volumes were boosted when companies started to use swaps to manage their existing assets and liabilities. This prompted more banks to enter the arena to service the hedging needs of their corporate banking relationships. The result was increased liquidity in the market. This allowed dealers to "warehouse" swaps (i.e., make markets and run trading books), which in turned fueled growth in the swaps markets.
- At one time, U.S. dollar swaps essentially dominated the market. Today, the U.S. dollar is still the largest currency but accounts for less than 35 percent of total trading volume. Yen and euro swaps are the next most important currencies with shares of roughly 12 percent and 13 percent, respectively.
- The International Swaps Dealers Association—renamed the International Swaps and Derivatives Association in 1993—was founded in 1985 to provide a framework and establish business standards for the swaps markets. This organization introduced master documentation that has become the market standard for swaps transactions.
- Structured and exotic derivatives, such as derivatives embedded in a cash instrument or different asset classes linked, came in vogue in the early 1990s. Bond investors played a key role in the development of this

market and became active users of structured products to leverage their positions and increase their portfolio returns. Structured derivatives also helped to take advantage of legal, accounting, and tax loopholes.

■ In 1994, the derivatives markets suffered a severe setback when interest rates rose unexpectedly and some end users and dealers alike lost significant amounts of money. The heaviest losses made front-page news, and derivatives quickly became known as dangerously risky. Many users cut way back on their use of derivatives, or stopped buying them altogether.

■ Tighter regulations and increased safety requirements, combined with an increased understanding of derivatives products, are responsible for the rebound in the derivatives markets. Today, they are bigger than ever before. Total over the counter (OTC) interest rate derivatives outstanding amount to $54 trillion. They are now very much a commodity product and trade at razor-thin margins in the major currencies (e.g., less than one basis point in the U.S. dollar).

■ Although many banks now offer capabilities in swaps and other derivatives, the concentration of business is astounding. In the United States, the seven largest banks combined account for roughly 95 percent of the total notional principal amount outstanding.

■ The rankings of the leading dealers have changed dramatically in the past 9 years, as Tables 3.1 and 3.2 show.

All these dealers have a significant commitment to the derivatives business and have made huge investments to be among its leaders. In many ways, they are responsible for the success of derivatives. Their creativity has

TABLE 3.1 Leading Interest Rate Derivatives Dealers—United States*

1990 Dealer	Penetration	1999 Dealer	Penetration
Citibank	29%	Bank of America	45%
Merrill Lynch	20	Chase Manhattan Bank	36
First National Bank of Chicago	19	Citigroup	36
J.P. Morgan	19	J.P. Morgan	28
Bankers Trust	18	Goldman Sachs	25
Salomon Brothers	18	Morgan Stanley	20
Chase Manhattan Bank	15	Deutsche Bank	18
Security Pacific	15	Merrill Lynch	16
Continental Bank	14	ABN AMRO	15
Lehman Brothers	13	Credit Suisse First Boston	12

* Dealers' derivatives penetration with liability managers.

TABLE 3.2   Leading Interest Rate Derivatives Dealers—Continental Europe*

1992 Dealer	Penetration	1999 Dealer	Penetration
Citibank	33%	Deutsche Bank	48%
J.P. Morgan	29	J.P. Morgan	30
Credit Suisse	28	Société Générale	28
Credit Lyonnais	27	Chase Manhattan	27
Société Générale	26	Citigroup	27
Deutsche Bank/Morgan Grenfell	23	Dresdner Kleinwort Benson	26
Banque Paribas	22	ABN AMRO	25
BZW/Barclays Bank	22	Credit Suisse First Boston	22
Swiss Bank Corporation	22	Paribas	22
Union Bank of Switzerland	20	UBS Warburg	21

* Dealers' derivatives penetration with large liability managers.

provided companies and investment managers with the vast array of tools they've needed for hedging exposures and taking positions. And by and large, these dealers have been substantially rewarded for their efforts. But derivatives is a constantly evolving business, as our worldwide research continues to document. What has been an effective sales program in the past, or is even effective now, may not work so well in this new era of increasing consolidation. Those dealers that are successful will provide strategic applications targeted to customers' real needs as well as a strong service component intended to help the customer understand derivatives for what they are: arguably the most creative, versatile, and influential innovation of recent decades and the most important achievement in modern finance. Because of derivatives, you may not be able to predict the weather, but you *can* now hedge against it.

DERIVATIVES REACH HIGH AND WIDE

Perhaps the most important feature of derivatives is that their unique character extends well beyond derivatives into many cash markets and the real economy. They can help a company to compete more effectively against international competitors, provide access to funding that otherwise might not be available on the same favorable terms—and so make a real impact on a company's bottom line.

Since derivatives are *derived* from an underlying asset—be it currencies, bonds, equities, or commodities—derivatives and cash markets are closely linked and tend to move in tandem. In fact, derivatives prices can drive the cash markets as much or more than the underlying cash markets impact derivatives. Thus new issues of corporate bonds often are "swap-driven" and the expiration of futures contracts can create havoc in the "cash" bond and equity markets. (The press even claimed that the use of futures for program selling was one of the key factors triggering the meltdown in the stock market on Black Monday, as the *Wall Street Journal* reported on October 19, 1987: "When portfolio insurers rush to sell futures, the futures prices often become depressed relative to stocks. At that stage, arbitragers begin buying what they regard as 'cheap' stock-index futures while selling offsetting baskets of the underlying stocks. These 'sell programs' can help drive stock prices even lower, creating a vicious circle for a while.")

Because of the close link of derivatives with so many financial assets, they have fundamentally changed the working life of those executives who both buy and sell financial services. Here are some fundamental changes derivatives have brought about on the sell-side of the business:

- Account officers, already well versed in lending money and understanding the credit needs of their corporate customers also need to know how to swap a floating rate loan into a fixed interest rate loan.
- Bond salespeople need to know the futures and swaps markets to have a thorough understanding of bond prices and to provide better service to their customers using derivatives. To some degree, the same holds true in equities.
- In foreign exchange, customer dealers that know second or third generation currency options can be more helpful to their customers and make more money for their employer than salespeople who focus on spot and forward transactions.

The impact on buyers of financial services overall is at least as large:

- The CFO and the CEO are now expected to understand derivatives and be fully "in the know" about their company's use of them. It is now well understood that derivatives can have a major beneficial impact on a company's financial results; it is also understood that derivatives can cause substantial damage if used imprudently.
- On an operational level, the corporate assistant treasurer must be well versed in currency options, interest rate swaps, and other derivatives to be really effective.

These broader job requirements also provide advantages. Here are some of the benefits specific to liability managers:

- Currency options provide the short-term benefit of covering anticipated payables and receivables denominated in foreign currencies. They also can be used to manage economic risk and protect a company from the impact of currency fluctuation on its international competitiveness.
- Swaps are an important instrument for managing the interest rate exposure of existing liabilities as well as for borrowing money efficiently and cheaply. They allow companies to swap an existing floating rate loan into a fixed-rate obligation if they believe that interest rates will rise.
- Equity derivatives such as stock options are used to link executives' performance to shareholder value and to manage the liabilities arising from employee stock owner plans. Companies also use them for strategic purposes such as mergers and acquisitions (M&A) to protect themselves against a drop in their own share price or an increase in the share price of the target company. Managing the exposure from corporate cross-share holdings is another important application.

Asset managers benefit from the use of derivatives as well. Hedging of price volatility is the most obvious benefit, but there are others specific to investors:

- Changing investors' asset allocation quickly and cheaply. When the asset allocation committee of an investment institution decides that the model portfolio is overweighted in equities or has too much exposure to foreign bonds, it can typically make tactical adjustments more easily with derivatives than through transactions in the cash markets. Since the derivatives market is more liquid and transparent than the cash markets, and the spreads are more narrow, derivatives make for a nimble portfolio management tool.
- For the same reasons, it tends to be more efficient to use futures to invest large new pools of money under management. A successful fund manager who has attracted large new inflows cannot afford to sit on this new cash without detrimental effects on performance. But he or she can even less afford to invest hastily in cash securities without doing the rigorous homework necessary to pick the securities that offer the best return for the risk profile of his or her new investors. Derivatives allow a fund manager to "park" the moneys in a portfolio that is approximately right for the client while taking the time to make the specifically right investment decisions for the long term.
- One of the early uses of derivatives was to arbitrage between different markets and to exploit any inefficiencies in pricing. One of the more common plays is to buy futures and sell the underlying cash instrument or vice versa to profit from differences in pricing. These days, the

markets have become so efficient—precisely because of the good work of such arbitrageurs—that, at least in the major markets, it is more and more difficult to find pricing inefficiencies.

- Due to local regulations or tax regimes, international investors are sometimes prohibited from investing in a market (typically one of the emerging markets) that can offer high returns as well as diversification. Dealers have offered investors a helping hand by constructing derivatives, such as equity swaps, that pay investors the return on the performance of a foreign market in exchange for a fixed rate payment.
- The opportunity to capture incremental yield is one of the more exciting, but also one of the more dangerous uses of derivatives. Investors can buy derivatives that leverage their positions so that an expected decline in interest rates boosts their return by several times the resulting increase in bond prices. But, beware the lesson of 1994: When rates move in the other direction, investors can get hurt doubly.

THE LESSON OF 1994

That is exactly what happened in 1994. Bond investors, corporations, and many other investors were fully expecting that rates would continue to trend down. But early in the year, the Fed became concerned with inflationary pressures and nudged up short-term rates several times in a row. Long rates shot up and many were caught by surprise. The result was front-page news. A series of losses, each seemingly greater than the last, were well publicized. Among the big losers were Orange County, Procter & Gamble, Gibson Greetings, and even one dealer, Barings, which had to be taken over by ING Bank. As Figure 3.1 shows, investors and corporates exited the market in droves.

In all cases, the losses appear to have been the result of insufficient risk management controls combined with an overly aggressive use of derivatives, especially because some users did not fully understand what they were buying. With hindsight comes clarity, and both the sellers and buyers of derivatives realized that their management procedures and computer systems for tracking risk were sorely lacking. The downside of the derivatives risk had been made clear to all, and even the most enthusiastic users became advocates for major change.

The Group of Thirty—a private, nonprofit group established in 1978 to deepen understanding of international economic and financial issues—put together a broad cross-section of industry participants to survey and document derivatives practices and performance. They established standards and guidelines for prudent use of derivatives, and their highly publicized

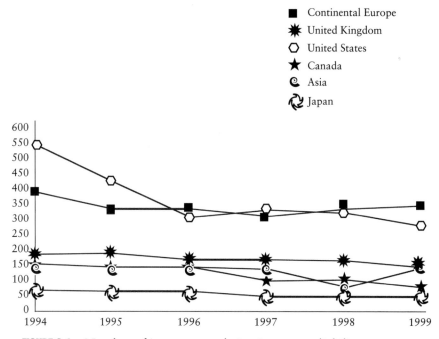

FIGURE 3.1   Number of interest rate derivative users—liability managers.

and well-received recommendations can be found in the study group's publication, *Derivatives: Practices and Principles*. Many of their recommendations apply to both dealers and end users:

- Understand derivatives before buying them.
- Value derivatives positions and analyze exposures to risk on a regular basis.
- Have adequate systems in place to perform these analyses.
- Employ staff that is expert in derivatives and systems.
- Establish reporting lines into senior management to keep them fully informed.
- Enroll top management in "crash" derivatives courses.
- Use netting agreements.

Many dealers and end users alike heeded these recommendations and have taken steps to reduce operational risk. Value at Risk (VaR), which estimates the expected potential loss over a given period with a specific degree of confidence, has become the norm for measuring risk. This change alone is a big step forward from the days prior to 1994 when "back of the envelope" calculations were standard. Other across-the-board improvements include investment in better software to measure risk and implementation of more direct and frequent reporting lines.

Dealers have also taken steps to reduce counterparty risk. A significant proportion of business is done on a collateral basis with one or both counterparties to a swaps transaction posting collateral that is released when one of the parties defaults. Credit-sensitive users such as government agencies are the most enthusiastic users. Other improvements include more frequent use of netting agreements so that each swap counterparty is exposed only for the net amount that they owe for all the transactions between them. Netting agreements have an added benefit of allowing dealers to free up their credit lines with other dealers and important customers. Sell-side firms also improved their service to customers by providing them with regular mark-to-market updates of their derivatives' positions.

HOW TO WIN THIS NEW GAME: TRUST AND SERVICE

Trust and service are key factors in derivative sales today. While it's no secret that derivatives dealers are in the business to make money, many customers around the world tell us they feel dealers are *only* in the business to make money. Customers question the spreads they are being offered, and worry they'll be sold a product without a thorough explanation of the risk. They question dealers' integrity, and wonder if there is any genuine interest in helping them advance their own business plans. In short, many customers do not trust their dealers, and they voice their feelings clearly and bluntly: "Dealers are not keeping their word," says one. "Dealers often deceive clients on spreads," says another. Still others complain that dealers breach confidentiality and worry that dealers will take advantage if they reveal their trading intentions.

Winning a customer's trust is a powerful lever and creates a kind of closed circle that is hard for other dealers to infiltrate. When customers are willing to share their problems with dealers they trust, those dealers are then in the best position to understand customers' needs and recommend appropriate solutions.

Trust may seem like an intangible "you either have it or you don't" attribute, but our experience with clients shows that dealers can take specific action steps to build trust. Following are key steps to earn a customer's trust . . . one deal at a time:

■ Educate important customers about the ways derivatives can be customized to solve their particular problems. A good derivatives salesperson acts as a filter, and tells customers what is important to them, why, and what they should or should not do with the information. The on-going demand for outside experts to help manage derivatives illustrates that customers have a genuine desire to know more about how to use them.

Taking the time to educate a customer shows your commitment for the long term, and will help alleviate customers' concerns that dealers only call to make a quick deal. This is a key way to provide real value.

■ Educate yourself about your customers' needs and concerns. This "bottom line" information is critical to a dealer's ability to recommend appropriate derivatives instruments, and again reinforces that the dealer is not just there for the quick sale. With this investment of time comes the implication of a dealer's real concern for how well the derivative works for the customer. This goes a long way toward creating a partnership mentality, and with it, trust.

■ Remember the customer at the end of the day and at the end of the deal. Provide ongoing service, such as updates on the markets, risk exposure analysis, and changes in the positions of customers' derivatives. We advise our clients to provide *daily* updates to their most active customers.

Much of the derivatives business today is in plain-vanilla products such as short-dated swaps and options, or in floating rate agreements. We advise our clients that when there is no differentiating factor in the *product* (and derivatives is increasingly a commodity business), then the key differentiating factor among dealers is *service*. Outstanding service gives dealers a competitive edge when customers perceive all other factors to be equal. And while product differentiations can still be made, it has become an increasingly difficult sales strategy because of the large numbers of dealers competing for the same business and the resulting shortening of product cycles.

It is the irony of the derivatives business that the hallmark of an innovative, successful derivatives product is that it has become commoditized. What is a new and high margin product today will be copied by competitors within a few months or even weeks, and as a result will become more of a commodity and thus a less lucrative product. For example, many banks and firms now trade constant maturity swaps and lookback options, but once they were thought of as leading edge instruments that very few could price correctly.

In this type of market, not just good service, but *great* service, becomes key. Users of derivatives tell us that "great service" means the following (note how some of the responses overlap with those elements required to build trust):

- Quote quickly, competitively, consistently, and in large sizes. Competitive quotes are increasing in importance as product becomes more commoditized.
- Offer advice that reflects an understanding of a customer's needs and provides real solutions to their problems. Customers are not willing to pay dealers for commodity-type products, but they do reward handsomely those who help address their key problems.
- Periodically check in with phone calls to ask how their needs have changed, or to see if there are any problems. Calling only to push product smacks of insincerity.
- Complete customer-friendly documentation in a timely manner. Equally important is a reliable and efficient back office that produces accurate confirmations and is "on the ball" with periodic payments that need to be made.
- Conduct *effective* relationship reviews on a regular basis.

Relationship reviews deserve special mention because rarely are they done effectively. How to do a good relationship review? In a word: Prepare. And follow up and follow through. Know the customer's balance sheet or securities portfolio, their cash flows, their exposures, their outstanding derivatives positions, their understanding of and appetite for more advanced products. Come prepared with specific suggestions based on an astute analysis of their exposure. Know who the senior decision-makers are and include them in the meeting. If the meeting is with a high-level customer, include the equivalent from your firm, such as the head of the Derivatives department.

We suggest the following agenda for a superior relationship review:

- Both sides recap what was promised at the last review meeting.
- Both sides review what actually has been done and by whom—on each agenda item.
- Both sides state what they expect to accomplish by the next meeting.

This agenda can typically be accomplished in something like an hour. Since customers tend to work with so many dealers, we advise our clients to conduct a relationship review no more than once per quarter. These reviews can go a long way to fulfilling both the service component and the trust obligation critical to deepening relationships.

At some point, the everyday working relationship begins to take on more of the qualities of a partnership. Trust and service, built over time—*one deal at a time*—provide incremental leverage until the combined effects of trust and service dovetail and become what we term "Very Important relationships."

THE IMPORTANCE OF VERY
IMPORTANT RELATIONSHIPS

Many banks and firms offer competitive pricing capabilities in mainstream and exotic derivatives and now offer customers a wide choice of alternatives. In this kind of competitive environment, excellent service is key, as discussed earlier, but strong relationships count for just as much.

Very Important relationships matter for several reasons. On average, three different dealers are asked for a price quote. Often, the strength of the overall relationship between a customer and a dealer is the decisive factor in who gets the first call and the best opportunity to win the deal. Many liability managers tell us their overall banking relationship with a dealer is of paramount importance when they decide whom to use for a particular derivatives transaction. In fact, as Table 3.3 shows, only competitive pricing is mentioned more frequently as an important dealer selection criterion.

Not only do customers tell us that banking relationships are important, they also act accordingly. Most users of structured derivatives solely rely on dealers that they also use for other, more commodity-types of derivatives. And 40 percent of a dealer's banking customers typically use the same dealer as one of their main providers of derivatives. The hammer-over-the-head implication is that derivatives dealers that are able to cross-sell product and fulfill customers' other banking needs, have a huge competitive advantage.

Derivatives customers typically use many different dealers, but they concentrate most of their business with their Top-3 dealers. For example, in continental Europe, liability managers rely on more than eight dealers for their derivatives needs, but almost 70 percent of their business is awarded to their three most important dealers. And even within that select group of dealers, the distribution of business is not "fair." The lead dealer garners more than 35 percent of a typical customer's business, the second dealer 20 percent, and the third dealer just over 10 percent. Not only does the lead dealer get more

TABLE 3.3   Most Important Dealer Selection Criteria—By Geographic Area

Criterion	United States	Canada	United Kingdom	Continent
Ability to provide competitive quotes	63%	74%	78%	74%
Depth of relationship with bank	47	27	51	43
Ability to provide prompt quotes	26	23	35	38
Understanding and acting on company's needs	22	36	30	19
Product and market knowledge	30	39	22	25

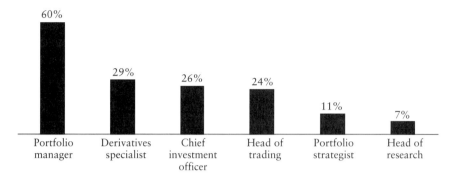

FIGURE 3.2   Asset manager executives discussing derivatives (with dealers).

business from its customers, but that dealer is also more likely to earn their especially attractive business, such as structured derivatives.

Building relationships that lead to Top-3 dealer status depends on a combination of trust and service, and also on developing that trust and service through relationships at all different levels of the customer organization. Figures 3.2 and 3.3 show which executives to target at asset managers and at corporations in the United States.

It is plain risky to build a customer relationship based on just one contact within a company. Doing so leaves the dealer vulnerable to executive turnover and can be a serious hindrance when trying to cross-sell products. Instead, focus on building deep *institutional* relationships within the different levels of a customer organization (as illustrated in Figures 3.2

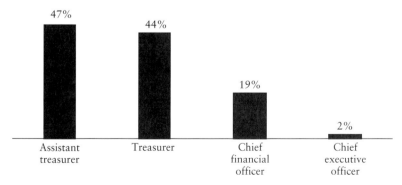

FIGURE 3.3   Corporate executives discussing derivatives (with dealers).

and 3.3). This not only improves opportunities for cross-selling, but these across-the-board contacts have important implications for dealers' selling strategies.

SELLING STRATEGIES: HOW TO BECOME A LEAD DEALER

The key change in derivatives sales today is change at the top. Selling derivatives has become much more complicated than it was in the early 1980s. Products were more straightforward then, and most customer organizations had just a single buyer requiring coverage. Today's users no longer consider just the components of derivatives risk; they also consider their overall business risk and use derivatives for *strategic* risk management.

As such, derivatives have become a *strategic* concern at large organizations. And financial engineering has reached a point where it is no longer left to asset or liability managers alone. Both policy *and* strategy are being decided at the senior executive level. There are two reasons for this change: One is the tremendously heavy and negative publicity attached to derivatives losses in 1994, the other is that users have a better appreciation of derivatives' potential benefits.

On one side, because no chief executive wants to stand before the board or shareholders and announce the loss of a substantial sum in derivatives, he or she needs to be involved in the whole derivatives process. On the other, quite a few chief executives have come to realize that successful use of derivatives can do as much for earnings as the construction of a new plant or the downsizing of a few thousand employees. Similar arguments apply to investment management firms that operate under the "prudent man" rule but want to take advantage of financial innovation to increase risk-adjusted returns for their plan sponsors. (Also, a successful derivatives strategy can make a powerful difference to an organization long term, which is why institutional equity analysts scrutinize these strategies.)

Try to implement sales strategies that focus on the key decision makers at customer organizations. The traditional buyer of interest rate swaps (a company's treasury function), for example, is not likely to be the logical buyer of a product that protects revenue or operating cash flow, which is more typically the concern of the line manager. Dealers will have the most impact when they discuss their customers' strategic view with these customers' top-level executives, and pitch how derivatives can reduce cash flow volatility and increase shareholder value for them. And dealers should keep portfolio managers and assistant treasurers up-to-date on new market and product developments.

Selling derivatives in this way—from the top down—gives a dealer a genuine understanding of customers' overall needs, and positions them to be the first "port of call" when customers need a solution to an important problem. In a very real sense, we advise dealers to go back to the educational selling techniques used in the early years of derivatives marketing, but this time aimed at a much higher level in customer organizations.

SEGMENTING THE MARKET

Substantial investment of both time and money are required to build strong relationships. Selling strategies are more involved, and deep selling requires considerable resources. The cost of those resources—in terms of people, capital, and computer systems—continues to rise. Professionals within the business are commanding and getting salaries that are commensurate with the complexity of the derivatives they're charged with designing and selling. Capital charges are becoming more onerous, making it more important than ever that capital be doled out astutely and for selected customers. And the growing number of transactions, as well as the need to price increasingly exotic instruments, demands powerful, state-of-the-art computer systems to keep up with it all.

To use their resources in the most efficient way possible, we advise our clients to "fish where the fish are." This means differentiating between those customers with the potential to become really important and those that are a second or third priority. Wasting resources is not an option because, while volume has increased, there are fewer customers today than in 1994.

In some markets, this astonishing level of concentration of customers is greater than even the traditional 80/20 rule. Table 3.4 shows the proportion of total customer derivatives business generated by the 20 percent most active users worldwide and in three major regions.

TABLE 3.4 Customer Derivative Business by Most Active Users

	Percentage of Total Derivatives Volume
United States	92%
United Kingdom	82
Continental Europe	90
Global	89

Effective focus requires a *rigorous* segmentation of the market. One obvious and important segment of the market is the really big users of derivatives. But these big buyers have significant requirements and are not ideal customers for all derivatives dealers. When defining their focus and choosing their target customers, dealers should ask themselves the following questions:

- Do we have sufficient capital to accommodate the large flows of business that active users generate, often in large, bulky trades? If not, then focus instead on smaller, but still frequent, derivative users that do not require as much capital commitment. The trade-off will be exposure to lower flows.
- Is our credit rating strong enough to be an acceptable counterparty for active users, who are especially credit sensitive because their counterparty exposures are bigger? Government agencies in particular are notorious for being choosy about dealers' financial strength and credit rating. Institutions rated AA or lower will be acceptable to fewer agencies and large users. A low credit rating can be worked around by creating a credit-enhanced vehicle, but these vehicles can be an expensive use of capital, and posting collateral for each trade done with a higher rated counterparty ties up capital in low-risk and low-yield securities. Are the benefits worthwhile?
- Are our product capabilities in line with the needs of active users? Do they range across all the currency denominations our important customers tend to use? Active users of over $1 billion per year transact, on average, in 6 or 7 different products versus 3 to 5 for smaller users. And they tend to be bigger users of exotic and structured derivatives. In the United States and Europe, the major users account for roughly 95 percent of all structured business.
- Do we have a strong institutional relationship that can be leveraged to advantage? Do we lend money, or are we a preferred dealer/broker in cash bonds and equities? If so, coordinate your relationships closely with the relationships of account officers and bond and equity salespeople. This coordination will give you a better understanding of each customer's overall needs, and highlight opportunities to cross-sell products. Coordinated coverage also ensures a customer is not contacted by different people in your organization during the same day—with different messages.
- If you do not have a strong relationship with a prospective customer, what can your firm offer that other dealers do not? If you cannot answer this question convincingly, the buyer certainly will not be able to answer it for you. If you cannot provide more *product* value than a

relationship bank can provide, do not waste precious resources attempting to capture "hard-to-win" business.

■ Do we have sufficient high-quality staff to carry out our goals? If we don't have them, do we have a hiring plan in place? Can we afford the level of traders and salespeople that our business goals suggest we need?

THE INNOVATION LIFE CYCLE

Since that first swap between World Bank and IBM, innovation has continued to propel the derivatives market. With good reason. Profits are highest at the beginning of the product life cycle. Since there is no copyright or patent protection on derivatives, no sooner is a "winner" out on the market than other dealers begin to focus all their efforts on duplicating it. As duplication multiplies, margins are driven down and spreads narrow. The better the derivative, the more duplication and the narrower the margins.

Today, the product life cycle of even the most complex derivatives can be as little as a few months or even weeks. Plain vanilla and short-term derivatives make up more than 90 percent of the market now, and trade at margins of as little as one basis point. Compare this with the early 1980s, when swaps demanded up-front fees in addition to spreads of 25–35 basis points. As customers become more educated about the use of derivatives and competition among sell-side firms continues to increase, this product life cycle is bound to shorten even more, guaranteeing that yesterday's hot new products will be tomorrow's old news.

The clear message to dealers is to put substantial resources into developing profitable new products. But the investment required to do so is high. The very complexity of the products makes those able to develop them an exclusive group. PhDs from top schools are required, and these folks come with a price tag to match their brain power. And there's no guarantee that the new products these "rocket scientists" develop will be winners. Some products are instant best-sellers, others never catch on, and some take years to become widely used. This was arguably the case with interest rate futures. It took five years for them to become popular, and now they are traded in huge volumes in many different currencies at many exchanges around the world. Catastrophe insurance options is an example of a potentially sound product that has not yet gained acceptance. These options, specifically designed to help insurance companies offset risk, first began trading in September 1995. In 1996, 14,678 were traded; three-fourths of the way through 1997 11,537 were traded. By the end of 1999, they effectively stopped trading.

No dealer has a 100 percent success rate in developing new product. Such a rate is a red flag that signals the dealer is not generating as many new products as it should, and thus has less chance of finding a real winner. However, with preparation, product development can be taken out of the realm of the "crap shoot." The best way to improve the winners-to-losers ratio is to do the following:

- Carefully listen to customers' needs and focus new product development efforts to address those needs. This ensures a fertile market, because customers increasingly want solutions to their finance problems. They reward creative problem-solving, and pay little attention to dealers that offer an assembly-line product that has little or nothing to do with their specific needs.
- Be first. The dealer first to market will reap substantial benefits, financial and otherwise. Margins are only large in the early stages of a new product, because with new derivatives product, "shopping around" is not an option. Customers understand the large value being offered to them and that there is no other alternative.
- Know when to "hold 'em, when to fold 'em." Sometimes products are introduced ahead of their time, as with interest rate futures. It is hard to know when to continue investing money in marketing a product, and when to give up trying. To avoid getting "stuck" on marketing only one product, hedge by developing several products simultaneously. This ensures that there is always one or more new products in the pipeline. With several "eggs in the basket," there is a greater chance for one to "hatch" over time.
- Follow through. Marketing a product effectively is critical to its success, and distribution power is key to successful marketing. Distribution power, in turn, is driven by strong relationships and enough high-quality human resources to service them. Selling new derivatives products today, more than ever before, requires bright salespeople who understand the complicated structures and can explain their benefits to the customers.
- Establish a first-class reputation. This will attract customers, and also act as a powerful lure for employees. In a business reliant on the best and the brightest, competition to get them is fierce. It is only natural that the most talented people are attracted to the top firms. This presents a catch-22, however, since those same highly talented people are required to establish a firm's reputation in the first place.

These recommendations apply to all derivatives dealers, not just the largest ones. Being a follower rather than an innovator can be a sensible goal for firms unable (or unwilling) to meet the high costs of innovation.

Some dealers place themselves second *strategically*. They are able to accept that they will never be on the cutting edge, and use their lower development costs and lower personnel costs to compete effectively in more mature and lower margin instruments.

STRUCTURE: COMBINE OR INTEGRATE?

Being truly global is a requirement for dealers that want to be among the leading dealers worldwide. A global orientation lets dealers service their customers better, as well as manage their own risks more effectively. Many of the customers that dealers serve (or hope to serve) compete in markets around the world and have exposures to many currencies and yield curves. A dealer able to help its global customers with their needs in each local market has the potential to score a big win over competitors without this capability.

Being truly *global* has been the buzzword of the 1990s. Every large dealer says it is global, or that it wants to be global. But what does "global" really mean? In derivatives, it means coordinating coverage so that each sales representative working with an account knows what his or her colleague on the other side of the globe is doing with the same account. This is important, for the following reasons:

- A coordinated approach will give a dealer a global view of all the transactions it has done with a customer, its total credit exposure with that customer, and the transactions currently being worked on or proposed. Customers benefit from this approach, because their central treasury can receive updates not only on individual transactions of various operating units around the world, but also on the overall effect of those transactions.
- Being global allows a dealer to add more value because of exposure to derivative markets around the world. This gives a significant edge in market knowledge which a dealer can pass along to its customers. A global dealer not only will have up-to-the-minute knowledge on the domestic market in Germany, but also will know about important developments in the United States.
- Global dealers are first to spot trends, understand local differences better, and more quickly link events in various markets. This gives a dealer critical insights for advising its customers and also is advantageous for running its own positions.
- A global trading book makes it easier to manage risks and monitor trading limits, since the book is passed along across time zones as local markets close and open.

- A global book also provides the advantage of centralizing all market knowledge, which is essential to successful positioning. Dealers also get more "bang for their buck," since a *global* book allows a dealer to run one book that is much larger than each individual *local* book would be for the same commitment of capital. This, in turn, enables a dealer to provide more liquidity to its customers and quote tighter spreads.

Whether global or not, all dealers face the issue of how to structure their operation. One way is to integrate all derivatives activities *across* such different asset classes as interest rates, equities, currencies, and commodities. Another organizational structure is combining cash and derivatives activities *within* each asset class, such as currencies or "rates."

Both structures have their advantages; choose the structure that best matches your firm's goals. Housing cash and derivatives capabilities together seems to make sense for the majority of firms, for the following reasons:

- Buy-side executives often have combined cash and derivatives responsibilities and find it easier to speak with one sales representative who covers them for both product areas.
- Such a generalist representative is better positioned to understand and act on each customer's needs than separate cash and derivatives representatives who need to coordinate coverage.
- Management will have a much clearer picture of the cross-sell opportunities when the dealer follows an integrated cash/derivatives strategy, and will be much more effective in leveraging its customer relationships. This is critical because dealers' cash customers often offer tremendous opportunity in derivatives products.
- It's advantageous from a trading perspective to keep cash and derivatives traders in close contact since cash markets can drive derivatives prices and vice versa.
- Banks and firms that offer "one-stop shopping" are more likely to "make the cut" as customers continue to consolidate their dealer lists.

Integrating cash and derivatives capabilities starts at the top. Management designs the internal structure to support the firm's strategy. This strategy needs to be "sold" to the troops all the way through the firm, with special emphasis on the individual sales reps who are in daily contact with customers. They are the critical link for implementing the concept, and the task is a demanding one. They must understand cash and derivatives instruments, be current on both markets, and cover both the cash and derivatives needs of their customers. To make the sales job less daunting, try to rely on a combination of generalists and specialists—generalists to cover the majority of the transactions, and specialists to help out with the complicated derivatives structures typically used by those active users on the buy-side that employ derivatives specialists themselves.

While the trend is to combine cash and derivatives activities within an asset class, integrating derivatives across more than one asset class also has merit, and can be very profitable for those few dealers able to do it successfully. Some of the advantages are:

- For dealers that want to focus on structured business in derivatives offering returns linked to more than one asset class, it is comparatively much easier to develop, structure, price, and sell these high-margin products when a firm's derivatives capabilities are all integrated rather than being included with each underlying cash business.
- Dealers that employ derivatives specialists on their sales desk are better able to provide value to derivatives specialists at large end-user organizations. Sophisticated users want to speak with true derivatives experts on the sell side.
- Firms with an integrated derivatives strategy are able to help educate end users' top management on how to use derivatives for managing strategic risks that require highly innovative solutions.

Creating cross-asset derivatives is not easy, which is why they can be so very profitable. We caution clients that innovation of this sort requires outstanding product development and structuring capabilities, as well as highly qualified and highly priced talent, not only to structure the derivatives but also to be able to explain them to customers. Highly structured derivatives are relatively uncommon events, so the playing field for them is small. This approach can work well—and currently is working well—for those few dealers with leading-edge capabilities.

Whichever structure dealers choose, a consistent approach is key. Frequent change is costly in terms of internal turmoil, and can also create havoc with customers, who prefer stable and rewarding relationships.

DERIVATIVES DOWN THE ROAD

Given the extent to which the derivatives business has changed since its inception, and the scope of the future changes that likely will occur, consider how the following may impact your firm:

- Providing leading edge solutions will continue to be critical to stay ahead of the pack. But staying ahead is becoming increasingly difficult.

Product life cycles will continue to shorten as structures innovated by one dealer are replicated quickly by other firms, which will then offer them at increasingly competitive prices. In this environment, how is your firm poised to compete in an increasingly commodity-oriented business?

■ As the economies and capital markets of Asia, Eastern Europe, Latin America, and Africa develop, currencies that are currently illiquid and thinly traded will become much more commonplace. While still volatile, their real economies—each in its own way—seem to be increasingly well positioned for growth. As their economies grow, so will their need for capital. As they open up and liberalize their capital markets, this in turn will fuel demand for derivatives. (And this does not preclude growth from more stable economies such as North America, Europe, and Japan, which have tremendous potential for derivatives growth.) How is your firm preparing to take advantage of these long-term and exciting growth opportunities?

■ In recent years, committed derivatives users have become ever more active and have generated larger and larger volumes. But the most promising prospect for future growth could well be among the astonishingly high numbers of companies and investors that still do not use derivatives at all. In the United States, the number of derivatives users among large corporates currently stands at approximately 300, well below the peak of 550 in 1994. What strategies does your firm have to target this still-large prospect pool?

■ Increased regulation will likely raise the cost of doing business due to the capital requirements laid down by the Fed and the BIS. FASB Statement No. 133 by the FASB (Financial Accounting Standards Board) possibly will have a chilling effect on customers' derivatives activities. The extensive disclosure requirements and higher standards for internal risk management are good for the long-term health of the business, but also raise the cost of participation. Expenditures on technology are also bound to increase. It is a requirement of doing business to have state-of-the-art systems to analyze and track exposures, to quote clients competitively and quickly, and to develop and structure innovative products. Does your firm have a plan in place to meet these increased costs? Will your firm survive the rash of consolidations these increased costs are likely to bring about?

Some dealers wonder if product innovation is still possible, since so many great ideas have already been discovered. A pessimistic view is that derivatives have completely matured and that even exotic products have become mainstream. However, dealers' creativity should not be underestimated. Consider these products, both developed quite recently:

- Perhaps the most exciting product innovation is the application of derivatives to new "underlyings," such as electricity, allowing companies to manage strategic risk. These instruments are different from swaps and other mature instruments because they enable companies to hedge their revenues rather than their expenses.
- Credit derivatives are increasingly being used to manage a credit risk associated with an asset that already functions as an underlying for more established derivatives, such as interest-rate risks.

There continues to be opportunity in this business. And, because of the seemingly contradictory combination of growth and consolidation, there is *increased* opportunity for those dealers that can lead with innovation and support it with superior service to a select group of customers. True, derivatives dealers may not be able to come up with another innovation as big as swaps, but smaller innovations will likely always be in the pipeline. That is the very nature of the financial markets, and of the derivatives business in particular. Innovation is what gave birth to the "new" derivatives market, and it is what will continue to drive it.

CHAPTER 4

Corporate Banking

Allan F. Munro, Donald M. Raftery,
Steven C. Busby, and David D. Fox

The Decline of the Banker and the Rise of the Relationship Manager

Relationship banking is not what it used to be. And both banks and their customers benefit. The term *relationship banking* is as old as corporate banking itself, but the definition has changed greatly since the days when the relationship manager was primarily and principally responsible for credit. As the duties of that role enlarged to keep pace with the changes in large corporate banking,[1] a new breed of relationship manager emerged, who acts as an adviser as well as a provider. But what is being provided is not capital, but services. This change has redefined the whole concept of relationship banking.

To put this changed concept in perspective, here are some key events in corporate banking from the past 25 years that have contributed directly to the new definition:

■ Disintermediation occurred on a massive scale: Bank certificates of deposit and commercial paper rose sixfold in volume, from $180 billion in 1973 to well over $1.2 trillion in 2000. Commercial paper multiplied

---

Allan F. Munro wrote "The Decline of the Banker and the Rise of the Relationship Manager," Donald M. Raftery and Steven C. Busby wrote "Corporate Cash Management," and Allan F. Munro and David D. Fox wrote "The Challenge of New Business Solicitation in Middle Market Banking."

20 times, from $41 billion in 1973 to over $900 billion in 2000. Money market funds depleted commercial banks' low cost retail deposits, escalating from $0 in 1973 to $2.5 billion one year later and expanding nearly 50 times to almost $1 trillion in 2000.

■ Aggressive foreign banks entered the domestic lending business and their lower cost base—on a marginal cost basis—put pricing pressure on domestic loan margins.

■ As credit (and cash management) became more "commoditized" and profit margins narrowed, banks moved to fee-based businesses to remain profitable.

■ The evolution of electronic data interchange (EDI) reduced the need for multiple regional commercial banks to serve corporations' cash collection and distribution needs as they concentrated more business with the technologically advanced commercial banks.

■ "Marginal cost of funds" pricing evolved to "risk-adjusted rate pricing." As advances in information technology made it possible for banks to determine the low profitability of once treasured "house corporate customers," banks' strategies changed accordingly. They put in place more focused market penetration objectives and, rather than going for volume lending and an ever-escalating pursuit of customers, sought to develop relationships that were far more important and profitable.

■ The deemphasis on traditional institutional lending relationships and the boom in acquisition loans, buyout finance, and junk bond business created a greater "transaction" thrust.

■ With the creation of the "Section 20 affiliate" (which allowed banks to underwrite securities), commercial banks began to challenge investment banks in areas previously off limits, such as the underwriting of commercial paper, mortgage-backed securities, corporate debt, and securitized receivables.

■ Banks sold corporate loans to get assets off their books and relieve pressure on regulatory capital requirements and spread risk across a managed portfolio. This has led to asset securitization and the recognition of loans as marketable securities.

Pressure on profits prompted banks to expand into other areas. While increasing their product and services offerings, banks took a closer look at their existing operations. As they tightened up what had been rather loose pricing structures and began to demand pricing agreements, the banking environment all across the country became much more businesslike and rationalized in strategy and in daily operations. Corporate treasurers became equally businesslike and transactional—and less relationship dependent.

When LBO and MBO borrowing exploded in the late 1980s, supply was pressed to meet demand. Finding themselves in the buyer's seat for the first time, corporate treasurers felt they had a new freedom—and a serious responsibility—to shop around for whichever bank would give them the best price and the fastest money. Speed became a new priority. Whereas in the early 1980s, borrowers considered 10 days an acceptable turnaround time for a major loan decision, by the end of the decade the drive to meet LBO and MBO demands reduced that expected time frame to just 24 hours. The pace of activity was extraordinary as bankers scrambled to meet the fast-changing rules of the game.

Adding to the upheaval was the acceleration of bank mergers during the 1980s. When a recession hit, banks with capital problems due to bad lending had to be absorbed. Other banks that did not have the capital to invest in technology—a requirement for staying competitive and critical to understanding profitability—were also absorbed. "Capacity," then later "shareholder value" became the new watchwords. If a bank wasn't large enough to survive on its own, or if its return on investment was too low to attract investors, the solution was simple: Get bigger—fast!

As a result of this mind-set, of the 25 main providers of corporate banking services in 1978 only a third survive today. The decrease in providers at a time of increased volume did little to augment the customer base of those banks remaining, even though the number of large corporations being served remained steady.[2] In fact, many banks saw a reduction in their customer bases.

Table 4.1 shows how many banks disappeared as a result of merger, acquisition, or outright failure to compete. Even many of the survivors (boldface entries in the table) did not post considerable customer gains. In fact, of the top 25 banks in 1978, only Bank of America and Bank of New York have substantially greater customer positions today after mergers.

In addition to Bank of America and Bank of New York, mergers have vaulted three regional banks—PNC BanCorporation, FleetBoston, First Union and SunTrust Banks—barely visible in 1978 onto today's list of top banks. And NationsBank, which ranked 27 in customer penetration in 1978 under the name of North Carolina National Bank, has leapfrogged to the number one ranking thanks to its merger with Bank of America. Other banks that had been highly successful in the 1970s, such as Security Pacific Bank, Manufacturers Hanover, and Continental Bank, have disappeared altogether.

Table 4.2 shows the top ranking U.S. banks serving large corporations today. Of these top-ranking banks, three of these four regional banks had the greatest percentage of customer gains as a result of mergers, as Table 4.3 on page 104 shows.

TABLE 4.1   Market Penetration—Then and Now*

1978 Institutions—United States	1978	Customers 2000	1978 to 2000 Change
Citibank	64%	48%	−10
Chase Manhattan	62	58	−4
Bank of America	55	75	20
Continental Illinois Bank	53	—	—
Morgan Guaranty	53	25	−42
Chemical Bank	52	—	—
Manufacturers Hanover Trust	48	—	—
Bankers Trust Co.	45	—	—
First Chicago	43	—	—
Security Pacific Bank	39	—	—
Mellon Bank	35	35	0
Wells Fargo	31	29	−2
Irving Trust	30	—	—
Harris Bank	30	—	—
First National Bank, Boston	30	—	—
Crocker National	28	—	—
United California Bank	28	—	—
Republic National	26	—	—
Wachovia	25	34	9
Northern Trust	22	22	0
First Nat'l Bank, Atlanta	24	—	—
Citizens & Southern	24	—	—
Bank of New York	22	42	90
Philadelphia National (CoreStates)	22	—	—
National Bank of Detroit	22	—	—
Marine Midland	21	—	—

* Based on the largest 1,700 corporations and nonbank financials in the United States of America.

FOREIGN BANKS FOLLOWED SUIT

The experience of foreign commercial banks mirrored that of their U.S. counterparts. By the mid-1990s, they had made significant inroads into the United States large corporate market as active providers of domestic credit. They were able to increase their customer bases significantly, as Table 4.4 on page 105 shows.

TABLE 4.2   Market Penetration*—Now

2000 Institutions—United States	Customers
Bank of America	75%
Chase Manhattan	58
BankOne	58
Citibank	48
Bank of New York	42
First Union	36
Mellon Bank	35
Fleet Boston	35
Wachovia Bank	34
Wells Fargo Bank	29
J.P. Morgan	25
Sun Trust Banks	23
Northern Trust	22
PNC Bank	22
US Bancorp	13
Key Bank	13
National City	10
Union Bank of California	10
Comerica Bank	9

* Based on the largest 1,700 corporate and nonbank financials in the United States of America.

This increase in customers was not enough to assure profitability. And in any case, the increase was short-lived. The foreign banks were slow to recognize and adapt their strategies to the evolving U.S. credit market. Former credit bankers, wedded to the *product,* were blind to the changes in the market. Poor analysis of long-term profitability both because of and compounded by even poorer management information about customer profitability soon had many foreign banks reeling from the market dynamics in the same way as had their U.S. counterparts. The difference was, they didn't know why.

It wasn't until some banks, such as Barclays Bank and National Westminster Bank, faced financial challenges on their home turf that they began to recognize the profit futility of lending money overseas. Moving to measure success based on "return measures" rather than on revenue (a strategy the largest American commercial banks had begun to implement a few years earlier) focused foreign banks on the truly low returns of a domestic

TABLE 4.3   Market Penetration after Mergers*

	Customers		
	1978	2000	Change
Bank of New York	22%	42%	90%
(Including Irving Trust)			
Bank of America	18**	75	317
(Including National Bank of North Carolina,			
C&S Bank, First National Bank of Atlanta,			
NationsBank, Continental-Illinois, and Security			
Pacific)			
BancOne	18	35	94
(First National Bank of Chicago)			
Pittsburgh National Corporation	17	22	29
(Including Pittsburgh National Bank, First National			
Bank of Louisville, and Midlantic Bank)			
First Union	11	36	227
(Including Philadelphia National, CoreStates)			
Fleet National	7	35	400
(Bank Boston, Shawmut Bank)			
(Including Industrial National Bank of			
Rhode Island, Shawmut Bank, NatWest USA)			
Sun Trust Banks	5	36	620
(Including Crestar)			

* Based on the largest 1,700 corporations and nonbank financials in the United States.
** 18% represents North Carolina National Bank. Bank of America's 1998 customer penetration was 55%, which is a 36% change from 1998.

credit-driven strategy. And, since foreign banks had not developed other products to complement their credit strategies, they were left in the late 1990s with few choices—acquire new product capabilities or retrench in the market. Some chose to exit entirely those relationships that did not provide good "return measures." Others, such as some Canadian and Swiss banks, simply shifted their focus to more lucrative market segments. Canadian Imperial Bank, for example, acquired Oppenheimer & Company, a U.S. stock-brokerage firm, and with it Oppenheimer's investment banking focus on smaller, noninvestment-grade U.S. companies.

Those foreign banks that had experienced such significant customer increases soon posted equally impressive decreases. Just as had happened with the domestic banks, the population of the top 25 foreign banks

TABLE 4.4   Market Penetration—Then and Now*

1982 Institutions—Foreign	Customers			Change
	1982	1998	2000	
Royal Bank of Canada	19%	24%	17%	−11%
ABN Amro Bank	11	37	34	209
Canadian Imperial Bank	17	22	12	−30
Bank of Montreal	14	32[1]	23	64
Bank of Tokyo	11	25[2]	17	55
Scotia Bank	18	24	19	6
Deutsche Bank	8	40[3]	33	313
Credit Lyonnais	20	23	15	−25
Société Générale	10	24	14	−40
Barclays Bank	19	18	15	−22
Banque Nationale de Paris	14	22[4]	18	28
Credit Suisse	14	16[5]	19	14
Fuji Bank	9	—	10	11
Swiss Bank	16	19[6]	8	−50
Sumitomo Bank	7	—	8	14
Sanwa Bank	8	15	6	−25
Commerzbank	7	14	10	42
Industrial Bank of Japan	9	15	10	11
National Westminster Bank	19	12	12[7]	−36
HSBC Midland Bank	6	11	17	183
Dai-Ichi Kangyo	5	13	8	60
Long Term Credit Bank	7	10	[8]	—
Standard Chartered Bank	4	7	7	75
Westdeutsche Landesbank	5	8	7	40
Union Bank of Switzerland	13	1[9]	[9]	—

*Based on the largest 1,700 corporate and nonbank financials in the United States of America.
[1] Includes Harris Bank.
[2] Includes Bank of Tokyo-Mitsubishi.
[3] Includes Bankers Trust.
[4] Includes Banque Indosuez.
[5] Includes Credit Suisse First Boston.
[6] Includes SG Warburg and Dillon Reed and Union Bank of Switzerland.
[7] Includes RBN NatWest.
[8] Terminated Business.
[9] Included in Swiss Bank, USB Warburg.

changed dramatically. Table 4.5 shows the European banks with the greatest downward shift in corporate banking and lending strategy in the past eight years (1992–2000), and the effects of those shifts on their respective customer bases. (Note: ABN Amro Bank and Deutsche Bank are the only foreign banks to broadly expand customer penetration during the period with acquisitions and active marketing strategies as shown in Table 4.4.)

Where the U.S. and European banks had found adversity, the volume-oriented Japanese banks saw opportunity. They entered the U.S. market leading with domestic credit provision and, planned to fill the void left first by the U.S. banks, then later by the European banks. In 1997, several Japanese banks, among them Bank of Tokyo-Mitsubishi, Fuji Bank, Sumitomo Bank, and Sanwa Bank ranked among the top 20 foreign banks in the United States.

These rankings also were short-lived. By 1998, to no one's surprise but their own, financial problems directly related to return on capital and risk-adjusted return objectives precipitated a fast retreat from the U.S. corporate market by all but Bank of Tokyo-Mitsubishi. The decline in market penetration continued into 2000, with Bank of Tokyo-Mitsubishi joining the trend.

Table 4.6 shows the dramatic changes since 1997.

TABLE 4.5 Market Penetration—Foreign Commercial Banks

Greatest Changes in Strategic Direction			
	Customers		
1992 Institutions—Foreign	1992	2000	Change
National Westminster Bank	33%	12%	−64
Barclays Bank	30	15[1]	−50
Royal Bank of Canada	30	17	−44
Canadian Imperial Bank	30	12	−30
Toronto Dominion Bank	25	12	−52
Union Bank of Switzerland	25	8[2]	−68
Westpac	22	8	*
Credit Lyonnais	21	15	−29

[1] Includes BZW Barclays.
[2] Includes Union Bank of Switzerland, SBC Warburg Dillon Reed.
* Less than 1%.

TABLE 4.6 Market Penetration—Japanese Commercial Banks*

	Change in Strategic Direction					
	Customers					Change from
1998 Institutions—Foreign	1996	1997	1998	1999	2000	1998
Bank of Tokyo-Mitsubishi	29%	29%	29%	25	17	−42
The Fuji Bank	23	26	18	14	10	−45
Sumitomo Bank	23	27	18	13	8	−56
Sanwa Bank	21	24	15	11	6	−60
Industrial Bank of Japan	20	20	15	14	10	−34
Dai-Ichi Kangyo Bank	16	18	13	12	8	−29
Long-Term Credit Bank	16	16	10	**	**	**

* Based on the largest 1,700 corporate and nonbank financials in the United States.
** Terminated business.

THE TRUE IMPORTANCE OF BEING TRULY IMPORTANT

The size of a bank's customer base is not nearly as important as its composition. Our research shows that a typical lead bank (and, it is the customer who determines which is the "lead" bank) earns 28 percent of the total amount spent on banking services. But a typical second-tier bank earns only 9 percent of the total amount spent on banking services and the numbers drop precipitously with each subsequent tier.

Table 4.7 illustrates just how important it is to be a *lead* relationship bank. Just as the revenue opportunity drops off sharply with each drop in relationship tier importance, the opposite is also true. Figure 4.1 illustrates how *any* improvement in relationship importance brings incremental benefits. The typical lead bank earns *sixteen* times the revenue of a fourth-tier bank. In dollar terms, this translates into revenues in the millions versus revenues in the thousands. And the compression of profits is even greater, as Figure 4.1 shows.

Enticing though these incremental increases can be, resist the temptation to try and uptier all your existing relationships. Trying to be all things to all people is always far too costly. Expanding the number of customers or enhancing lots of relationships is never as profitable as leveraging relationships with a well-defined group of companies where the bank has a real chance to become truly important.

TABLE 4.7   The Importance of Being Important

	Corporate Banking		
Relationship Tier	Percentage of Revenue Earned per Tier	Number of Banks Cited per Tier	Percentage of Revenue Earned per Bank
Lead	54%	1.9	28%
Second Tier	19	2.1	9
Third Tier	13	2.8	5
Fourth Tier	14	7.8	2

It is not sufficient to become the lead bank. Key to success is becoming the lead bank, and sustaining that lead, to those specific corporations where the bank has the skills, resources, and relationships to excel with those products that bring acceptable returns to build the bank's shareholder values. This usually means actively exiting those relationships where there is little chance of being the lead bank for its products of choice. Doing so frees up capital and people to concentrate fully on those customers that can, with the requisite commitment, be made into mutually beneficial lead relationships. Leading banks know that the dark side of "the importance of being truly important" is the high cost of being unimportant. Wasting time and skills and resources yields no profits and only incurs professional frustration.

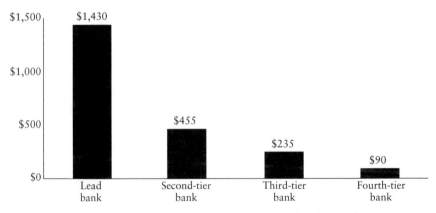

FIGURE 4.1   Revenue opportunity increases with relationship tier.

A NEW LOOK

Those banks that survived the fallout from dwindling customer bases and decreased profitability finally got the message that to ensure their continued survival, they needed to be more capable managers, more informed about their customers, and more careful in their investments into customer relationship building.

Both foreign and domestic banks began to focus on those customers with whom they had the best chance of becoming a lead or second-tier bank, and with whom they could earn the greatest levels of return on capital.

Advances in cost accounting and control made this easier. Bankers for the first time could pinpoint just where their profitability was coming from. They began to see how concentrating all the bank's resources on those chosen *existing* customers that held the most promise for evolving into long-term *leading* relationships could be much more profitable than the old way of striving to cultivate numerous new relationships. As a result, the number of solicitations targeted to *prospective* new customers dropped rapidly. Whereas in 1978 a large corporation received, on average, solicitations from 11 banks with which there was no relationship, today that same corporation receives just 2 such solicitations. Figure 4.2 shows how the mean number of commercial banks soliciting new customers continues to decline.

As banks concentrated more intensely on developing relationships with their most promising corporate customers, they also wisely cut back on unpromising and marginal customers.

Those customers that found themselves suddenly out of favor with some of their banks in turn became more selective in their choice of banks. By reducing the number of banks in their stable, they were able to attract

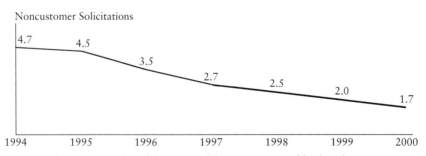

Note. Based on mean number of domestic and foreign commercial banks soliciting a new customer relationship.

FIGURE 4.2 The declining number of banks soliciting noncustomers.

better providers because they could compensate them with a greater share of business. The result was an overall decrease in the number of banks used, and a proportionate increase in importance for those banks they did use.

In 1978, customers considered 9.2 banks as "important" providers of banking services. By 2000, this number had dropped to 7.9. Figure 4.3 illustrates how the overall decline in commercial banks used continues. Mergers have contributed to the decline in the numbers because there are now fewer banks from which to choose.

Typically, of the 7.9 important banks used, slightly more than four-in-ten are foreign banks. This proportion increased in 1995 when the Japanese and French banks were willing to provide credit at a time when the American banks were not. When American banks resumed normal lending and some foreign banks reduced their positions in the United States, the ratio reverted to prior year patterns.

The trend to concentrate more banking business with fewer important banks occurred throughout the market, although the number of important banks any given corporation needs varies depending on the type of industry or the size of the company.

Table 4.8 shows how the number of important banks used differs by industry. And Table 4.9 approximates how the trend is broken down by size of company. This decrease in banks used and the decrease in banks' customer bases is occurring when corporate loan volume is at an all-time high, and continues to grow enormously. Yet fewer banks are willing to make those loans. And those banks that do make the loans immediately sell them

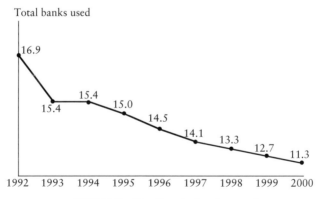

FIGURE 4.3 Decline in banks used.

TABLE 4.8 Number of Important Relationship Banks Viewed
by Industry

Important Bank Relationships			
	1977	2000	% Change
Industry Segments			
Utilities	9.7	8.0	−18%
Insurance	8.5	6.6	−22
Retail	10.5	7.1	−32
Transportation	9.1	7.2	−21
Finance Companies	12.9	13.7	6
Total Industrials	9.2	7.3	−14
Chemicals	10.0	7.6	−24
Food, Tobacco	9.1	7.6	−16
Machinery, Equipment	9.2	7.9	−14
Paper, Forest Products	9.0	6.9	−23
Oil and Gas	9.4	9.9	5
Total Companies	9.2	7.9	−14

to the syndicated loan market, the only way for them to serve their customers' credit needs without incurring the penalty of low returns on capital. The syndicated loan market is mirroring the explosive growth of corporate loans, multiplying from $137 billion in 1987 to well over $1.2 trillion in 2000.

The upshot of all these scenarios is that large corporate banking has become an extraordinarily competitive environment. Key not only to

TABLE 4.9 Number of Important Banks Used
by Industrials

Rank by Revenue	1977	2000	% Change
Over $5 billion	12.5	10.4	−17
$2.5–$5.0 billion	9.8	8.7	−12
$500–$2.4 billion	6.7	6.6	−2

success, but even to mere survival, are the modern relationship managers. In their new, redefined role, they ensure that those customers the bank *does* have—no matter how diminished their number—are the customers the bank *should* have.

QUALITY RELATIONSHIPS, NOT QUANTITY

Far more important than the number of customers in any bank's portfolio is the quality of its relationships with those customers. Table 4.10 shows how the customer portfolios of two leading banks have changed. Even though both banks deliberately brought about a decline in their customer base over a 20-year period, today each bank is *more* profitable, simply because a higher proportion of their customers are lead relationships.

For Citibank, lead relationships have gone from 29 percent to 55 percent of its reduced customer base. For Chase Manhattan Bank, lead relationships have gone from 23 percent to 52 percent. The impact on profitability has been even more dramatic.

Take a closer look at Citibank's customer base. Over 20 years, the total number of accounts plummeted, while the *proportion* of lead relationships increased by more than 90 percent. Its customer portfolio now has the potential to be significantly more and more profitable. In contrast, two mergers have served to keep Chase Manhattan's customer base stable. Its lead relationships, however, have more than doubled as a proportion of total customers.

TABLE 4.10 Changes in Customer Portfolios

	Citibank			Chase Manhattan		
	1978	2000	Change	1978	2000	Change
Total Customers	65%	48%	−17	60%	58%	−2
Lead	29	55	26	23	52	29
Second Tier	29	17	−12	25	20	−5
Third Tier	29	18	−11	28	20	−8
Fourth Tier	13	11	−2	24	9	−13

THE EVOLUTION OF THE RELATIONSHIP MANAGER

Relationship managers today are responsible for divining who the right key customers are. As if that were not enough, they are also responsible not just for maintaining but for always elevating the importance of those relationships by providing more and more services. This level of responsibility is a far cry from the days when credit was the relationship manager's primary responsibility. Credit may still be an important component of the job, but it is now only one piece of an increasingly complex amalgam of services and values.

In the 1960s and 1970s, relationship managers were primarily credit officers. Their careers depended on making the bank an important lending institution for a large number of corporate customers who looked to the relationship manager to predict economic conditions that would change the cost and availability of credit. Trainees were given intensive credit training, and all were familiar with the admonition: "It takes a lot of interest to make up for a bad loan." While relationship managers were encouraged to sell the bank's other products—such as corporate trust, trade, foreign exchange, overseas branch services, and the emerging cash management services—they were not required to know a whole lot about those products. The real emphasis of their job was on managing the credit relationship because, thanks to firm pricing and low-cost funding, corporate loans were very lucrative.

In our 1974 research, corporate treasury officers cited "Knowledge of company's needs" and "Knowledge of overall business conditions" as the two most important requirements of a relationship manager. Those requirements began to change as alternatives to bank credit came in and the profitability from credit began to diminish. The largest lending banks—mostly those in major U.S. money centers—recognized the inherent profitability risk of depending solely on credit and were highly motivated to change their product mix before it was too late. The number and variety of financing products began to increase exponentially. Not only did lending, cash management, and foreign exchange products multiply, but a host of new products, such as derivatives, capital raising products and highly complex structured financings, were added to the mix. Whereas in the 1970s our clients required that we provide information on only eight credit and cash management products, today our coverage has increased nearly tenfold, and includes the following extraordinary range of products:

▪ *Corporate Banking Credit Services.* Foreign local currency credit; syndicated loan financing; receivables financing; project financing; tax-advantaged products; loans for acquisitions; recaps, restructurings, or LBOs; short-term trade services and finance (without government support and including settlement of trade transactions; documentary collections, letters of credit, and acceptances refinancing); long-term structured trade finance (including government-supported export financing).

■ *Investment Banking Services.* Public or private underwriting of common stock, preferred stock, or convertible issues; repurchase of common stock; public offering of bonds, including domestic straight bonds, 144(a) offerings, and Eurobonds; bonds backed by assets, such as mortgages, loans, or credit card receivables; issuing dealer for your company's domestic or Eurocommercial paper programs; medium-term note program; private placement of term debt securities; advice on domestic acquisitions or divestitures for a fee; advice on international acquisitions or divestitures for a fee; advice on takeover defense; advice on major corporate restructuring, including recapitalization, or leveraged or management buyouts.

■ *Specialized Services* (Insurance companies, brokerage firms, or dealers). Standby letters of credit; securities lending.

■ *Cash Management Services.* Cash management consulting; lockbox; account reconciliation; domestic money transfer; cash balance and information reporting services; concentration account; international (cross-border) money transfer; zero-balance account; remote or controlled disbursement; automated clearinghouse (ACH); check-imaging applications; corporate purchasing/procurement cards; electronic payments (EDI); payables outsourcing; receivables outsourcing; short-term investments; local but non-U.S. cash management; multic-urrency product; international/cross-border ACH; interstate banking services.

■ *Foreign Exchange Services.* Foreign currency options of less than one month in maturity; foreign currency options of one month or more but less than three months in maturity; foreign currency options of three months or more in maturity; barrier options (including knock-out and knock-in options); average exchange rate options; foreign currency options.

■ *Interest Rate Derivatives.* Interest rate swaps of less than two years; interest rate swaps of two years or more but less than seven years; interest rate swaps of seven years or more; interest rate options, caps, collars, or floors; Swaptions; interest rate swaps denominated in different currencies; interest rate or currency swaps linked to a bank loan; interest rate or currency swaps linked to a debt issue; cross-currency swaps of two years or more; customized or exotic derivatives (e.g., barrier options, quanto or diff swaps, constant-maturity or swap rate swaps); derivatives structured to address tax, accounting, or regulatory issues; interest rate futures or exchange-traded options; OTC bond options, commodity swaps, options, or futures; equity derivatives, such as equity warrants or equity index options or futures; credit-related swaps (credit, default, index, and total rate of return swaps); unwinding or repackaging of derivatives positions; asset swaps.

■ *Investment Management.* Administrative/record-keeping services for master trust, defined benefit, defined contribution (e.g., 401(k)), or custody assets; active investment management services for pension and employee benefit plans (excluding short-term or excess balance investments).

More product specialists were brought in to handle the tremendous increase, and the formerly all-important product—credit—became one of many product offerings. By 1989, with credit availability even more strained and banks' financial conditions under question, credit became a particularly significant offering, and a relationship manager's ability to convince his or her bank to provide that credit—and provide it quickly—became the *most* important requirement of a relationship manager.

Yet, ironically, so great is the change in the structure of relationships that today, credit is no longer under the relationship manager's control. Large U.S. commercial banks pulled responsibility for credit products out of relationship managers' portfolios to provide them with more time for "sales management." Credit became its own product specialty group, with credit judgments centralized and managed by credit product specialists. This change signaled the end of the relationship manager as the credit manager. The relationship manager is now expected to manage relationships across all product lines without responsibility for any one product.

A NEW DEFINITION

From a product-specific, quantitative job of advising on interest rate movements, the relationship manager is now a full-range financial service adviser, with a "softer," more qualitative emphasis on overall profitability and customer management. The new mission is to earn access to the treasury office by acting in an advisory capacity to the CFO and the treasurer while becoming fluent in the full financing needs of a corporation—from short-term borrowing to structured finance to long-term debt underwriting.

Many new electronic cash management products along with a wide range of derivatives and other complementary products have brought added complexity to the job. Since these are products on which relationship reliance tends to be built, relationship managers are expected to identify the customers' needs in these areas as well. While they don't have to know the products in-depth (an impossible task anyway), they need to know enough about their customers' needs to be able to recommend the products in the first place, and introduce the appropriate specialists. And, after making recommendations, relationship managers also coordinate the interactions of the bank's numerous product specialists to make sure the job gets done efficiently, harmoniously, and always with profitability and the long-term interests of the relationship in mind.

An ability to listen, to learn, and to offer creative ideas and solutions has become an integral part of the relationship manager's job. Yes, credit is still important, but so are these other, less easily quantified skills. In the late 1980s, corporate treasurers cited the "ability to convince the bank to provide credit" as the most important attribute of a relationship manager. But "ability to provide creative ideas and solutions" came in such a close second as to be a statistical tie.

Table 4.11 shows how corporate treasury officers' expectations changed between 1974 and 1995.[3] "Creativity," now considered so critical to the relationship manager's effectiveness, is by its nature difficult to define. Figure 4.4 shows how corporate treasurers define creativity.

Customers no longer want their relationship managers simply to fulfill their credit needs, they want them to act as advisers and help them identify *all* their needs. In the ideal mutually reinforcing scenario, the banker who invests time in a relationship and knows the customer's needs is best qualified to create the product and advisory support that helps the customer achieve its own business success.

TABLE 4.11   Most Important Relationship Manager Requirements

	Rankings		
	Mid-1970s	Late 1980s	Mid-1990s
Knowledge of overall business, financial and economic conditions	2	5	10
Knowledge of your company's needs for banking services	1	4	3
Ability to convince bank to meet credit needs	6	2*	1*
Ability to provide creative ideas and solutions	na	2*	1*

* Statistical tie.

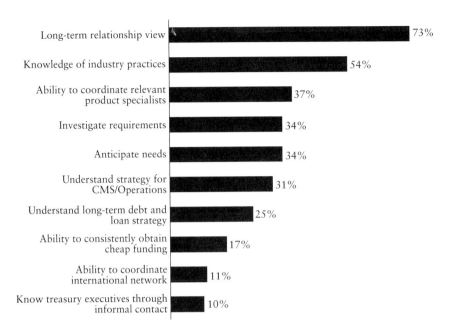

FIGURE 4.4 Factors differentiating innovative and creative relationship managers.

That is why taking a long-term view is by far the leading factor differentiating relationship managers. Relationship managers can only provide real value when they know their customers well. And customers expect the banks that work with them over time will understand and pay the closest attention to their particular servicing requirements.

This expectation increases with the bank's importance to the customer. Our research shows that 85 percent of all lead customers perceive they have a relationship-driven connection with the bank. Seventy percent of second-tier customers think this way, and only 40 percent of third-tier customers believe this is so.

CROSS-PURPOSES

The new definition of the relationship manager's role did not go unchallenged. As bank senior management began emphasizing customer-centered "solutions" relationship management over bank-centered product knowledge, and added new product groups to augment the relationship management delivery groups, the pressure to establish competitive positions caused the new relationship management ideal to butt heads with the old product specialist orientation. Product specialists were miffed as they saw relationship managers encroaching on their proprietary territory. Relationship managers were frustrated as they saw their efforts with customers stymied by uncooperative product specialists. Each felt their way was the one "right" way, when in truth neither an exclusive specialist approach nor an exclusive relationship orientation can fully satisfy customers while also maximizing product profitability.

Specialty groups are expensive because of the natural tendency of any group, once established, to create its own infrastructure to meet its needs. Since each feels its needs are unique, there is a strong instinct for self-preservation; and potential synergy between bank and customer can easily be overlooked as specialists by definition focus on their narrowly defined responsibilities. By choosing to reap the short-term benefits of completing a product transaction, they can miss the greater benefits that come from a long-term view of how the product, or an alternate product, will benefit the customer.

The cost of the tunnel vision that comes from a purely product-oriented strategy is largely invisible in boom times. But eventually most products experience either a decline in volume as markets become saturated or replacement products arise, or a narrowing of margins as the product's life cycle takes it closer to commodity pricing. When many major product areas turn down at the same time, there is a big opportunity cost as multiple product groups lose contact with key customers. And once removed from the information loop, the product-oriented banks are poorly positioned to benefit from subsequent upturns.

As each product specialist works to sell product, he or she is not sensitive to, or necessarily even aware of, how any particular product fits into the bank's overall strategy for that customer. In the "Segmentation" section later in this chapter, we explain how to determine an appropriate marketing strategy for each customer. For now, Figure 4.5 illustrates how a purely product-driven marketing strategy can be beneficial for selling specific products because each product specialist manages each customer contact independently, but is not concerned about elevating the overall share of relationship "wallet."

Yet a purely relationship management orientation also has its drawbacks, among them problems in allocating and maintaining the appropriate human resources for marketing to groups whose demands are ever-changing, as are the profit margins they provide for banks.

Even so, our clients' internal reviews reveal that relationship customers show the highest profits consistently over time. And most often, those customers are in a lead position. Even where banks have a successful product

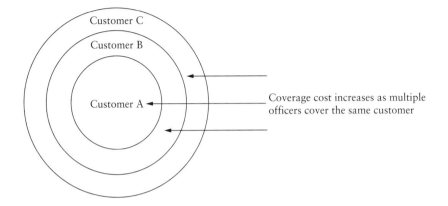

- Product specialists manager process
- High share of product "wallet"
- Undetermined share of relationship "wallet"
- Unpredictable relationship "returns"

FIGURE 4.5 Product coverage.

strategy based on their ability to price, execute, and identify opportunities in the market better than their competitors, our research proves out that where price and execution are ranked the same, it is the *relationship* that wins.

Figure 4.6 shows how relationship coverage provides the most efficient use of resources. The delivery cost is managed by a relationship manager who employs a strategy unique to that customer and coordinates the product specialists accordingly. In some cases, the appropriate delivery strategy may be product specialist coverage only, but only the relationship manager can make this determination, after astute analysis of each customer's needs. This kind of analysis is discussed later in this chapter.

FROM COMPETITIVE TO COOPERATIVE— THE NEW, INTEGRATED RELATIONSHIP MANAGEMENT STRATEGY

There is no denying that conflict can be an integral part of the relationship manager/product specialist alliance, especially when it is reinforced by inequitable rewards and accounting systems. Winners, however, adopt a team approach (and support it with fair compensation schemes) that emphasizes the very best of both strategies and allows relationship managers and product

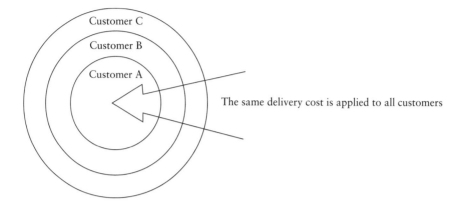

The same delivery cost is applied to all customers

- Relationship manager process
- Multiple product specialists involved
- High share of relationship "wallet"
- Long-term view of relationship
- Continuum of "returns"

FIGURE 4.6   Relationship coverage.

specialists to work together toward goals beneficial both to them and to their customers. When managed this way, the inherent tensions between the two groups can be creative, dynamic, and constructive.

So even though each orientation appears at odds with the other, in truth each is more effective when used to support the other. The issue is not *whether* to use a relationship strategy or a product strategy, but rather *when*. Like a star tennis player equally adept with both forehand and backhand, good relationship managers are equally adept with a relationship management approach and a product specialist approach. They understand when each is most effective for getting the job done and can harness and orchestrate, in a positive, coordinated way, the bank's resources to service their customers.

It is a big job. Here are some of the key strategic components of a successful relationship management strategy:

- The bank's product mix matches the customers' product requirements.
- The products the customers need match with those products the bank is particularly good at providing.

- The relationship manager knows the customers' needs thoroughly, and has enough of a working knowledge of the bank's products to identify opportunities.
- The relationship manager disseminates enough information about the customers' needs to allow the bank's specialists the chance in turn to identify opportunities.
- There is mutual trust. The relationship manager has confidence in both the products and the product managers. The product specialists trust that the relationship manager knows enough about the products to recognize opportunities for their use. The relationship manager, in turn, has confidence that the information he or she is providing to the product specialist will result in a compelling, informed proposal at that all-important first presentation.
- There is flawless execution.
- A managed, consistent interaction exists between the relationship manager and the product specialist.
- There is a good, up-to-date database for coordinating *all* the bank's activities with the customer. This enables the relationship manager to take a holistic view of the way the bank is serving customers' overall needs, while also providing details of specific transactions.

SEGMENTATION: BREAKING DOWN TO BUILD UP

Segmenting customers by both their product needs and the bank's expertise at providing those products can ease inherent tension between relationship managers and product specialists because it clarifies, on a customer-by-customer and product-by-product basis, whether relationship managers or product specialists should lead the coverage. And when the relationship manager and the product specialist work together to develop such a plan (and we strongly advise that they do), they are driven by the customer's needs rather than divided by proprietary needs to everyone's benefit. That's not to say product transactions will be guaranteed—they are judged on their own benefits in the context of a longtime, mature relationship—but it does position the bank well, as Table 4.12 demonstrates.

Segmenting your customer base is a clear-cut way to determine which customers hold the most potential for becoming lead relationships and which do not. Segmentation begins with a rigorous customer profile analysis, a three-step process designed to segment customers based on ideal future returns. The process seems simple, but we caution our clients not to underestimate the challenge.

TABLE 4.12 Means of Rewarding Relationship Banks

Rewards of Relationship-Oriented Relationships	Frequency of Reward	
	Always or Often	Rarely or Never
Offering more frequent opportunities to bid competitively for business	82%	6%
Awarding a transaction in the event of a tie	77	5
Accepting their offer even if marginally more expensive than the most competitive offer	24	26
Offering business on an exclusive basis	14	55
Allocating higher margin business	23	40

First, sort your customers into three or four "return categories" of your own choosing. (We do not care so much which return categories are used, only that our clients be rigorous in assigning their customers to the groupings they've chosen.)

Second, segment your customers based on ideal future returns, and eliminate any customers that hold little opportunity of meeting those ideals. The objective here is to make the segmentation decisions based on future goals, not past experience. This is where the process can become difficult. A customer returning 11 percent on the return measure may rank among the top 10 percent of the bank's customers, but if the bank's ideal return is 15 percent or higher, then that customer cannot and *should not* be placed in the "highest return" category. Many of our clients resist this rigid requirement because it winnows so many customers from their top tier positions and they feel vulnerable publicizing such small numbers. Painful though it can be, it is critical to become aware that customers you regard as your "top customers" may not be all that important.

Third, after "getting it right," be patient—and persistent. Do not allow the list of names in each category to change more than 3 to 4 percent each year for the next 2 to 3 years. Changing the customers in each category based on the events of a single year creates an undisciplined management process.

Once the profile analysis is complete, create another set of customer groups based on the type of delivery method needed to maximize return from each customer. Our clients use various nomenclatures to describe the groupings, but we have found that most customers fit into one of these four categories:

1. *Partnership Customers.* These are your bank's core customer group and represent a limited number of top-tier customers. They are loyal for *reasons* and provide the highest levels of profit through multiple product dependency. They are well worth the high quality and costly relationship management they require. We recommend that first-rate relationship managers service all these accounts.

2. *Potential Partnership Customers.* These customers represent a broader customer base. While they are slightly less profitable than partnership customers, they still require a high level of relationship management because they have the potential to become partnership customers. First-rate relationship managers should service these accounts also.

3. *Annuity Customers.* Often the largest customer group, these companies produce predictable and steady revenue flow from a few core products. The relationship management returns are marginal, and analysis shows there is little opportunity to expand the relationship. Nevertheless, these good, steady customers warrant servicing by a solid account person to maintain information flow.

4. *Product Customers.* This last group of customers falls outside the profile of relationship customers. Usually only one product in which your bank has a particular expertise anchors the business. However, since these customers often represent the bank's broadest customer base, there is potential for transitioning at least some of these product-based customers into long-term, partnership accounts. Your best product specialists should be placed on these accounts to exploit the opportunity on a product-by-product basis, with the objective to build a critical mass of "share of product wallet" in that business line. Periodically, the bank should monitor the transactions to see if enough synergy has been built by the various product managers to transition the customer from that one-product orientation to more of a multiproduct partnership. The bank can then determine when to apply relationship management resources to help develop that partnership relationship.

THE VALUE OF A PLAN

Once the partnership groups have been created, we advise that the product specialists and the relationship managers continue to work together to devise an account plan, a product plan, and an action plan for each customer within the various partnership groups. Such a detailed business plan can be a powerful tool for focusing and coordinating sales efforts.

As you begin to form the customer plans, keep in mind the importance of superior execution, discipline, and consistency. Each builds on the other. The absence of just one of these three elements puts the other two at risk and threatens to damage your customer relationship. The following three definitions make up the foundation of truly good service:

1. *Execution.* The relationship manager is dependent on the product specialist to execute consistently, time after time. Doing so is in everyone's best interest, because a customer's satisfaction in one product area improves the chance of success in selling other products.
2. *Discipline.* Look carefully at how your customers are being serviced. If not carefully monitored, high-profit customers can be overlooked in the pressure to address the more pressing demands of lesser accounts. A mistake in either direction, whether assigning a primarily transaction-oriented customer to a relationship manager, or pairing a customer with real, long-term potential with a product specialist, comes with a huge opportunity cost.
3. *Consistency.* Don't underestimate the value of a familiar face. The most frequent customer complaint is "failure to meet more often with those bankers who contribute real value." Frequent turnover in relationship managers can have a negative impact that can last for years. But if you work closely with your customers well in advance of the inevitable relationship manager turnovers, it will ease the transition for both bank and customer. Our research shows that 92 percent of customers agree that the relationship manager should have a personal style that works well with their finance department.

Here then are our recommendations for how to create an account plan, a product plan, and an action plan for each of your customers.

The Account Plan

A superior account plan is made up of the following:

■ A relationship tier goal, arrived at by estimating the bank's current importance to the customer. This goal should specify a specific level of relationship (from "lead" down to "fourth-tier") as well as a time frame for achieving that level.
■ A review of the 3-year volume *and* profitability of business being done with the customer, and a stated 2-year objective.

■ A credit exposure/credit commitment analysis, evaluating the amount of credit risk your bank is willing to take for the customer versus the amount of credit commitment required by that customer to qualify as one of their primary credit providers. For the few customers without credit requirements, this assessment should still be made to prepare the bank to meet surprise requests.

■ An analysis of the opportunities to provide each of your products of choice. With the product manager as guide, the relationship manager will know enough about the product opportunities and objectives to integrate the product sales strategies without fear, and can introduce the product manager at the appropriate time. The product manager benefits because he or she comes to the first meeting briefed, well prepared, and further up the sales curve than other product managers making initial sales calls.

As we advise our clients, the account plan should be a unique reflection of your institution, showing simply and accurately the business goals and strategies for each individual customer.

An effective account plan relies heavily on a bank's information management system. Recording accurate volume, profitability numbers, and global product transactions is the greatest challenge. Determining how to allocate resources based on those global numbers is the next-greatest challenge.

We recommend using a table, similar to the one shown in Table 4.13, to develop an account plan for each customer.

The Product Plan

Product specialists are just as committed to building business relationships as are account officers. When product specialists develop product plans, it helps facilitate a sense of teamwork and shared goals. In addition, a product plan helps the product specialists focus on a disciplined approach to product execution and business development. As product specialists put in place specific plans for each product, these plans in turn reinforce account officers' confidence that the products they are selling are, in fact, deliverable.

The product plan works in conjunction with the account plan. A good product plan consists of the following elements:

■ A thorough analysis of your bank's current product execution, development capacity, and capabilities compared with that of each of your direct competitors.

TABLE 4.13 Account Plan

3-Year Actual

	Tier Provider Rank	Revenue Volume	Profit Volume	Credit Limit Required[1]	Credit Limit Available[1]	Product Clusters Planned	Product Clusters Earned
1997	3	$1,200,000	$ 60,000	$30,000	$50,000	3	2
1998	2	2,400,000	170,000	40,000	50,000	6	5
1999	1	3,600,000	325,000	50,000	60,000	7	7

[1] In millions of dollars.

2-Year Plan

	Tier Provider Rank	Revenue Volume	Profit Volume	Business Strategy Summary[2]
2000	1	$3,600,000	$325,000	1. Present debt capital raising capabilities to CFO and capture co-lead on next issue (6/00) 2. Raise international credit facility commitment by 20% (3/00) 3. Conduct CEO anniversary dinner (12/00)
2001	1	4,200,000	400,000	

[2] The business strategies listed here are merely examples. A much broader strategic plan should be written for each customer, listing target dates and person accountable for each element of the plan.

- A plan for allocating specialist resources, based on the account plans, across conflicting demands of business development, product development, and execution support.
- Accountability for specific events—with dates—to measure product specialist performance against the product plan.
- A review and profitability plan that is tied in with the account plans.
- A sign-off by team leaders and senior management.
- A strategy for introducing the appropriate product specialists to their customer counterparts and getting it right on their product-specific strategy, including how it fits into the overall relationship strategy.
- An analysis of each competitor's strengths and weaknesses, along with tactics for taking advantage of any vulnerabilities as well as defending against their strengths.

TABLE 4.14   Product Plan

	Product Cluster—A			Product Cluster—B		
	Tier Provider Rank	Revenue Volume	Profit Volume	Tier Provider Rank	Revenue Volume	Profit Volume
3-Year Actual						
1997	3	$ 85,000	$ 5,000	5	$106,000	$ 5,000
1998	2	115,000	10,000	4	150,000	8,000
1999	1	250,000	25,000	3	200,000	20,000
2-Year Plan						
2000	1	300,000	25,000	3	200,000	20,000
2001	1	350,000	35,000	2	250,000	30,000

Note: "Provider rank" is the desired goal to maximize the bank's share of its customer's expenditures on any given product. In many cases, the provider rank is based on the judgment of product specialists but can, with customer cooperation, be a mutually agreed on actual rank.

A table such as the one shown in Table 4.14 helps quantify the opportunity for each customer in each product, in both monetary and probability terms. It also acts as a tool to ensure coordination and cooperation between the relationship manager and the product specialist.

Use this table in the following way:

- Based on the past 3 years' experience and revenue earned, the relationship manager and product manager work together to set forth the 2-year objective. It is based on revenue but is heavily influenced by the bank's provider rank and the perceived opportunity for that bank to move higher up the ranking.
- Product A in the table utilizes a retention strategy. The bank has achieved in 1998 first-tier provider rank and as such should control 50 to 60 percent of the revenue opportunities.
- Product B utilizes a strategy of new business building, since the bank is a number 5 provider and likely earns only 5 to 15 percent of the product revenue.

The Action Plan

The action plan helps ensure that the account plan and the product plan get implemented. Here are recommendations for creating a superior action plan:

■ Determine a target number of meetings to be held in the coming year. List the names and titles of the individuals with whom you plan to meet, as well as potential meeting dates. State the purpose of each meeting. A typical entry looks like this:

Customer ABC
Meetings to be held between June 1 and December 15

Date of each meeting	Purpose of meeting
Meeting 1 June 1	Review overall plan for the year
Meeting 2 August 1	Assess customer needs in FX
Meeting 3 December 15	Review our operations and cash management accuracy over past six months

■ Set a schedule for the target number of original ideas to bring to the customer.
■ A schedule to meet with the bank's product specialists to determine product opportunities and assign responsibility for visits and product transaction closes.
■ Agree with product specialists on a revenue goal for each product.

JUDGING THE PLAN'S EFFECTIVENESS

A plan is only as good as its execution. As we consult with our clients, we see too few senior managers using specific criteria for judging the success of their relationship managers. Too often, they judge them on the latest deal and *not* on the real criteria for success: the ability to create a long-term, mutually beneficial relationship, even if the "deal payoff" is less immediate. Here are a few measures for evaluating the success of relationship managers:

■ Test your relationship manager's knowledge. Do the customers' actions align with the objectives set forth in the account plan? Do the clients that the relationship manager identifies as partnership customers behave as partnership customers? Do they invite the relationship manager to advise before transactions are publicized? Is he or she asked to help shape the request for proposal (RFP)? Does the relationship manager often receive the "right of first refusal?" A negative answer to any one of these questions indicates that, even though the relationship manager may think it is a partnership relationship, it may not be.
■ Ask your customers what the bank and its bankers can do specifically to enhance understanding of their business and needs. Formal and informal relationship reviews are the standard method for achieving this,

but few bankers and few customers ever put in writing specific actions to be taken to enhance understanding. We suggest creating such a document; when signed off by both parties, it becomes the "partnership agreement" for the year and serves as a valuable benchmark against which to compare the progress of relationship managers.

Ultimately, it is the responsibility of senior management to reinforce to the customers the advantages of using the relationship manager as a *partner*. Some customers are skeptical that the relationship manager, whom they perceive as being paid for transactions, can truly function as an adviser separate and apart from the bank's own short-term business interest. Senior management must be intimately involved to assure the customer that the relationship manager *can* effectively switch roles from advocating his or her own bank's products to advising on the "right product" from the "right supplier," even if that supplier is not his or her own bank.

AN IDEAL PARTNERSHIP

It is the very breadth of the relationship manager's role that gives it strength. Those banks that use the relationship manager to the full capacity of both the job and the individuals performing it will find themselves with a distinct competitive advantage, and uniquely positioned to weather the changes in an industry where customers' needs are ever-changing. With the relationship manager now acting as a true adviser as well as a provider, "relationship banking" has evolved into a meaningful partnership relationship that benefits both bank and customer.

Corporate Cash Management

Corporate cash management in America has become a concentrated business along three dimensions:

1. Each corporation concentrates its business with a few suppliers.
2. The leading cash management banks hold large market shares relative to their competitors.
3. The leading banks are differentiating themselves in the recognized quality of service delivered.

Looking at the details behind these three propositions, our annual research shows that the typical allocations of revenue among a large

corporation's important cash management banks follow this pattern of
concentration:

First bank	55%
Second bank	21%
Third bank	10%
Fourth bank	6%
Fifth bank	3%

In brief, the first bank gets over half of all the business and the second bank
gets nearly half of the rest; 92 percent of a typical large corporation's cash
management business is concentrated with just four service providers.

Differences driven by company size and industry are evident. For example, gas utilities (which serve geographically concentrated markets) concentrate 75 percent of their business with their first cash management bank
while telecommunications utilities (often serving larger territories) concentrate only 46 percent with their first bank.

Larger companies concentrate their cash management business less
than do smaller companies, but the difference is not proportional, as shown
in Table 4.15.

The second type of concentration is in market penetration among the
1,700 largest corporations. As shown in Table 4.16, the market leaders are
strong as measured by market penetration, and they are getting stronger in
both scale of operation and delivered service quality.

A large number of mergers have reshaped the competitive landscape of
cash management providers. The mergers at Bank of America and Chase
Manhattan—as well as those at Wells Fargo, FleetBoston, Bank One, and
First Union (each barely visible in cash management in 1993)—have significantly changed the list of leading banks by market position among today's

TABLE 4.15   Share of Wallet Received by Top 5 Banks

Company Size	First Bank	Second Bank	Third Bank
Over $5.0 billion	46%	21%	12%
$2.5–$5.0 billion	54	22	11
$1.0–$2.4 billion	61	20	9
$650–$999 million	67	19	8
$500–$649 million	69	23	2
Total Companies	55%	21%	10%

TABLE 4.16 Cash Management in 2000

	Market Penetration
Bank of America	62%
BankOne	44
Chase Manhattan	42
Citibank	32
First Union	26
Wachovia Bank	26
Mellon Bank	25
Wells Fargo	24
Fleet Boston	20
PNC Bank	18
U.S. Bancorp	13
Bank of Montreal—Harris Bank	13
Bank of New York	12
Northern Trust	12
SunTrust Banks	11
ABN AMRO	12
American Express	9
Merrill Lynch	9
KeyCorp	8
Deutsche Bank	8

top cash management banks. Other banks that had been highly successful in the 1970s and 1980s, such as Security Pacific Bank, Manufacturers Hanover, First Interstate, Chemical Bank, Continental Illinois, Crocker National, United California Bank, Republic National, and Irving Trust have disappeared altogether.

Of the top-ranking banks, five had substantial gains in customers as a result of mergers, as shown in Table 4.17.

The relative importance of cash management banks is not fully measured by *penetration*. For example, these three leading banks have a larger proportion of their respective cash management customers counting them as particularly *important* for either domestic or international cash management: Bank of America, Citibank, and Chase Manhattan.

On the third type of concentration, we are seeing the emergence of a cash management bulge bracket, similar to that in investment banking. Bank of America, Citibank, Chase Manhattan and, to some extent, Bank One are differentiated from other leading cash management providers in

TABLE 4.17   Impact of Mergers*

	Market Penetration		Percent Change
	1993	2000	
Bank of America	43%	62%	44
(Including National Bank of North Carolina, C&S Bank, First National Bank of Atlanta, NationsBank, Boatmen's, Continental Illinois, and Security Pacific)			
First Union	11	26	136
(Including Philadelphia National, CoreStates)			
Fleet National	6	20	233
(Including Industrial National Bank of Rhode Island, Shawmut Bank, NatWest USA, and Bank of Boston)			
Chase Manhattan	24	42	75
(Including Chemical and Texas Commerce Bank)			
Wells Fargo	7	24	242
(Including Norwest and First Interstate)			
BankOne	9	44	388
(Including First Chicago and NBD)			

* Based on the largest 1,700 corporations and nonbank financials in the United States.

terms of both the number of customer relationships and the quality of the service delivered. (While specialists such as Mellon Bank and Wachovia compete favorably in terms of quality, they lack a large customer franchise.)

Given the capital-intensive nature of this business, which is only increasing due to e-commerce product development initiatives, there is a question of whether the smaller competitors can afford to keep up.

When evaluating banks' cash management services, as shown in Table 4.18, company executives who specialize in cash management emphasize three factors:

1. Strength or credit relationship.
2. Quality of customer service.
3. Price.

As is so often the case, price is more important in the decision making of larger corporations. And price is given great importance in the comparative "bake off" through which a new cash management bank is selected. But, while price is often key to *winning* business, service quality is far more important in *keeping* business. And in the cost-competitive business of cash management, profit margins are narrow, so customer loyalty is essential for

TABLE 4.18   Cash Management Bank Selection Criteria

	Degree of Importance
Strength of credit relationship	59%
Quality of customer service	57
Price	53
Service accuracy	40
Regional needs	36
Tailoring of services to needs	23
Quality of operations personnel	12
Superior Internet or electronic interface	6

long-term success and profitability. Make sure you will keep any business you compete to win. Don't lose what you've won!

The three main reasons banks *lose* cash management relationships are:

1. Customer service support.
2. Accuracy of service.
3. Price of service.

Looking backward, the main reasons new cash management banks have won new corporate business are led by *price*, as shown in Table 4.19.

TABLE 4.19   Why Banks Win Cash Management Business

	Degree of Importance
Price of service	36%
Customer service support	24
Accuracy of service	17
Willingness to customize services	15
Product feature of function	14
Global cash management capabilities	14
Ability to provide innovative ideas and solutions	13
Quality of specialist	11
Commitment to business	10
Internet/electronic banking capability	5

Looking ahead, two changes in the market are important. First, over the past several years, more and more banks and corporations have been pricing their relationships on the basis of longer-term agreements. And selection decisions are driven by quality of customers; quality of operations; and quality of cash management specialists. (Price comes in fourth.) Second, more and more corporations are using the Internet to select the banks they will use for cash management.

The Challenge of New Business Solicitation in Middle Market Banking

Lending to midsize companies[4] within the middle market is the heartland of traditional wholesale banking. This large, diverse, and profitable business of financing the growth of companies too large for proprietors to finance by themselves and too small to use public capital markets is ever changing, as each year companies grow into it and others expand and grow out of it. This market is becoming increasingly important, yet most commercial banks remain alarmingly unskilled—both in tactics and in strategy—at soliciting the new business they both want and need for profitable growth.

An effective new business solicitation program matters now more than ever to banks competing in this market. Here's why:

- *Serving midsize companies is a big business.* Approximately 195,000 midsize companies headquartered in the United States account for an estimated $218 billion in borrowing and $170 billion in cash balances.
- *It is a profitable business.* Many successful banks earn returns in this market of 18 to 22 percent on equity versus a typical commercial bank's overall return of 12 to 15 percent.
- *It is (almost) a captive business.* Roughly 95 percent of midsize companies are privately held, so few have access to public capital markets. They depend on commercial banks for their working capital and long-term debt financing. Today, the great majority—76 percent—of midsize companies use only one bank as their primary source of financing, 23 percent use two banks, 8 percent use three banks, and only 3 percent use more than three banks.
- *It is an attainable business.* Many middle-tier banks have been eliminated due to mergers and many large banks are no longer willing to provide personalized service to their smaller, less-profitable customers. With fewer banks for midsize companies to choose from—or,

more accurately, with fewer large banks willing to provide the high level of personal service those companies demand—opportunities open up for smaller banks to expand their positions. Their lower-cost infrastructure enables them to deliver the "high-touch" that midsize companies want at profit levels that are still attractive. Nonbank financial providers, such as investment banks, insurance companies, and emerging dot-com companies are also making the most of this opportunity.

AS CALIFORNIA GOES, SO GOES THE NATION

California has more midsize companies than any other state. What is occurring there is indicative of what is—or soon will be—happening across the nation as mergers proliferate and eliminate the middle-tier commercial banks. Here is a brief history of what has happened to California banks serving midsize companies over the past 25 years.

In 1974, Bank of America dominated the California midsize market principally because of its extensive and unchallenged branch network. Back then, banks located their branches based on retail customer potential, not midsize company potential. Nevertheless, Bank of America's retail branch network also gave it an advantage with midsize companies, since such companies required geographically convenient branches to serve their day-to-day needs. The other California commercial banks, which did not have the benefit of Bank of America's extensive branch network, confined their solicitation efforts to companies within their immediate geographic markets.

From the mid-1970s through the late 1980s, largely as a result of inflation, the number of companies that qualified as midsize increased approximately 35 percent, expanding the market at a faster rate than the Tier One banks, such as Bank of America, Security Pacific, Wells Fargo, and a few others could add new customers. As a result, the Tier One banks' share of *total* customers declined relative to the market's growth.

Yet, despite the increased opportunities inherent within the newly expanded midsize market, the second-tier[5] commercial banks in California *at that time* did not step in immediately and develop strategies to exploit this growth and expand their midsize company business. They chose not to act right away for two reasons:

1. Their focus was on retail business. Their business officers were not encouraged to reach outside the limited geographic market of their branch systems.

2. Not only did many second- and third-tier banks not compete with the first-tier banks across a broad market, they collaborated with them within their own market and often brought them in as participants on loans that exceeded $1 million to hedge their own credit exposure risk. Most of these loan collaborations occurred as a company's sales entered the $25 million to $50 million sales range and moved higher. Since a midsize company's loan size grows in proportion to the company's growth, a first-tier bank would take over the relationship—with little or no resistance from the second-tier bank—as the company's volume of credit needs expanded.

Tier One banks, on the other hand, did not so much fail to embrace the opportunity of the expanded midsize banking market as they made a calculated business strategy to become more discerning in pursuing it. They had begun to realize that many of their midsize banking relationships were not profitable enough to warrant the intense relationship manager servicing they required. The "hands on," in-person service of the relationship manager had simply become too costly, and it was no longer profitable to handle these smaller relationships in such a manner. Bank of America began to move away from using one-on-one relationship bankers to service customers with sales of less than $10 million. Other Tier One banks soon followed.

They developed branch servicing, 24-hour toll-free numbers, and other lower cost delivery channels to service these midsize companies more cost-effectively. Using $10 million as the cutoff, prospects that were less than promising, as well as customers whose profitability would not support coverage by a relationship manager, were now serviced by these less personal, more economical means. Tier One banks' customer penetration in the midsize market dropped accordingly, as shown in Figure 4.7.

Due to the sheer size of the overall midsize company market in California (55% of the midsize companies had sales of $5–$10 million), banks in that state were the quickest to recognize the benefits of resegmenting this market for relationship manager coverage. But other banks were quick to catch on. Chemical Bank made a similar move in its tristate market of New York, New Jersey, and Connecticut. And in 1990, Greenwich Associates redefined its California midmarket definition from $5 million–$50 million to $10–50 million to match this shift.

Wells Fargo Bank, however, took a different, "bottoms up" strategy. It had low customer penetration in southern California, where two-thirds of the midsize companies in the state were headquartered. It launched a "face-to-face" campaign with these midsize companies and it paid off—big time. By 1995, Wells Fargo Bank matched Bank of America as the statewide leader in customer penetration with companies with sales of $5 million–$50 million.

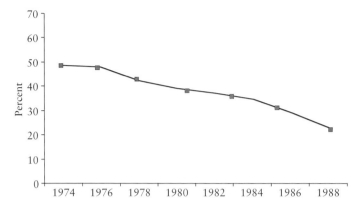

FIGURE 4.7 Customer penetration among tier one banks in California—$5 million to $50 million, 1974–1988.

Figure 4.8 illustrates this closing of the gap between these two banks. By the late 1980s, the number of Tier One banks serving the midsize market had declined, and the banks that had previously enjoyed Tier Two status had virtually disappeared due to acquisitions. But the number of third-tier banks serving this same market began to rise. They soon graduated to Tier Two status and neatly filled the gap created by the departed Tier Two banks.

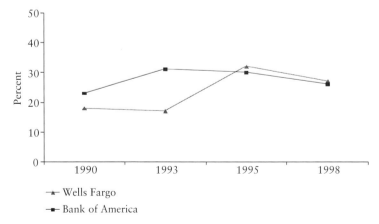

FIGURE 4.8 Customer penetration: Bank of America and Wells Fargo Bank in California—$10 million to $50 million, 1990–1998.

By this time, the smaller banks had grown to have enough loan capacity to meet clients' needs and no longer needed to collaborate with Tier One banks, as had been their custom. They began to hold onto the loans, and since the high-touch approach this market demanded remained financially viable for them, soon came to recognize just how inherently profitable the midsize market could be.

And thanks to mergers among the Tier One banks, these freshly minted second-tier banks were able to hire mature and experienced bankers who specialized in serving midsize companies, providing them with an instant group of officers who could—and did!—bring in the midsize company business.

These changes in strategy, by Tier One banks as well as by the second- and third-tier banks, had a dramatic effect on the customer penetration rankings over the next 10 years.

After Wells Fargo's acquisition of Crocker Bank in 1984 (the first in a string of major bank acquisitions), there were five first-tier commercial banks[6] serving the California market. By 2000, there were only three first-tier banks serving this market, as Table 4.20 shows.

During this same period there were four second-tier banks with a market penetration of 3 to 8 percent. Now there are nine banks at or near this level, as shown in Table 4.21.

Of this list, only Sanwa Bank of California has not expanded its customer penetration extensively. And today's short list of banks for the first time includes a nonbank, as Merrill Lynch is now a competitive second-tier provider of financial services to midsize companies. These firms, and a plethora of smaller community banks, now aggregate a significant customer

TABLE 4.20   Tier One Banks

Customer Penetration	1990	2000	Rate of Change
Bank of America	23%[1]	30%	30%
Security Pacific	14	—	—
Wells Fargo	17	28[2]	64
First Interstate	11	—	—
Union Bank of California	11	16[3]	45

[1] Includes Security Pacific Bank.
[2] Includes First Interstate Bank.
[3] Includes Bank of California.

TABLE 4.21   Tier Two Banks

Customer Penetration	1990	2000	Rate of Change
Bank of California	3%	—[1]	—%
Sanwa Bank California	4	5	25
Comerica Bank	—[2]	5	—
Imperial Bank	1	6	500
Merrill Lynch	—[3]	5	—
City National	2	5	150
Citigroup	—[3]	5	400
Mellon First Business Bank	2	3[4]	50
California Bank & Trust	2	3[5]	50
Silicon Valley Bank	—[3]	3	—

Note: Percentages based on total interviews in California.
[1] Merged into Union Bank of California.
[2] Did not operate in California.
[3] Not covered in our research in 1990.
[4] First Business Bank acquired by Mellon Bank.
[5] Formerly Sumitomo Bank California.

penetration and a serious threat—as a group—to the first-tier banks' long-term position. Overall, and adjusting for overlapping customer relationships, the new second-tier banks currently hold approximately 32 percent of the midsize company banking relationships in California.

These dramatic changes are not unique to California. They are now occurring nationwide, creating unprecedented opportunity for those smaller banks that recognize just how profitable this market can be and are willing to do what's necessary to capture their fair share of it.

FEW BANKS ARE CONSIDERED, FEWER ARE CHOSEN

Our research shows that one midsize company in four considers adding a new bank. In most instances, this consideration is driven by company expansion. Growing companies begin to recognize their need for more financial providers just as their sales levels begin to make them more attractive to competing banks.

Larger companies are more inclined than smaller ones to add a new bank, as shown in Table 4.22. And as companies grow and take on additional

TABLE 4.22 Companies That Consider Adding a New
Bank, by Size of Company

Sales Volume (in millions of dollars)	Consider Adding a New Bank
$20–$50	31%
$10–$20	25
$5–$10	20

Note: Based on total companies interviewed in each sales
range.

banking relationships, they are that much more likely to add yet another
one, as Table 4.23 shows.

In most cases, companies change banks because they have outgrown the
product scope of the bank or feel the bank's fees are being raised unreason-
ably. But while companies often state "fees" as the key reason for leaving a
bank, there are often other underlying product and servicing issues that
cause them to feel they are not receiving good value.

Table 4.24 presents the five key reasons companies consider adding a
new provider. Note the high dissatisfaction levels among smaller companies
with servicing and among larger companies with product scope.

Yet, despite the high levels of expressed dissatisfaction, only half of
the 24 percent of companies that say they are considering adding a new
bank actually do so. When you recall that 76 percent of the midsize companies are *not* considering adding a new provider, you begin to get a sense
of the challenge and difficulty banks face in their ongoing efforts to convert prospects to clients. And the challenge remains the same whether a
company is looking to change its existing bank or add another one. New

TABLE 4.23 Companies That Consider Adding a New
Bank, by Bank Usage

Profile of Company	Consider Adding a New Bank
Using only one bank	16%
Using more than one bank	33

Note: Based on total companies interviewed in each
category.

TABLE 4.24   Reasons Companies Consider Adding a New Provider

Reason	Sales Range		
	$20–$50 mil.	$10–$20 mil.	$5–$10 mil.
Insufficient product scope	38%	33%	23%
Dissatisfaction with the account servicing or "people capabilities" of the current provider	24	48	40
Raising fees or rates	24	16	17
Existing bank merged or no longer exists	9	2	7
Insufficient geographic scope	7	17	16

Note: Based on the 24% of companies considering adding a new banking relationship.

business solicitation programs must be truly compelling so companies will see the benefits of making a change.

THE SORRY STATE OF SOLICITATION

Because most customers feel that their current bank is no better nor worse than any other bank, they fail to see the benefits of changing banks, or adding an additional bank. They will continue to think this way until competing banks give them one or more specific reasons to think otherwise. Thus far, banks have been astonishingly ineffective at communicating to their prospective customers just what it is they do best.

To win the business, it is up to the bank to give prospective customers *specific* and motivating reasons why they should choose it over competing banks. Otherwise, why expect customers to change banks if the banks themselves cannot offer compelling reasons to do so?

Table 4.25 lists the criteria companies deem most important when choosing a new bank. Smaller companies place more emphasis on the quality of the relationship manager than do the larger companies, which tend to be more interested in a bank's willingness to lend.

Those banks best able to communicate the ways they meet these top selection criteria are the banks that should, and *do*, win the most business. It seems a simple formula. But, often a bank does match most of the criteria a company is looking for, or even all of the criteria, yet fails to communicate the reality and importance of this happy circumstance. Our interviews with midsize companies across the United States shows that there is remarkably low recognition among them of how—and how specifically—the banks soliciting them for business are going to add much value.

TABLE 4.25 Criteria Used in Selecting a New Provider

Company	Sales Range		
	$20–$50 mil.	$10–$20 mil.	$5–$10 mil.
Quality of relationship manager	42%	56%	50%
Willingness to lend	51	49	51
Low credit pricing	42	44	44
Strong operations	40	38	46
Cash management capabilities	35	41	37
Innovative ideas or solutions	25	32	30
International capabilities	14	13	14
Investment banking services	15	18	17
Defined contribution	9	10	9

Note: Based on total companies interviewed in each sales range.

Across the country, even a Top Ten bank with high customer penetration has difficulty distinguishing itself in its solicitation efforts. This is because, despite all those banks out there soliciting, few are doing it well. A typical Top Five bank has noncustomer recognition levels for its solicitation coverage well below 15 percent. And the "practice leaders," those banks with the most memorable solicitations, had a visibility among noncustomers of only 15 to 20 percent in 1998, even though the bank's prospect call reports showed significantly higher rates of active solicitation. Banks may be soliciting actively, but all too often they are not soliciting effectively, and in many cases fail to meet with the right buyer for the services they are selling.

Figure 4.9 demonstrates the low levels of recognized, in-person solicitations among noncustomers for the typical top five California banks over an

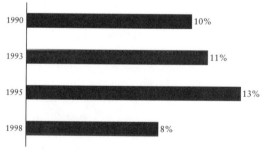

Note. Based on noncustomers recognizing an in-person visit to their office by a bank.

FIGURE 4.9 Solicitation recognition by noncustomers in California—$10 million to $50 million—top 5 bank mean.

8-year period. The low numbers reflect that, even though a soliciting officer may have called on the customer, the sales call was not remembered.

While Figure 4.9 is specific to the California market, California is typical of many geographic markets in that solicitation recognition rises when credit availability tightens (as it did leading into 1995) and eases as it becomes more available. Midsize companies pay less attention and undervalue solicitations when credit is readily available.

The "high/low" spread in Table 4.26 highlights how noncustomers who receive in-person solicitations have a difficult time differentiating among the one to four (on average) soliciting banks that visit them annually. In six of the eight criteria we measure, only 10 or fewer percentage points separate the "best banks" from the "worst banks." That isn't much of a spread. The one area where banks are most effective—and where the companies clearly are paying attention!—is with "willingness to lend." This not only ranks as the number one differentiating criterion, by far, but also earns the greatest differentiation among soliciting banks.

WHAT WORKS

Because the prospect opportunity is so large, bankers use a variety of approaches to solicit the market and try and increase their penetration. Table 4.27 lists some of the more popular methods used. And Table 4.28 lists the results.

It is not surprising that, in a market that places a high value on the high touch of a relationship banker, a scheduled, in-person sales call produces by far the most effective results in requests for further information and actual purchases. While this is an effective approach, it is also a pricey one. Dozens of prospects called on multiple times adds up to significant time and money

TABLE 4.26 Bankers Have Difficulty Creating Dramatic Differentiation in Their Solicitation Effectiveness

	Top 10 Mean	Low/High Evaluation Range	Low/High Spread	Differentiation Rank
Willingness to lend	34%	28–47%	19	1
Low credit pricing	19	17–27	10	3
Quality of relationship manager	26	19–32	13	2
Initiates new ideas	21	17–26	9	3
Cash management capabilities	23	18–28	10	3
International capabilities	15	12–22	10	3
Defined contribution plan capabilities	8	5–10	5	7
Investment banking	16	13–18	5	7

TABLE 4.27   Strategies Banks Use to Try to Win Relationships

Strategy	Frequency
Unsolicited sales letter or brochure	33%
Unsolicited phone call	31
Scheduled in-person sales call	31
Unscheduled in-person sales call	10
Unsolicited letter with preapproved loan offer	9
Unsolicited e-mail or Internet contact	2

Note: Based on companies experiencing a solicitation.

spent in pursuit of customers who, as we have seen, are not likely to notice most of the effort.

One bank we consult with developed a different strategy to avoid this expense. Rather than funding the high cost of sending their bankers door to door, the bank instead hires new business development officers whose sole job is to get new business. Their annual salaries are low, which keeps costs down, but when they successfully bring in new customers their compensation can rise as high as $400,000 per year.

Another bank set out to buck the low recognition trend and implemented an in-person contact strategy with a targeted group of their highest priority prospects. Within 12 months of those meetings, over 50 percent of the companies solicited were able to comment favorably on the bank's ability to deliver against the nine main criteria used by companies when considering a new bank. Many said they would consider adding this bank next.

This is a dramatic improvement when you note that only 35 percent, on average, of companies receiving in-person solicitations say they would

TABLE 4.28   Effectiveness of Actions Taken by Banks to Win Relationships

$5–$50 Million Action	Requested Further Information	Purchased One or More Services
Unsolicited letter or brochure	12%	2%
Unsolicited telephone call made by bank officer	19	4
Conducted scheduled, in-person sales call	36	14
Conducted unscheduled, in-person sales call	16	7
Unsolicited letter with preapproved loan offer	11	3

Note: Based on companies receiving each type of solicitation.

consider adding the bank. In contrast, an effectively targeted solicitation program will raise the bank's "odds" for being considered from the average of 35 percent to over 50 percent—a 40 percent increase!

THE BENEFITS OF BENEFIT STATEMENTS

The best solicitations begin not with a letter or a phone call, but with a concerted internal effort to train the officers what to say and how to say it.

We recommend designing benefit statements that address those criteria specified by companies as most important in their choice of a new bank. Well-crafted and explicit benefit statements can be a valuable tool to help calling officers describe easily and clearly the bank's areas of expertise so that each prospect, in turn, will understand and appreciate the bank's capabilities to deliver. Benefit statements are especially effective when the bank officers or new business development officers are actively engaged in helping create them and feel real ownership and full understanding of them.

Bankers lacking this training are naturally reluctant, and in many cases, even unable, to say exactly what needs to be said in a sales call to win. Calling officers need to be taught how to address those questions that are critical components of a company's selection process. Since "willingness to lend" and "quality of relationship manager" are the most important criteria, make sure your bankers are well prepared to show exactly how they are able to meet these criteria and score on other expectations as well.

Bank officers must learn how to say, with clarity and conviction:

- "We will lend to you," when they know little about the company, which is often privately held.
- "I am high quality," when they aren't comfortable describing personal qualities.
- "We will be low price," when they don't know comparative pricing or risk pricing levels yet.
- "We have high quality, error-free operating services," when they see their bank making operating mistakes every day.

The answers to these selection questions are not as difficult as some bankers perceive them to be. After all, the customer is merely looking for explanations of the bank's processes to gauge what the company needs to do to deserve the loan at the right price. All that is required is for bankers to answer the questions succinctly and honestly, describing how they have the authority and responsibility to "deliver the bank," assuring the speed and ease of the process for resolving operating errors, and explaining the requirements the company must meet to obtain credit approval: For example, a banker could answer the preceding questions this way:

- In addressing the bank's willingness to lend, the banker need only lay out the specific information he needs about the company, and the criteria the company must meet to receive the loan commitment. The banker should also explain the process he must undergo to get the loan approval, as well as the timing involved.
- In addressing the personal qualities and integrity of himself as a banker, he can subtly weave examples of his experience into the conversation, ideally highlighting examples where he has succeeded on a customer's behalf.
- In addressing price competitiveness, he need only reveal the bank's pricing strategy based on companies meeting the proper requirements.
- In addressing operations quality, he can address the bank's speed and resolution at correcting errors. Customers expect errors, after all, and wouldn't believe an officer who insisted his bank was error free.

Answering the selection questions really is as simple as that. But, it is a requirement for success.

There is more to an effective sales call, however, than strong answers to these threshold selection questions. Bankers must also be able to answer yet another set of questions if they are to truly distinguish themselves from all the other competing bankers who are just as personable, just as intelligent, and just as sincere as they are:

- What explicitly sets your bank apart from other banks the company is using already or is considering using?
- How, specifically, will you prepare yourself and your prospect for this particular sales call?
- How will this particular sales call showcase a specific, persuasive, and relevant example of your bank's expertise?
- What are the one or two topics you will discuss at the meeting?
- What new or different—and company specific—idea can you offer?
- How will you follow up promptly after this call?

HOW TO DEVELOP A PROSPECT LIST

It is not enough simply knowing what to say. Bankers will want to spend considerable effort creating a prospect list to ensure that the officers, now well-versed in stating the bank's benefits correctly, are making those statements to the right people.

Most calling officers would achieve more long-term success if they did more homework to prepare themselves well for action. Bearing in mind that not all "prospects" should be prospects, we advise developing a list of targeted customers based on the following guidelines:

■ Work with readily available lists of companies provided by service organizations such as Dun & Bradstreet[7] to generate a list of potential prospects based on location, size and industry. At the early stages in a selling campaign, this list will be large. Assuming 20 percent of the names on the list are already your customers, pare the remaining names using the following criteria:

  • Delete based on industry. Eliminate those industries that do not fit your bank's loan portfolio and/or business strategy.

  • Delete based on location, depending on the scope of your delivery capability and whether your bank is a holding company, a unit bank, or a branch bank.

  • Delete based on risk. Eliminate companies that are a poor credit risk.

  • Delete based on profiling. Review your current customers to determine the amount of business generated by each one. From this, create a profile of the most desirable customers and use this profile to identify and target prospects most likely to generate similar revenue.

  • Delete based on revenue potential. Eliminate companies that do not match the bank's "hurdle rate" for minimum revenue, which for many banks ranges between $50,000 and $100,000.

The purpose of this exercise is to: delete as many "poor bets" as possible. Then you can concentrate your most valuable strategic resources—your new business calling officers—on achieving the success with their best prospects. These will be companies your bank most wants to work with and that would surely want to work with your bank if they only knew how well your bank could deliver the services they most want and need!

Segment the selected best prospects into the following three groups:

1. *High-priority prospects.* Cover these prospects with the same intensity of skill, communication, and management attention reserved for your existing customers. Depending on the size and complexity of the companies in this group, we advise our clients that these high-priority prospects represent 15 to 20 percent of the bank's target group.

2. *Medium-priority prospects.* Market to these companies based on periodic visits and direct mail solicitations. Look for reasons—at each company—to discontinue the effort (and free up time to devote to the more promising prospects) as well as reasons to "pour it on" for the best prospects within this group, as you discover how attractive they really are.

3. *Low-priority prospects.* These are the companies that are unwilling to meet with you due to a close alliance with another bank. Some of our clients have had success with periodic direct mail solicitations to keep their bank's name in these prospects' minds should an opportunity arise. But remember, there is only a 6 in 100 chance of having one or more of your bank's services purchased as a result of this effort.

Winnow your high-, medium-, and low-priority prospects still further by evaluating the strength of the prospect's current banking relationships and assessing the human and financial resources required to enter the relationship and displace the present bank. Do not underestimate this task; it can be tricky and time consuming. Achieving change must be done as quickly as possible to avoid undue expense, both financial and nonfinancial. The cost/benefit analysis of pursuing a particular prospect can only be divined through a series of new business sales calls intended to reveal, at the earliest possible opportunity, whether the company is being managed for growth or value. Growth companies offer a greater opportunity because they use more and more providers and are often—even when they don't yet realize it—looking for additional providers. Remember that only 16 percent of companies using one provider typically replace that provider or add another bank each year, while 33 percent of companies using more than one provider add another provider. That's a difference between six years and three!

THE POWER OF ONE GOOD SALES CALL

Since only 5 to 10 percent of a typical bank's customers report dissatisfaction with their bank, it is incumbent on the soliciting bank to create that dissatisfaction by effectively showing the company just what they may have been missing. Here are some ways to do this:

- Send a letter of introduction enumerating the benefits of using your bank and the reasons that justify a visit. Suggest a specific meeting time.
- Once you've succeeded in setting up an initial meeting, confirm it, in writing, with an explicit focus on what you and your bank can do to help this particular company.

- Make sure the solicitation visit is a substantive one that makes good use of the prospect's valuable time. Don't linger. A well-focused first meeting is your best way to get that second meeting.
- Create a short, written plan for the first visit, including appropriate information you hope to glean from the company, and the value and information you in turn will leave them.
- Know in advance what will make the meeting worthwhile for the prospect to help ensure that you will be welcome back.
- Determine what knowledge you have that could be helpful to the company. Can you provide insight into interest rate movements, or offer an observation on their particular industry? If you have reports or other research materials to offer, do not hand them over at the meeting. Instead, *tell* the prospect what is in the report, then a day or so later mail the report along with a brief personal note. This type of "bridge calling" turns one sales call into two, and is a highly effective way of ensuring that the calls build on each other toward a *relationship* and a *transaction*.
- Early in the meeting, either introduce one well-chosen good idea or offer the prospect the opportunity to select a topic from an array of three or four choices. Concentrate entirely on that most promising idea, and make the most of it! Establish expectations for the time frame of your reply as well as the format of that reply (such as a phone call, letter, or personal visit). Then, meet or beat that expected commitment— so you'll be seen to be even better! This can be a tangible and credible means of demonstrating your interest and commitment.
- Trumpet what your bank does best. Many bankers hesitate to laud their operations because they know the bank is not perfect. But *no* bank is. If you want your sales call to be remembered, walk in the door espousing your bank's key, real virtues and continue from there.
- Always remember: The purpose of the first sales call is to assure a good second call with a specific purpose that is important and useful to your prospect.

We recommend the following timeline as a tool for evaluating progress with prospects. Within the three (yes, 3!) years that it typically takes to convert a prospect into a customer, certain milestones should be reached within specific time periods. These "fish or cut bait" benchmarks can help you know early in the solicitation process if the company being approached is in fact worth the investment of time, expenses, and resources.

The timeline suggests two to three times as many meetings as a typical banker would feel are "necessary." But this type of saturation marketing is an invaluable tool for determining the prospect value sooner, rather than

TABLE 4.29 Timeline: Target Benchmarks for Turning Prospects into Customers

6 Months	18 Months	24 Months	3 Years
2–3 meetings to: Verify company's current bank(s) Verify strength of company's current bank(s) Verify sales size and net worth (D&B is not always accurate) Verify decision makers and strength of influencers	4–6 additional meetings to: Meet company owner See financial statements Qualify product needs Determine other soliciting banks	3–4 additional meetings to: Introduce bank senior management Employ product specialists Introduce to satisfied bank clients	Close
Terminate or continue	Terminate or continue	Terminate or continue	

later and is ultimately cost-effective. To win "share of market," you must first win "share of mind."

Table 4.29 shows the benchmarks we recommend as you work to convert prospects to customers. We suggest that at the end of each 6 to 12-month time frame, the soliciting banker and his or her immediate supervisor conduct a formal review to determine whether the relationship should be terminated or continued.

In addition, you can broaden the scope and effectiveness of in-person solicitation efforts by cultivating referral sources. There are two sources of referrals: those within the bank's market and those outside it.

Business friends and accountants within a bank's market can recommend the bank to their suppliers. We recommend our clients host functions peopled with a mix of clients and prospects, giving clients ample opportunity to say good things about the bank.

Bankers are often asked by their customers to refer banks in other markets as their business needs expand. Cultivating these out-of-state banks is usually a word-of-mouth process. But we advise being more proactive. Make a formal presentation to heads of corporate banking in cities where there is a *correspondent* banking relationship. This presentation should describe the bank's relationship management process, products of choice and profiles of attractive businesses. Just one strong local business bank with a leading market penetration position can provide a flow of opportunities.

TABLE 4.30 Influential Sources When Adding a
New Provider

Existing banker	43%
Acquaintances/friends at other businesses	42
Accountants	32
Local business periodicals	14
Lawyers	14
Independent consultant	11
Other	9

Note: Based on companies citing sources used for referrals.

As Table 4.30 shows, there is tremendous opportunity in cultivating these referral sources, both within a bank's market and outside it.

KEEPING A GOOD THING GOING

Here are additional recommendations to help ensure that prospects evolve into lasting, mutually beneficial relationships.

Take a long-term view of the prospect portfolio and manage it actively. Credibility with prospects is created over time. Our research shows that very little new business—and virtually no *good* new business—is won on a single sales call. Rather, the invitation to participate as a relationship bank is the result of a *managed series* of calls that build on previous contacts and experiences. When done correctly, this relationship-building process can take up to three years. All too often, our research shows, customers complain of "hummingbird calls," where a soliciting officer stops by briefly but quickly departs when there is no immediate sales opportunity. A "linked," sequential calling process is critical, because it builds momentum over time, creates recognition of value, and allows the bank to differentiate itself in the ways necessary for success.

Maintain a fixed prospect portfolio to ensure that valuable human and institutional resources are carefully put to best use and not wasted in on-off-on-again or hit-or-miss scrambles. When additions and deletions are made at the whim of the soliciting officers, it undermines the disciplined and consistent process necessary for long-term business development. This is only effective, however, when the originally selected prospect portfolio is a fertile one. So, take care to be sure you are "fishing where the fish are."

Establish tactical and strategic selling goals, and then manage to activate them. Many soliciting officers have well-defined and measurable targets for achieving their goals in the near term. (Greenwich Associates defines "near term" as one year.) But it can take up to three years before the initial sales call is translated into actual business. If "quick hits" are rewarded over strategic calling agendas, transaction selling takes precedence over relationship building and leaves little opportunity for developing the good new business that will prove enduring. As management shapes the factors that influence and motivate soliciting officers, implement a platform that rewards strategic new business development behavior as well as tactical behavior.

Create a transfer process for active prospects. When an officer leaves a set of customers, considerable time is spent transferring these customers to the officer's successor. The same should be done with active *prospects*. In many banks, the emphasis is on transferring active customers and little attention is given to transferring active best prospects. Yet customers and prospects both represent significant assets. The customer represents a value currently being realized; the prospect represents a substantial investment already made but not yet realized. It is incumbent on the officer who is moving on to provide an up-to-date, complete file on each and every prospect and to introduce each new prospect to his or her successor to ensure that the solicitation process continues seamlessly.

Develop cross-selling strategies for each major prospect. Often bankers' product presentations are based on trial and error or a series of "Do you use?" questions. They do not carefully assess and address the prospect's business. By involving product specialists in advance of the solicitation, more effective and specific presentations will raise the bank's opportunity to succeed.

Maintain a consistent presence. Active prospects, or the 15 to 20 percent of the prospect portfolio that the bank has determined offer the highest opportunities for good new business, should be managed as intensely as the bank's most important customers. After all, if you must dislodge an established bank and beat all competitor banks, you'll want to be seen to be your very best! Employ the same actions reserved for top customers, such as access to upper management, invitations to special events, reviews of yearly offerings, "season's greetings," and a series of specific, relevant, well-presented "good ideas."

Determine competitors' organizational coverage of your prospects. Midsize companies are dynamic. They are constantly growing up and out of the $5 million–$50 million market *and* growing out of the delivery system their banks are providing. As a branch manager's skill and product knowledge are outstripped by the needs of a fast-growing midsize company, there is a high risk of losing that customer to a competitor. By determining the skill set of the officers in charge of the competing relationship, based on the delivery unit he or she represents, the soliciting banker can achieve insight into the competitors' vulnerability that it can then exploit.

THE THREAT OF NONBANKS

Getting the solicitation piece right matters now more than ever:

- A relatively small proportion of companies in any geographic market adds a new financial provider each year—only one company in eight.
- The group of nonbank competitors is broadening. Savings banks, investment banks, insurance companies, and other nonbank financial providers, such as emerging dot-com companies, to name a few, are each soliciting the same clients for the same business.

Of those companies planning to add a new financial provider, fewer than half are considering a commercial bank. Table 4.31 shows the current distribution. Companies planning to add a new financial service provider use criteria for making the decision not unlike the ones they use to select a commercial bank—pricing and product scope matter most, as shown in Figure 4.10.

Nonbanks now provide specific services to more than 30 percent of midsize companies. Thus far, their success has been in specific product competencies such as 401(k) plans, stockbrokerage, leasing, and insurance

TABLE 4.31   Commercial Banks—The Choice of Only Half of the Companies Planning to Add a New Financial Service Provider

Type of Firm Being Considered	
Commercial bank	46%
Finance company	27
Investment bank	21
Insurance company	15
Savings bank	10
Foreign bank	10
Diversified financial firm	4

Note: Based on companies considering adding a new financial service provider.

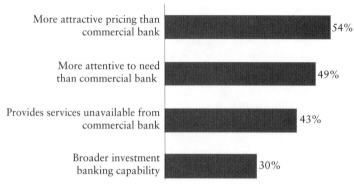

Note. Based on companies considering a nonbank financial service provider.

FIGURE 4.10 Most important factors in selecting a nonbank financial service provider.

products that most commercial banks are not offering or are only beginning to develop. Not coincidentally, these same product areas are fast becoming important to midsize companies.

Some of the product ambitions are likely too great for this market to bear (the expectations of small companies are often unrealistic, as they tend

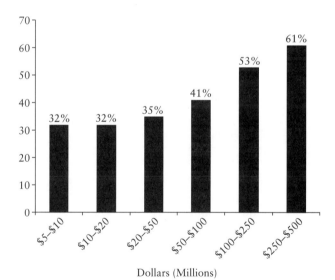

Dollars (Millions)

Note. Based on companies interviewed in each sales range.

FIGURE 4.11 Companies using nonbanks.

to be colored by the bigger markets); nevertheless, they illustrate the willingness of midsize companies to diversify from their once exclusive use of commercial banks. In 1998, our research showed as many as 18 percent of private, midsize companies were considering taking advantage of the attractive phase of the capital markets with initial public offerings of their stock, and nearly 25 percent were thinking about public offerings of long-term debt.

For now, the nonbanks have been more successful in penetrating the upper-end companies that are more likely to use more financial service providers because of their own growth and expansion, as Figure 4.11 shows.

But the middle market[8] is by no means immune to the advances of nonbanks, as 33 percent of the companies use nonbanks for products not actively embraced by many midmarket banks. While the nonbanks may not yet pose a threat to the traditional midsize banking business, they are—or should be—a real concern to banks planning to expand into those product areas that are now the stronghold of nonbanks and often offer greater fee and return opportunities than the traditional business of lending and cash management.

This increase in competitiveness among banks and nonbanks is an indicator of the growing importance of the midsize banking market. Those banks able to elevate their solicitation efforts to a level commensurate with their abilities will have the best chance of winning a healthy share of it.

In summary, advancing customer penetration is not easy in the midsize company market, but those banks that have developed disciplined approaches to new business solicitation with intensely trained officers have the best opportunities to succeed at the expense of competitors.

CHAPTER 5

Investment Banking

Phillip S. Kemp, Jr., John G. Colon, James A. Bennett, Jr., and
Robert C. Statius-Muller

Winning Is Now Everything

In investment banking, there is no glory—and not much profitability—in
second place. Whether an investment bank is a well-established firm or one
new to the business, real success in investment banking in the United States
comes only to those firms that become the *number one* investment bank to
each of a carefully chosen group of client companies. The group must be
large enough for the firm to sustain a good and profitable business while re-
liably delivering the array of services the investment bank excels at delivering and that the client companies want and need.

This is not so easy to do in today's intensely competitive investment
banking environment, where companies are always comparison shopping
among investment banking services in search of more and better service or
lower cost. And investment banks are always striving to add new customers,
or gain greater importance or do more business with the corporations they
already serve.

It wasn't always this way. There was a time—quite a long time—when
the business of investment banking was a gentlemanly one. Bankers and
their customers adhered strictly to unwritten, but no less stringent, rules of
behavior whereby a company committed to use one bank for all its banking
needs. But back then, the volume and scale of those banking needs were

---

Phillip S. Kemp, Jr., and John G. Colon wrote "Winning Is Now Everything," James
A. Bennett, Jr., wrote "Investment Banking in Canada," and Robert C. Statius-
Muller wrote "Project Finance."

small. So the investment banking business was small. Corporations came to the banker's office seeking capital and advice. Rarely, if ever, would a bank officer solicit business. In fact, they disdained doing so—particularly from another firm's clients. It simply wasn't done. There was little innovation or motivation for offering anything other than the bank's stock set of services. This environment made for a low key and comfortable professional lifestyle, where being "smart and clever" was not nearly so important as being "well connected."

This changed during the 1960s and 1970s as institutional investors became more important in the capital markets and investment banks became more aggressive in soliciting new business. By the 1980s and 1990s, the clubby atmosphere had long bowed to a no-holds-barred competitive environment. Investment bankers were forced to roll up their monogrammed cuffs and earn business based on demonstrated merit in open and direct competition with all comers. Today, companies are no longer beholden to one bank, but rather pick and choose from a stable of banks that best suit their needs.

In this decidedly new business environment, there is little tolerance for second place or second best. Because, as we will show, only the winners really win. Here's why:

- Winners take all—or just about all. Of fees paid for investment banking services, 60 to 65 percent go to the company's lead investment bank, while the second most important bank receives a mere 20 percent of the fees. And the numbers for the third, fourth, and lower-tiered banks drop even more precipitously. Though the second- and third-tier banks are able to survive, banks that fall below that level are likely losing money, particularly after bearing the opportunity costs of not "pouring it on" to become a winner with another company.

When all the costs of developing a major relationship are factored in, being "*not* number one" takes just about as much effort and cost as being number one. Therefore, it's important to concentrate your skills and efforts on companies where you can and will win: "Do not play to play; play to *win*."

Figure 5.1 shows just how sweet the rewards can be when you do win.

- The stakes are rising. Now, not only do winners take just about all; they are taking "just about all" of increasingly higher fees. An average company[1] that now pays $9.5 million annually in investment banking fees paid less than half that amount just 10 years ago. And the fees paid by

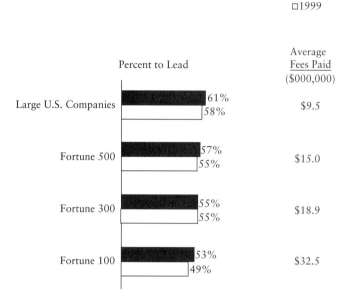

FIGURE 5.1   Fees to investment bank.

Fortune 500 companies have risen even more as, on average, a Fortune 500 company that paid fees of $5 million in 1990 paid $15 million just 9 years later. For Fortune 500 companies, these numbers translated into merger and acquisition (M&A) fees of $400 million paid in 1990, which went on to almost quadruple—to nearly $2.0 billion—by 1999. And the *total* M&A fees paid have exploded, from just over $1 billion in 1990 to close to $3.5 billion in 1999. Hard to believe that as recently as the 1950s investment bankers did not charge "extra" for M&A advice!

■ The winners tend to remain winners. And it's no wonder why. If your firm were earning 60 to 65 percent of the numbers just listed, you'd be motivated to stay on top, too. Our latest research shows that once a bank becomes a lead bank it tends to remain in the lead for a long, long time. The typical company retains the same lead investment bank for 8.5 years. Fortune 500 companies exhibit even greater loyalty and retain their lead investment banks, on average, for 11.3 years.

Table 5.1 gives the average duration of lead bank relationships by size of company.

TABLE 5.1 Average Length of Relationship with Lead Bank

	Lead Bank
Fortune 500	
Fortune 1–100	13.3
101–200	12.6
201–300	11.4
301–400	9.4
401–500	9.2
Sales Size	
Over $2.5 billion	11.5
$1.0–$2.4 billion	8.9
$500–$999 million	7.0

- Capital of major firms has grown from millions of dollars to billions. Most firms, including venerable Morgan Stanley Dean Witter and Goldman Sachs, have chosen to be publicly owned to have access to larger pools of permanent equity capital.
- Competition is intensifying. Companies are flooded with solicitations from a spate of investment banker "wannabes." Drawn by the potential profitability of the M&A, equity, and high-yield debt side of the investment banking business, the many new entrants to the market often compete on price as they struggle to gain a foothold.
- The size and types of transactions have become increasingly complex, and the staffing required to support those transactions has multiplied exponentially. Merrill Lynch, Morgan Stanley Dean Witter, Citigroup (including Salomon Smith Barney), Credit Suisse First Boston, J.P. Morgan, and Goldman Sachs each employ over 10,000 people worldwide.
- It is a global business, conducted across multiple borders and time zones. Most major firms have regional headquarters in at least three or four different countries.

In short, the investment banking business *now* is markedly different from what it was just one generation ago, when investment banks controlled the information flow and institutions did not. Today, many institutions are bigger than the banks servicing them. And while investment bankers remain a source of information, they are now one of many sources.

Technology has made it possible to attain information easily and inexpensively. This, along with the growth of an increasingly sophisticated group of institutional investors and corporate CFOs, is driving a "manage it yourself" investment banking mentality in corporate America.[2] Not only are investment bankers in heated competition with one another, in some instances they now also count their own clients among their competitors.

CREDIBILITY AND CAPABILITY RESULT IN CONFIDENCE

Despite the dramatic changes that have occurred in investment banking over the past few decades, one constant remains: Credibility mattered then and it matters now. Close to 70 percent of the senior corporate executives participating in our research cite "credibility" as the single most important factor for becoming their company's lead investment bank. Just about as important is demonstrated capability in advising on important M&A transactions as well as in raising capital. Companies place high value on those firms that can "get it right" because an M&A transaction is such a high-stakes and irreversible proposition, both for the company and the CEO spearheading the transaction.

The investment bank in the fortunate position to be a company's primary M&A adviser already has the key ingredients necessary to become the company's lead investment bank. In both cases, it is credibility with the company's CEO and board of directors that matters most.

Table 5.2 shows additional criteria important for achieving lead bank status. Note how similar these criteria are to those required to become the chosen investment bank for M&A transactions, as shown in Table 5.3.

TABLE 5.2 Factors Determining Lead Investment Bank

	Most Important
Capability in advising on important M&A transactions	68%
Bank's credibility with the CEO and board of directors	67
Capability and continuity of the corporate finance relationship manager	53
Capability in equity research and equity underwriting	44
Capability in underwriting long-term debt issues	43
Capability and willingness to provide credit	24
Financial strength and credit rating of firm	12
Capability in advising or transacting in global risk management	8

"Capability" and "Credibility" rank highest on both lists. An investment bank cannot have one without the other, and both are critical. Capability is the lever a bank can use to ratchet the relationship to ever higher levels of credibility. This credibility, in turn, gives companies the confidence they need to grant increasingly important deals.

And confidence is what a company's CEO as well as its board of directors must feel about their advocate at the investment bank. Such confidence is not easily won, and most often is the result of years of intensive and effective coverage.

Many struggling start-up firms are now discovering this. It is not sufficient to hire a small group of star bankers and wait for the business to follow. It is *organizational* credibility, which can only be earned over time, that matters most. Key to earning this "trust over time" is cultivating those relationships that are most worth the time and effort of doing so. Begin with one transaction, perform it flawlessly, and continue to provide the highest level of service for all subsequent ones. Let your actions reflect a real understanding of the company as you propose numerous relevant ideas in a timely manner. Buttress this service with strong personal relations.

The best practitioners of the craft of relationship development are proactive about demonstrating to their clients that they are in the relationship for the long haul. They sell their product skills, certainly, but do so within the context of a clear understanding of the clients' goals. To win mandates: Listen actively to what the client tells you, and then show by your

TABLE 5.3   Factors Determining Mandate for M&A Advisory

	Most Important
Credibility with company's CEO and board of directors	51%
Capability of M&A specialists	49
Creative and innovative ideas	43
Understanding of company's M&A strategy	39
Understanding of industry	29
Capability of relationship manager	26
Historical relationship	24
Past record in structuring and closing transactions	21
Ability to arrange financing	16
Equity research capability	15
Lower fees	14
Execution support from M&A transactions teams	11
International expertise	5

actions how well you understand and how strongly you care about what the company wants to accomplish.

Active listening is, in fact, a powerful sales tool for earning the confidence of the CEO and board of directors, and helps nudge your firm ever closer to the coveted position of trusted adviser. While product capabilities and transaction "league tables" showing that you have the ability to execute a particular type of transaction do matter, they don't matter *most*. Which is why you need to spend time early in the relationship being a thoughtful and attentive listener rather than an aggressive seller.

Some firms have been able to hit a home run with *the* unique, compelling idea. Others have succeeded by developing a comprehensive analysis of what is required to get the deal done, including how to finance it as well as how to make sure that the shareholders of the target support the idea. But proven experience, combined with intimate knowledge of how a company operates and makes decisions, is how the majority of mandates are won. That's because the winners have the "unfair" competitive advantage of being in such a trusted position that they see the transaction coming even before the client does. The great relationship manager knows a lot about his or her clients, thinks about them all the time, and can anticipate the way the client thinks. With such a close relationship, is it any wonder that this relationship manager will be privy to information sooner than his competitors?

Corporate senior management determines whether an investment bank has that all-important credibility based on how well an investment bank performs in these areas, as shown in Table 5.4.

"Taking a long-term view of the relationship" is by far the most important factor determining a bank's credibility. Banks can't expect to raise their profile and gain credibility with a short-term, transaction-oriented approach to specific deals.

Corporate executives tell us that "taking a long-term view of the relationship" is not a single action, but actually a combination of many, such as:

- Eschewing an overt deal-by-deal mentality in favor of a partnership, relationship-oriented approach.
- Putting clients' long-term interests before your own short-term interests, such as advising *against* a deal even when that means losing a fee.
- Providing the same level of high-quality service regardless of whether the bank is playing a lead or co-manager role.
- Being willing to provide free analytical work on appropriate capital structures and acquisitions or corporate restructuring.

Personal relationships are also important, and we've already emphasized just how important a good relationship manager can be. But the

TABLE 5.4   Factors Determining Credibility

	Most Important
Taking a long-term view of the relationship	51%
Capability of corporate finance relationship manager	43
Direct M&A experience and track record	40
Personal relationships with CEO/board of directors	38
Historical relationship	35
Broad product capabilities	30
Equity analysts' relationship	24
Direct debt experience and track record	23
Length or continuity of banker coverage	18
Industry specialization	16
Direct equity experience and track record	16

power of one individual must be reinforced by a well-orchestrated plan to ensure senior level contact from the *organization*. The CEO wants to hear not just from the relationship banker, but also directly from the senior officers about the commitment, expertise, and prowess of the bank. He or she not only needs to hear it, but needs to see evidence of it—not with one transaction, or two, but over and over and over again.

THE POWER OF ONE GOOD ANALYST

Analysts play a strong role in winning equity mandates, as the power of their endorsement helps convince institutional investors to buy in volume and *now*. Although "institutional distribution capability" ranks as the most important factor in winning equity mandates, as Table 5.5 shows, "equity research capability" ranks second and is becoming increasingly important.

Good equity research analysts are increasingly—and increasingly often—important for winning mandates for mergers and acquisitions. Particularly with midsize or smaller companies, they often have a better relationship with the CEO of a company than the investment bankers do and tend to have a better understanding of the overall industry as well as a clearer vision of how two companies might work together. If a deal includes

TABLE 5.5 Factors Determining Equity Book-Runner Mandate

	Most Important
Institutional distribution capability	72%
Equity research capability and analyst relationship	61
Credibility with company's CEO and board of directors	34
Skill in structuring and pricing issues	28
Syndicate management capability	26
Historical relationship	24
Retail distribution capability	24
Capable equity capital markets specialists	19
Participation as manager in your past issues	19
Capable corporate finance relationship managers	12
Lower fees or spreads	9
Firm's trading volume in company stock	9
International distribution capability	6
Aggressiveness of bids for "bought" deals	2

a stock for stock swap, an equity analyst can help the banker and the client predict what the market reaction will be to a particular structure or price of a deal.

In addition, an analyst's strong reputation in a particular industry can give the impression that the firm, not just the individual analyst, is knowledgeable about that sector—an impression that quickly turns to reality as firms concentrate on capitalizing on analysts' expertise. Astute investment bankers spend time with those well-regarded analysts to learn more about the industries they cover (even as they, in turn, have a strong vested influence over what industries the analysts *should* be covering). The result is an increase in bankers' ability to offer creative ideas to their clients that, over time, further enhances the firm's reputation in that industry, improves the bank's credibility, and elevates the relationship.

HOW TO BECOME A LEAD INVESTMENT BANK

Today, most firms offer specific expertise within a traditional range of investment banking services. Often the temptation is to make that range as wide as possible in the hope of attracting the broadest scope of clients. This is a mistake. Instead, focus on those products and industries where your firm can develop real strength and be distinctive; and then market those strengths to a carefully selected group of companies. As the great coaches advise: "Plan your play and play your plan." Here are recommendations for doing this. Be aware that the first step is often the hardest.

- Make an accurate appraisal of your firm's current competitive position—your strengths and weakness in each product or service and with each client or prospect—and determine how you got there. What has worked unusually well for your firm and why? What has not worked well, and why not? A truly candid self-analysis can be instrumental as you develop your firm's strategy.
- Be realistic. It is worth taking the time and effort necessary to make sure that what your bank is known for is, in fact, what your bank should be known for and what the bank wants to be known for.
- Identify and list those products your firm knows best and is best known for. Be realistic. Do not list those products you *want* to be known for, or the ones you *hope* to be known for or might plan to develop in the future. List only those products your firm has a proven track record of delivering. Concentrate on dominating each of these categories, particularly with your own clients!
- Next, do the same for specific industries. Again, be realistic as you assess the status of your bankers and equity analysts. A reputation for "industry capability" requires both a banker known for his or her industry specialization *and* analysts who are well regarded in the particular industry. If you are missing either one of these two critical components, make the necessary adjustments by adding the right people and other resources *or* narrowing your market focus.
- Know the companies most in need of your expertise and receptive to working with your firm. Concentrate on specific clients and market segments. If your firm is to become the lead investment banker for a particular company, make certain you know that company's needs and interests *and* its strengths or weaknesses better than anyone else. And do all you can to make sure that each company *knows* you know them best.
- Be practical. While the largest companies might seem like the most attractive targets, remember that change happens slowly in many big organizations. You can be sure the incumbent lead investment bank, which has likely been the lead for a long, long time, will be aggressive in defending such lucrative turf. The likelihood of quickly unseating the lead bank is low. Smaller companies, on the other hand, have naturally

more dynamic relationships. As they grow, so do their investment banking needs, making them likely to be more willing to change bankers to get more new services, or to trade up to a larger, stronger investment bank. Be pragmatic as you select your targets. Some small companies may be too small for you to earn the fees that would justify the service commitment needed to become their new lead investment bank.

Prioritize your relationships based on the anticipated size of fees *and* the quality of the current relationship; then continue the focusing process as follows:

- Craft a clear marketing strategy, targeted to the high-priority companies. This will act as the firm's road map. *Make sure all your bankers understand the strategy, believe in the strategy, and all use similar language to communicate it.* In our consulting, we sometimes find that a bank's position is not always driven by a uniformly communicated message, but rather evolves piecemeal as bankers one-by-one articulate their *own* (not always accurate) version of the bank's position and capabilities. This is why candor in the first phase of this process is so important. When all the bankers in a firm are communicating the same message, it creates harmony rather than dissonance. Needless to say, we strongly recommend "one firm" harmony in everything an investment banker does. When the bank is clear on "who we are and what we do best," and when that message is communicated clearly and consistently, and acted on accordingly, the bank's message then ultimately becomes its definition.
- Set up a business development model that actively supports the prospect list and ensures that everyone in the company is working on the same prospects. Compensation is an important element here. The most effective schemes that we have seen take a two-pronged approach: Long-term relationship building is rewarded *and* losses are penalized. Ideally, compensation drives appropriate behavior and is the result of it.
- Service strong relationships vigorously. Your competitors are just waiting for you to make a mistake or leave an opening.
- Service strong *prospects* vigorously as well. In this "overbanked" market, your only hope of developing major new relationships is to target high priority prospects and impress them with service equal to that received by your top clients.
- Keep an eye out for vulnerable competitors. Remember that aggressors in the animal kingdom increase their chances for success by targeting the weakest in a herd.

- ▓ Track your calls, visits, and proposals to be sure your actions fulfill your plans.
- ▓ Be rigorous about reevaluating the prospect list on an ongoing basis. As a general rule, keep names on the list for two years to allow sufficient time to develop a relationship. There is no dishonor in removing names from the list, but this should not occur until progress (or lack of progress) with the prospect has been measured against the number of meetings held. It is natural that the list will change over time; just be sure that the criteria for creating and managing the list do not.

FROM "OUTSIDER" TO TRUSTED "ADVISER"

Investment bankers, particularly the superior ones, are always looking for ways to create and make bold use of an "unfair competitive advantage." They do this by getting close enough to the decision makers in a company to earn the position of trusted adviser. They are then more likely to receive or anticipate timely confidential information about the company, which in turn enables them to develop ideas that are *specific* to the client's objectives. Over time, this ratchets the relationship to increasingly higher levels until eventually the bank becomes that company's lead investment bank.

This presents a bit of a "chicken and egg" problem, because it is difficult to present creative and innovative ideas without having superior knowledge of the company and its business. That is why you need to focus on those companies where there is reasonable opportunity to become the lead investment bank, then work to strengthen those relationships with frequent, focused meetings. This is where time spent with a top-rated analyst can pay off, as incremental knowledge can help elevate these meetings from mere sales calls to more of a forum for the exchange of substantive ideas. Even one small assignment can have a big payoff. If handled flawlessly, by people in the bank more than qualified to do so, small transactions can become stepping-stones to larger ones when the firm demonstrates even more skill than the company anticipated.

Here are some additional recommendations for generating an unfair competitive advantage:

- ▓ Set your firm apart with the "best and the brightest." One highly regarded equity research analyst or product transaction specialist can have enormous influence.

▓ Make the firm a "greenhouse for excellence" by structuring an environment that fosters innovative thinking in a team environment. Establish
and maintain close coordination between relationship bankers and
product specialists to determine how to work best with each client. The
tug-of-war between a product transaction approach and a long-term relationship management approach can create difficulties, but corporate
clients expect a coordinated effort; and everyone is best served when
the investment banker figures out a way to give them what they want.

▓ Provide extraordinary service to help tip the scales in your firm's favor.
The complaint we hear most often from corporate executives is that
bankers do not take enough time to understand their needs. Only 30
percent of the clients participating in our annual research are happy
with the service they currently receive from their investment banks.

▓ Take a long-term view of the relationship. If you already take a long-
term view, take an even longer-term view. There is widespread feeling
among CEOs and other financial executives that bankers are becoming
overly transaction oriented. "Firms tend to be deal focused, rather than
focused on broader relationships," is a common complaint. "We are
seeing more emphasis on doing transactions at the expense of long-
term relationships," is another.

▓ To understand clients' needs thoroughly, listen actively. Probe, then
probe deeper. And prove you listened and understood by your subsequent actions.

▓ Work for free. As mentioned, this is an important way to show a client
that you are taking a long-term view of the relationship. CEOs are
looking for investment bankers who will act as strategic advisers. Assistance and advice—offered freely when appropriate—help cement the
impression that the banker is providing service, not just pitching transactions. Over the long run, those firms that enter into such partnership
relationships are the ones that ultimately earn lead-bank status. For
many corporate executives, the ultimate test of an investment banker's
sincerity is whether he or she will walk away from a deal, advising that
the transaction is a bad move, or one that does not require the bank's
services.

Bankers must be disciplined, however, about when to work for free and
when to refuse. Keep the long-term view in mind when you decide just how
much "free advice" you are willing to give. Bankers can't expect to get paid
for all the work they do for a client, and it certainly is a lot better to get the
call to do some free analysis than to learn that someone else got the call.

However, bankers need to be sure they do get paid back, at an appropriate fee level, eventually.

While you probably shouldn't expect payback after only one assignment, you should after three or four. But relationship bankers need to invest some real time in the relationship, supported by high-quality output, before they get a chance to collect a fee. Doing these free projects can be a tricky judgment call, but it is a good way to get to know the client. Such hands-on work often reveals some nitty-gritty details about the company not always conveyed in meetings.

- Hold more frequent, substantive meetings. Almost 40 percent of the Fortune 500 corporations participating in our annual research say they would like their investment bankers to meet with them more frequently.
- Link meetings to show creative and innovative ideas that are specific to a company's needs. Focus on intensive—rather than extensive—servicing.
- Provide stable but deep coverage, using several bankers and product specialists to provide dedicated service. Multiple points of contact between the company and the bank have many benefits: They help ensure everyone is kept in the information loop and build the relationship on an institutional, rather than a personal, basis. The challenge is to make the quality of service consistent across all the bankers on the team.
- Plan for the turnover in both corporate executives and in investment bankers that will inevitably occur. Customers are not going to be happy with personnel changes. In fact, such changes can be quite wrenching. If you anticipate change and actively manage the process, you can give customers the experience of seamless continuity of service. This ensures that the confidence they have placed in your firm remains intact.
- Make the best use of senior bankers' time by delegating the routine, day-to-day tasks to less senior bankers. Distributing the responsibility for clients across several key people ensures that senior bankers will not get spread too thin, and frees them to concentrate on deepening and broadening other relationships. The art to this is managing the clients' expectations and reassuring them that they are still in good hands, even if those hands do not always belong to the senior banker.
- Establish a client-centered internal structure where all team members take ownership of the client relationships. The key here is to spread the credit for transactions generously, and in such a way that productivity is not affected by worry over how the credit will be shared.
- Keep a pipeline filled with well-trained, ambitious, young bankers. Doing so guarantees there will always be enough high-level professionals to

meet demand and helps make leadership transitions seamless. Where possible, promote from within to retain valuable staff, ensure stable coverage, and maintain a consistent culture.

MANY TRY, FEW SUCCEED

With the potential for profits in investment banking greater than it has ever been, many commercial and foreign banks are attempting to enter the investment banking business. In fact, banks have been merging, diverging, and merging again at a record pace. Here are just a few recent acquisitions:

- Bankers Trust bought Alex Brown and was then acquired by Deutsche Bank. Though this is now one of the world's largest financial services companies, it still won't rank among the top investment banking firms serving large corporations in America.
- NationsBank bought Montgomery Securities.
- Bank of America bought Robertson Stephens.
- NationsBank bought Bank of America and sold Robertson Stephens to BankBoston.
- SBC Warburg bought Dillon Read, then merged into UBS to form UBS Warburg.
- First Union bought Wheat First Securities.
- Travelers bought Salomon Brothers and merged with Smith Barney to create Salomon Smith Barney. Travelers and Citicorp then merged to create Citigroup.

Despite these repeated and ongoing efforts to purchase some magic combination of product expertise and client relationships, most of the attempted transformations of commercial banks into investment banks have not gone well. Nor have the efforts of well-known commercial and merchant banks in Japan, Britain, and continental Europe as they try to penetrate the investment banking stronghold of the top U.S. firms.

As Table 5.6 shows, the names of the top 10 banks of today are not much different from those of 25 years ago. Some banks have dropped from the list due to mergers, but for every such instance there are dozens of other banks that have yet to make it onto the list because developing the business has proved more challenging than anticipated. Of the top 10 firms, three in particular—Goldman Sachs, Merrill Lynch, and Morgan Stanley Dean Witter—are distinguishing themselves as global leaders and reaping extraordinary rewards as a result.

TABLE 5.6   Top Ten Investment Banks—U.S. Market Penetration Then and Now

1978—Market Penetration		1999—Market Penetration	
Goldman Sachs	28%	Goldman Sachs	53%
Merrill Lynch	18	Merrill Lynch	46
Salomon Brothers	17	Morgan Stanley Dean Witter	42
Warburg Paribas Becker	15	Salomon Smith Barney	41
Lehman Bros. Kuhn Loeb	14	J.P. Morgan	28
First Boston	13	Credit Suisse First Boston	27
Morgan Stanley	13	Lehman Brothers	24
Kidder Peabody	12	Bank of America Securities	22
Morgan Guaranty	10	Chase Manhattan	20
Blyth Eastman Dillon	9	Donaldson, Lufkin & Jenrette	16

Those banks that have not endured failed primarily due to lack of resources, lack of focus, or a focus too narrow to sustain the firm when the chosen sector fell out of favor. Here are a few examples of strategies that failed:

- Warburg Paribas Becker lost credibility as they tried unsuccessfully to develop their commercial paper specialty into broader relationships. They were bought by Merrill Lynch in 1984.
- Drexel Burnham's prowess in high-yield bonds put them on the Top Ten list in the 1980s, yet ultimately got them into trouble. They were liquidated in 1990.
- With multiple mergers, Lehman Brothers became part of Shearson American Express, an organization that tried unsuccessfully to combine retail and wholesale. (Again independent, the firm is striving to rebuild its original Lehman Brothers brand and stature.)

In contrast, those that have succeeded have done so because each has been able to take a unique skill set to drive their success. The top firms may not all look alike, but in terms of their extraordinary product capability they are now more similar than ever.

NOT FOR THE FAINT OF HEART

With competition intensifying and three top firms pulling well ahead of the pack, how can new entrants to the investment banking business hope to

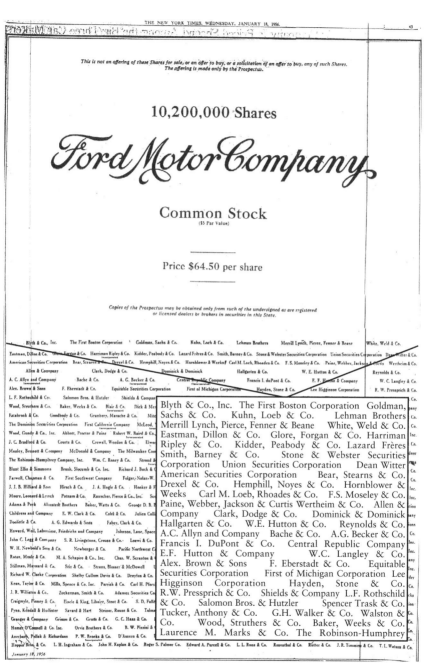

This is not an offering of these Shares for sale, or an offer to buy, or a solicitation of an offer to buy, any of such Shares. The offering is made only by the Prospectus.

10,200,000 Shares

Ford Motor Company

Common Stock
($5 Par Value)

Price $64.50 per share

Copies of the Prospectus may be obtained only from such of the undersigned as are registered or licensed dealers or brokers in securities in this State.

Blyth & Co., Inc.　The First Boston Corporation　Goldman, Sachs & Co.　Kuhn, Loeb & Co.　Lehman Brothers　Merrill Lynch, Pierce, Fenner & Beane　White, Weld & Co.　Eastman, Dillon & Co.　Glore, Forgan & Co.　Harriman Ripley & Co.　Kidder, Peabody & Co. Lazard Frères Smith, Barney & Co.　Stone & Webster Securities Corporation　Union Securities Corporation　Dean Witter & Co.　American Securities Corporation　Bear, Stearns & Co.　Drexel & Co.　Hemphill, Noyes & Co.　Hornblower & Weeks　Carl M. Loeb, Rhoades & Co.　F.S. Moseley & Co.　Paine, Webber, Jackson & Curtis Wertheim & Co.　Allen & Company　Clark, Dodge & Co.　Dominick & Dominick Hallgarten & Co.　W.E. Hutton & Co.　Reynolds & Co. A.C. Allyn and Company　Bache & Co.　A.G. Becker & Co. Francis I. DuPont & Co.　Central Republic Company E.F. Hutton & Company　W.C. Langley & Co. Alex. Brown & Sons　F. Eberstadt & Co.　Equitable Securities Corporation　First of Michigan Corporation Lee Higginson Corporation　Hayden, Stone & Co. R.W. Pressprich & Co.　Shields & Company L.F. Rothschild & Co.　Salomon Bros. & Hutzler　Spencer Trask & Co. Tucker, Anthony & Co.　G.H. Walker & Co.　Walston & Co.　Wood, Struthers & Co.　Baker, Weeks & Co. Laurence M. Marks & Co. The Robinson-Humphrey

January 18, 1956

FIGURE 5.2　1956 Ford Motor Company stock offering. (Used by permission of Ford Motor Company.)

compete? The truth is they may not be able to, at least not quickly. Becoming a lead bank, to whatever size company, requires a long-term commitment. And we do mean long term. It is one thing to note J.P. Morgan's growth—from 10 percent and ninth place in 1978 to 17 percent and seventh place in 1988, to 28 percent and fifth place in 1999. It is quite another to note that it has taken 20 years to achieve this growth.

To compete with the top investment banks in the United States, all of which are full service, a challenger has two options:

1. Commit to internal "organic" growth—with all the risks of not having the right strategy or organizational resources or sustained commitment or sufficient capital or the needed relationship or ability to attract and keep the necessary talent.
2. Purchase the necessary product capabilities, transaction experts, and coverage teams and face the very difficult task of integrating the at-odds cultures, strategic beliefs, personalities, and ways of doing business that lead to success in commercial banking versus investment banking.

Whichever option is chosen, the likelihood of failure is high. Take a look at this Ford Motor Company stock offering of 1956 (Figure 5.2 on page 173) and see just how many names you recognize from the over 700 underwriters.

And competition among investment banks—both at home and abroad—can only intensify. As banks aim to become competitive across all product capabilities, especially the higher margin products of M&A, equity, and high-yield debt, consolidation is likely to continue until just two types of investment banks will remain: a small number of extraordinarily large firms that are global in scope and capability, and a much greater number of firms highly specialized by geographic market, product, or client focus.

Regardless of which type of investment bank your firm is or aims to be, learn the valuable lesson provided by today's most successful investment banks. That is, enter to win. Commit 100 percent to the business, focus on client relationships, and make sure those relationships are with clients who present the best opportunity for your bank to become the lead bank. Not one of today's top investment banks plays to be number two. Whether you're competing globally or locally, neither should you.

Investment Banking in Canada

In Canada, the nationwide commercial banks have been able to maintain their dominance in long-term corporate finance for several reasons:

- Canadian bankers have long been known for their bold credit policies, particularly in longer-term lending.
- Canada's commercial banks have long been nationwide retailers with large capital bases and stable business platforms—a strong foundation on which to build.
- Canadian commercial banks acquired the leading securities dealers in the 1990s, and thus obtained the public capital markets capabilities in both debt and equity that balanced their traditional strengths in the private debt markets.

Historically, the giant international investment banks were discouraged from competing in Canada by the low profit margins of a very price-competitive market, the risks and costs of a "bought-deal" capital market, the difficulties of building distribution, and the relatively low volume of major transactions. Foreign competitors were daunted most particularly by the forceful combination of such home-team advantages as strong relationships, a strong Canadian preference, and dominance by Canadians of the Canadian debt and equity capital markets.

The importance of relationships—followed closely by recognized capabilities in mergers and acquisitions and in capital raising—are documented in Table 5.7. It shows the criteria that matter most in determining which of the investment banks servicing a corporation, province, or government agency will be chosen as the lead investment bank. The two most important factors are the *individual* capabilities of the relationship manager and the *institutional* credibility of the bank.

Selection of a lead investment bank is, of course, very important to the corporation or governmental units making the selection. The decision is *crucial* to the investment bankers for the powerful reason that, year after

TABLE 5.7 Factors Determining Lead Investment Bank

	Most Important	
	1999	2000
Capability of corporate finance relationship manager	60%	66%
Bank's credibility with the CEO and board of directors	59	54
Capability in advising on important M&A transactions	49	51
Capability in equity research and equity underwriting	43	45
Capability in underwriting long-term debt issues	38	39
Capability and willingness to provide credit	29	34
Financial strength and credit rating of firm	23	18

year, half of *all* the fees paid for investment banking services are paid to a single *lead* investment bank.

Investment banks that are not content to specialize in specific *products* (e.g., international, or non-Canadian, bond underwritings or international acquisitions) and want to build long-term, broad-based *relationships,* simply must focus on those clients with whom they can build strong, mutually beneficial relationships. In that way, they will earn the vital position as lead investment bankers.

To build lead or even colead relationships, we recommend to our non-Canadian clients that they focus on those corporations that are in such international industries as oil, pharmaceuticals, media, computers, and communications technology, where an investment bank's *global* industry expertise gives it that decisive unfair competitive advantage every firm is looking for. Similarly, we recommend to our Canadian clients that they concentrate on companies in those industries where their in-depth *Canadian* expertise and close long-standing and broad working relationships will give *them* the decisive, unfair competitive advantage. Broadly speaking, this strategic approach to market segmentation squares with the Canadian banks' dominance of capital raising and non-Canadian banks concentrating on M&A, particularly acquisitions outside of Canada.

As shown in Table 5.8, on six of the eight most important selection criteria, large international investment banks with special strengths in M&A can compete to win if they have a strong focus on companies in international industries. The three most important criteria are:

1. Creative and innovative ideas.
2. Credibility in M&A with the CEO and board.
3. Capability of M&A specialists.

TABLE 5.8 Factors Determining M&A Advisory Mandates

	Most Important	
	1999	2000
Creative and innovative M&A ideas	44%	51%
Credibility with company's CEO and board of directors	45	45
Capability of M&A specialists	37	44
Historical relationship	25	32
Understanding of company's M&A strategy	34	30
Understanding of industry	37	30
Ability to arrange financing	22	25
Past record in structuring and closing transactions	17	24

And the next three are:

4. Understanding company's M&A strategy.
5. Understanding company's industry.
6. Past record in closing M&A transactions.

As the largest international firms expand their commitments to investment research on Canadian companies for Canadian institutional investors, their comparative capabilities in M&A will get stronger, particularly for companies in international industries.

Meanwhile, the leading Canadian banks have acquired and are integrating into their organizations the research and capital-raising capabilities of the leading Canadian securities dealers in an effective "aggressive defense" of their home market, forcing the international banks to fight very hard for each transaction. At the same time, Merrill Lynch's strategic acquisition of Midland Walwyn—a retail stockbroker that was developing an increasingly strong institutional research and distribution business—is

TABLE 5.9 Investment Bank Penetration in Canada

Company	Important Relationships in 1987	Company	Important Relationships in 2000
Wood Gundy	32%	RBC Dominion Securities	67%
Dominion Securities	30	CIBC World Markets	66
Royal Bank	30	BMO Nesbitt Burns	57
McLeod Young Weir	25	Scotia Capital	56
CIBC	21	TD Securities	49
Burns Fry	14	Merrill Lynch	38
Bank of Montreal	17	Goldman Sachs	25
Toronto Dominion Bank	17	National Financial	21
Merrill Lynch Royal Securities	12	Salomon Smith Barney	19
Richardson Greenshields	6	Morgan Stanley Dean Witter	18
Nesbitt Thomson Deacon	8	Credit Suisse First Boston	14
Gordon Capital	7	Deutsche Banc Alex. Brown	12
Salomon Brothers	7	Citibank	10
Bank of Nova Scotia	6	J.P. Morgan	9
Citibank	6	Banc of America	9
Morgan Stanley	4	ABN AMRO	7
Morgan Bank	4	UBS Bunting Warburg	4
National Bank of Canada	3	Lehman Brothers	4
Levesque Beaubien	2	Peters & Co.	4
First Boston	2	Chase Manhattan/Chase H&Q	3

challenging other international firms to expand their strategic commitments in Canada.

Table 5.9 shows the market penetration of the 20 largest investment banks in Canada in 1987 and in 2000.

Canadian investment banks are in a strong position to dominate equity offerings other than those that must be international. With their dominant competitive positions in institutional distribution and research—the two most important factors in selecting book runners for equity underwritings—the leading Canadian banks are in a strong position to defend their turf, except for issuers that want or need to access the international equity capital markets. Table 5.10 shows the important factors in awarding book-runner mandates for equity underwritings.

In long-term debt, Canadian banks are strong two-fisted competitors: They are ready and able to offer a choice of either public or private debt, often right up until the "last minute." This compelling competitive advantage can be formidable.

In lead-managing long-term debt offerings, Canadian banks are in a strong position to meet the preferences of issuers, at least in part because issuers and underwriters of bonds can only access the market by conforming to it. Canadian banks have that always-wanted unfair competitive advantage of being strong on all the important factors, including aggressive pricing, as Table 5.11 shows.

TABLE 5.10   Factors Determining Equity Book-Runner Mandates

	Most Important	
	1999	2000
Institutional distribution capability	64%	59%
Equity research capability and analyst relationship	46	46
Credibility with company's CEO and board of directors	25	34
Skill in structuring and pricing issues	33	32
Historical relationship	17	31
Retail distribution capability	35	28
Firm's trading volume in company's stock	30	26
Participation as manager in past issues	23	21
Syndicate management capability	24	21
Capable equity capital markets specialists	13	12

TABLE 5.11 Factors Determining Lead Mandates for Long-Term Debt Offerings

	Most Important	
	1999	2000
Institutional distribution capability	50%	50%
Capable debt capital markets specialists	36	46
Skill in structuring and pricing issues	36	46
Lower cost or better terms	33	39
Historical relationship	33	34
Understanding of financing needs	34	31
Creative and innovative debt ideas	30	31
Syndicate management capability	36	23
Continuity of debt desk coverage	12	14
Participation as manager in past issues	9	13

Even as the leading Canadian investment banks have conducted an aggressive defense of their national market, the leading international banks have been committing more and more resources and have established stronger and stronger positions. The prospects are for continued vigorous competition.

Project Finance

The evolution of project finance is causing what may either be a pendulum swing or permanent change. As project financings increasingly adopt the characteristics of structures once reserved for less risky investments, project finance risk/return characteristics increasingly resemble those found in general corporate banking. This transition from "highly structured/high return" to "structured/average return" is changing the very nature of the business and marks the end of project finance as we knew it.

Project finance was developed as a way for companies to keep certain large and often risky investments—and more importantly the associated financing—off their balance sheets. Typical applications include the financing of large infrastructure projects such as toll roads and bridges, wastewater treatment plants, power plants, mines, and oil and gas extraction facilities. But by housing the risk of these investments in special purpose vehicles

(SPVs) and joint ventures (JVs) the owners could not reduce the risk—only transfer it to those financing the JVs and SPVs. The banks financing these projects in turn looked to protect themselves (and their depositors) with innovative financing structures and, as much as possible, insurance or loan guarantees from governments and export credit agencies.

Project finance is changing in two key ways:

1. *Disintermediation.* Rather than relying on the traditional sources of private credit to finance projects, corporations increasingly use the capital markets.
2. *Increase in competition leading to lower margins.* The increased number of banks providing project finance services drove margins down, making it both more difficult *and* less rewarding to compete. Our research shows that a typical project financing now involves six banks, up from four just 2 years earlier.

ADAPTING TO THE NEW REALITIES

As the industry changes, most banks and investment banks are adapting to stay competitive. Several years ago, the majority of our clients had separate Project Finance departments. But in the past 2 years, many banks have quietly disbanded these groups and reassigned staff to product groups (e.g., capital markets or syndications) or sector-specialized coverage units.

These changes in the business are reflected in the new criteria project sponsors now have when choosing their project finance banks. Our research shows that when selecting a bank for advisory services customers look for the following, in order of importance:

- Ability to structure deals.
- Level of experience.
- Creative ideas and solutions.
- Knowledge of local environment.
- Knowledge of capital markets.

And when selecting banks for arranging and underwriting, customer criteria are as follows:

- Attractive pricing and structure.
- Willing to hold major portion of the debt financing.
- Level of experience.

▩ Flexibility of lending specialists.
▩ Creative ideas and solutions.

Customers also have new criteria for the *type* of provider they want. Commercial and universal banks have made significant inroads into the project finance arena and now provide the lion's share of project financings as part of their ever-growing menu of "one-stop shopping" services. Whereas in the past, investment and merchant banks held roughly one-third of the top 10 slots, in recent years the universal banks have begun to dominate the top 15, as Table 5.12 shows.

Investment banks are striking back, however, and many provide a significant number of clients with senior debt in addition to capital markets financing. Reflecting the complicated structure of most project finance deals, sponsors favor experienced bankers, who are able to deliver creative solutions. The majority of project sponsors favor working with project finance specialists with substantial industry knowledge, but a noticeable minority of project sponsors prefer coverage by a generalist with ready access to project finance specialists. This trend is in line with the main theme of Chapter 4, which emphasizes the new role of relationship manager, and is nicely summarized by one corporate executive: "We prefer a corporate banker

TABLE 5.12 Project Finance Product Penetration

	Used for Project Finance
Chase Manhattan Bank	41%
ABN AMRO	35
Citibank	35
Deutsche Morgan Grenfell	28
Union Bank of Switzerland	26
Credit Suisse First Boston	24
Bank of America	22
Barclays Capital	21
J.P. Morgan	18
ING Bank (ING Barings)	16
Goldman Sachs	16
Société Générale	16
Bank of Tokyo/Mitsubishi	15
National Westminster Bank	14
Morgan Stanley	13

who is specialized in our industry and has a working knowledge of project finance because of his broader outlook and deeper insight. He can then co-ordinate project finance specialists as required."

To compete in this new project finance environment:

- Demonstrate strength in creative solutions.
- Be able to deliver capital market access as well as bank debt.
- Field experienced deal teams that can quickly win the client's confidence.

ONE STEP FORWARD, ONE STEP BACK

Our most recent research highlights some good news as well as an opportunity where the market is begging for improvement.

The good news is that the concept of single-firm use for advisory services and arranging is gaining acceptance. Only 13 percent of those project financing sponsors interviewed found this practice unacceptable, while 40 percent of firms, because of the perceived benefit of improved coordination and speed of transactions, had no objection to using one firm for

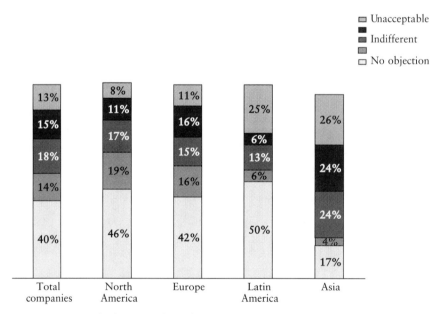

FIGURE 5.3 Single-firm use for advisory services and arranging of financings.

both advisory services and arranging. Figure 5.3 shows the level of acceptance of this practice by geography.

And the opportunity: Our research points up a need that is presently going largely unmet by project finance providers. Our qualitative research indicates that Export Credit Agency (ECA) knowledge and experience is an area sponsors consider *clearly* important, yet when judging the ECA services of the top 10 banks, a whopping 41 percent of project finance sponsors rank their services "marginal" or "negative."

This suggests a lack of capabilities by the project finance banks that translates into opportunity for those providers willing to embrace it. In the current project finance environment, there is not yet a clearly defined "bulge bracket" of leading providers. But as we study the industry, we see five organizations—two in the United States, two in Europe, and one in Asia—that provide high-quality project financing services on a global basis. This group stands poised to emerge as real leaders in this field, and we urge our clients eager to compete in this market to take a hard look at the quality and breadth of service these firms are providing and adjust their business strategy accordingly.

CHAPTER 6

Stockbrokerage

John G.M. Webster, James A. Bennett, Jr., John G. Colon, Lea B. Hansen, and Charles D. Ellis

Institutional Stockbrokerage: Continuous Competition

Institutional stockbrokerage is an unusually complex business requiring the skillful management of many components, both individually and in their interactive interdependencies.

Change—many kinds of change—is the persistent, dynamic, and dominant reality of this business. Consider these major dimensions of change:

- Share prices for several thousand companies—and the economic and business realities of these companies and investors' perceptions of those economic and business realities and potential realities—are changing all the time.
- Regulations change, sometimes profoundly.
- Technology changes, and so changes everything.
- Customers change. Institutional investors' portfolios are ever-changing: The average turnover of large portfolios is nearly 100 percent, which means that on average, every investment is changed every year as institutional

---

John G.M. Webster, James A. Bennett, Jr., and John G. Colon wrote "Institutional Stockbrokerage: Continuous Competition," John G. Colon and James A. Bennett, Jr., wrote "Stockbrokerage in Europe," Lea B. Hansen and John G.M. Webster wrote "Stockbrokers in Canada," and John G.M. Webster and Charles D. Ellis wrote "Japanese Stockbrokerage: Responding to Hyperchange."

investors constantly compete with each other for superior investment performance.

- And with changes in investment performance—favorable for this manager; unfavorable for that manager—money moves, sometimes with great force, as investors change the managers they want to manage their funds.

While most professionals will talk, almost longingly, about the great importance of long-term performance, their actions show how very important they believe short-term investment performance really is. The impact of investment performance differs from one type of institutional investor to another:

- *Mutual Funds.* Investment performance in the most recent quarter and year can dominate mutual fund sales, particularly at the margin, because investors (and stockbrokers) have so many alternative funds from which to select and switching funds is so easy to do. And investment performance is measured and reported daily.
- *Pension Funds.* With a remarkable 40 percent of large pension and endowment funds selecting a new investment manager every year—and over two-thirds of these large funds advised by investment consultants who specialize in advising on the selection of new managers (and thus contribute to the already intense pressure to perform)—investment performance is a dominating factor.
- *401(k).* Defined contribution employee benefit funds are rapidly gaining share of the nation's retirement assets. These funds are generally invested in mutual funds and can easily move at the Internet "click" initiative of the individual plan participants from one of the numerous funds offered by the typical plan to another, usually for performance reasons.
- *Hedge Funds.* Competition for customers' assets (and the chance to earn big incentive fees) depends directly on current investment performance. While the assets of most hedge funds are not terribly large, their superactive management generates a huge volume of transactions and makes them big customers for stockbrokers.

GROWTH BUSINESS

The growth in change has been enormous. As Table 6.1 shows, institutional trading has increased 50 times over the past 28 years we've been conducting our research on this business. And the nature of institutional trading has

TABLE 6.1   Growth in Block Trades

	Block Transactions	Total Shares Traded
1980	134,000	3,311,131
1990	843,000	19,681,849
1999	4,186,000	102,293,458

Source: NYSE Fact Book—1999.

changed even more rapidly, as measured by the growth in block trades of 10,000 shares, 50,000, 100,000, and 500,000 shares at a time.

We estimate total worldwide commissions to be $22.5 billion. Of this total, $12 billion (more than half) is generated by institutions in the United States—a very big business. In addition to the surging growth in institutional assets and the intensity with which these assets are managed, each and every institutional stockbrokerage firm constantly faces another even more commanding challenge: competition.

The repetitive and forceful strategic thrusts and tactical initiatives of all the other competitors, particularly the largest and strongest, challenge every stockbrokerage firm in every component of the business every day. And, the "strategic responses" of all the challenged firms multiply and magnify the challenge for all the other firms, who are thereby obliged to react promptly and boldly—which proliferates the challenges—and so the process goes on and on.

Here is how the institutional stockbrokers' competitive rankings have changed since our first research on this business in 1973. Back in 1973, Merrill Lynch and Morgan Stanley were not even in the Top 30. As Table 6.2 shows, most of the then-leading firms are now gone.

Importantly, the institutional stockbrokerage business is most certainly *not* an island unto itself: Powerful forces connect it to each of the other businesses of each major firm: investment banking, retail stockbrokerage, and investment management.

And as the larger American stockbrokerage firms have expanded internationally and developed important businesses in all the major markets of the world—in British shares, Japanese shares, European shares, Canadian shares, Southeast Asian shares, Australian shares, and Latin American shares, and so on—the complexity of the business and the strategic and operational challenges to the firms' business managers have become much larger, are far more complex, and are rapidly changing.

TABLE 6.2 Leading Institutional Stockbrokers

1974		1999	
Oppenheimer	64%	Merrill Lynch	91%
Mitchell, Hutchins	61	Morgan Stanley Dean Witter	87
William D. Witter	58	Salomon Smith Barney	84
Spencer Trask	56	Donaldson, Lufkin & Jenrette	80
H.C. Wainwright	55	Goldman Sachs	80
Drexel, Burnham	51	Credit Suisse First Boston	66
Baker, Weeks	50	Bear Stearns	66
Smith Barney, Harris Upham	49	Lehman Brothers	62
White, Weld	43	PaineWebber	61
Goldman Sachs	39	Sanford C. Bernstein	58
Merrill Lynch	38	Prudential Securities	50
Faulkner, Dawkins & Sullivan	36	J.P. Morgan	42
Loeb Rhoades	36	Deutsche Banc Alex. Brown	38
Donaldson, Lufkin & Jenrette	30	Schroders	37
C.J. Lawrence	29	CIBC World Markets	34
Becker Securities	29	Banc of America Securities	32
L.F. Rothschild	29	SG Cowen	32
Kidder, Peabody	28	Robertson Stephens	21
First Manhattan	23	Warburg Dillon Read	16
Bear, Stearns	22	Wit SoundView	14

THE STRATEGIC SWEET SPOT

Even with all this change, the strategic focus for a major stockbrokerage firm continues to be the "sweet spot" of the business: being *very important* to the *very important* institutional investors. This simple proposition is so important and so central to developing and executing an effective business strategy, we repetitively emphasize it in our consulting with senior management of the leading stockbrokerage firms. The proposition comes in two parts:

1. First, the very large institutional investors are *very* large. In our consulting with the leading stockbrokerage firms in America, we and they find it useful to focus our thinking again and again on the following key facts:

   The 100 largest and most active institutional investors account for 70 percent of *all* the trades done by *all* U.S. institutions.

The 50 largest institutions do 50 percent of *all* the trading done by *all* investors—individuals and institutions—on the New York Stock Exchange.

2. Second, the most important stockbrokers do a very large share of all the business done by any institution:

The five most important stockbrokers for the typical large institution do about 50 percent of that institution's *total* business.

The single *most* important stockbroker typically does 13 percent of the institution's business. The second broker does about 11 percent—and the next three brokers together do over 25 percent.

Figure 6.1 shows that even at the largest institutions (smaller institutions naturally concentrate their business and their buying power with far fewer stockbrokers), approximately 45 percent of their listed business is concentrated with their Top 5 stockbrokers.

And unlisted trading (sometimes called "OTC" for "Over the Counter" trading and sometimes called "NASDAQ" for National Association of Securities Dealers) is even more concentrated. The top 3 dealers do 40 percent or more of all the business by a typical large institution as shown in Figure 6.2.

The concentration of the "most with the best"—as *each* institution sees its own alternatives and selects its own dream team of stockbrokers—delivers the strategic imperative of the institutional stockbrokerage business: Be an important stockbroker to the important institutions. Or to generalize

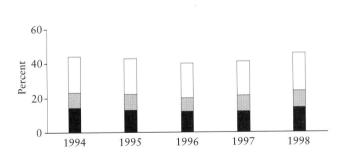

☐ Third, Fourth, and Fifth Firms
▨ Second Firm
■ First Firm

FIGURE 6.1 Concentration of listed business with top 5 brokers.

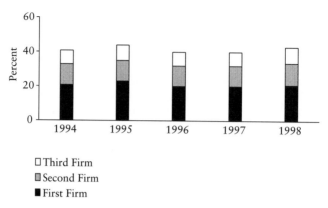

FIGURE 6.2   Concentration of NASDAQ business with top 3 brokers.

slightly: Be important enough for enough important institutions so your commission revenues more than cover the costs of your service proposition.

HISTORY AS COMPARISON

Thirty years ago, when retail stockbrokerage dominated the business and fixed rate commissions prevailed, the major variable to manage was simple: *volume*. Do a greater volume of business and you made more money. The important people in a stockbrokerage firm were, with genuine respect, called "producers" because producing more business was the business imperative.

But that was the *retail* stockbrokerage business. As institutional investors became more and more important, their very different wants and needs became steadily more important to all the major stockbrokers. Among the major firms, only those stockbrokers that could and would meet the needs of the institutional investors[1] would survive. Those large firms that for too long held onto their old ways of doing business virtually doomed themselves to failure. And, sadly, the failures were numerous.

Some stockbrokers recognized that, as intermediaries—when their customers' needs and wants were greatly changing, they would need to change greatly, too—and they undertook a series of actions:

- *Research.* Brokers competed for a larger share of institutional commissions by spending larger and larger sums of money to provide more—and more sophisticated—investment research "free" to those institutions that did more business with them.

- *Block trading.* Brokers used their own capital to buy all or parts of large blocks of stock—first 10,000 shares in a single block, then 100,000 shares in a block, and then even 500,000 shares in a block, hoping (and expecting) to resell the shares at a profit or at least not at a very large loss, but knowing they would sometimes have to absorb large losses as "the cost of doing business."
- *Give-ups.* Very large brokers would execute large institutional transactions and then "give up" or pay out part of the commissions to other brokers that the selling institutions wanted to compensate for selling mutual funds or for research services or for other purposes.[2]

In the late 1960s, the Justice Department and the Securities and Exchange Commission began investigations that led to the elimination of "give-ups" and to the staged elimination of the long-standing New York Stock Exchange practice of setting a schedule of fixed rates of commission that all member firms were then obliged to charge all their customers.

The fixed commission had made sense for the retail stockbrokerage business where most trades were for 100 shares or less. But if an institution wanted to buy 100,000 shares, why should it be obliged to pay a *thousand* times as much per trade? While the NYSE fought a delaying action, the inevitable result of the questions being posed and the business being examined were clear: Fixed rates were not appropriate for large volume, professional institutional investors. They would soon have to go.[3]

Today, with negotiated rates, volume continues to be important, but management's task and responsibilities have become far more numerous, complex, and important. (This is why the most capable individuals, who used to focus on leading research or sales or trading, now focus on *management,* where the greatest skills are now needed.[4]) Management's great challenge is to find and sustain the optimal mix of costs and revenues as the forces of change keep everything in turbulence:

- Revenues are a function of commission rates and trading volume calling for stockbrokers' management's attention both at each of 500 to 1,000 institutional customers *and* for all institutions as a group. Particular attention is required in managing the complex set of relationships between all their analysts, traders, sales professionals, and traders with their numerous counterparts at *each* of the nation's largest institutions.
- Commission revenue volume for any one stockbrokerage firm is driven, in large part, by the perceived value of the broker's research product plus research sales effectiveness.

■ Volume for any one firm is also driven by trading—a combination of market-making and risk-taking and the skills with which "position" traders commit their firm's capital to buying—as principals—large blocks of stock. Other factors are capital commitments by the broker-dealer and the working relationships between broker-dealers and institutional traders, plus the skills of sales traders.

■ Market-making and managing the execution of agency transactions is a function of many variables: capital available for taking large risks quickly; scale of activity; skill at pricing blocks; skill at hedging risks with derivatives; skill at reselling, by having immediate access to institutional traders across the country and abroad; and nerve.

■ Costs are a constantly changing mixture of fixed, semifixed, and variable costs that are *all* changing. Very few stockbrokers have ever been bankrupted by having too little *revenues:* The real harm comes to those firms caught in a low tide of revenues with too high *costs.*

Not only are each of these major component businesses individually highly competitive, their basic business characteristics are quite different from one another. Each stockbrokerage firm needs to find ways to harmonize their efforts and commitments in each component with their efforts and commitments in all the other components.

Adding to the managerial challenge is the remarkable reality that the working relationship between a large investing institution and a large securities firm can easily depend on 50 or even 100 different simultaneous, and quite separately conducted, person-to-person relationships between various pairs of specialized experts at both organizations:

■ In executions, a major firm will have at least one professional working with each institution in each of these roles:
  Listed sales trader.
  Listed "position" trader.
  OTC sales trader.
  OTC market-maker.
  International trader.
  Derivatives trader.

■ In research, there will be at least one professional in each of these roles:
  Equity strategist.
  Economist.
  Demographer.
  Technical analyst.

■ Industry analysts are required in 40–60 industries or "sectors."

■ And at each institution:

> Up to 20 portfolio managers, each with a different fund, a different portfolio strategy, and a different way of making investment decisions. 20–50 research analysts covering different industries. 5–15 senior traders.

These working relationships have an unusual characteristic: While large volumes of business are conducted involving large amounts of money and substantial risks to both parties, there are no contracts. As professionals, both parties know very well what they are doing, what they seek to accomplish, and what they want to avoid. They also know the "rules of the game" and what each can expect of the other. And both are well aware that the other party has alternative counterparties that are just as large, just as capable, and just as interested in winning the business. So, the competition—at the margin—is intense, even unrelenting.

Each component of the institutional stockbrokerage business will have its own "strategic imperatives for success," so in our consulting with our clients, we strive always to make our recommendations accord with the key factors for success in that particular component of the overall business. Also, our recommendations must differ from one client to another, so our advice is always in accord with the particular strengths and objectives of each client organization. The latter is crucial because each stockbrokerage firm *is* different, particularly in the all-important soft dimensions of culture and "ways of doing business."

While the hard dimensions such as dollars of revenues or costs of IT or office rents or dollars of capital committed to trading or the firm's office location may *look* dominant at any point in time, over the long run they are all changeable. What is constant and unrelenting is culture—what appears in the short run to be "soft."

The strength and the significance of cultural differences are so important in the stockbrokerage business that of the numerous mergers during the past 25 years—while typically erroneously announced as "mergers of equals"—none have succeeded in combining or blending the strengths of the two firms. Instead of "cross-fertilization," the usual experience is closer to "cross-sterilization"; stockbrokerage firms are culturally tribal and a merger of cultures usually leads to a fight to the finish—only one tribal culture can become dominant. The other culture has to be—and will be—expunged.

In the next sections, we concentrate on what it takes to succeed, based on what we've learned from our extensive research and our consultations over more than 25 years with all the major stockbrokers. We cover these crucial components: Research Services, Selling, Research, Institutional Sales, and Executions.

RESEARCH SERVICES

Research—on companies, industries, economies, countries and on every significant aspect of each of these spheres—is of great importance to stockbrokerage firms because knowledge is power: power in sales, power in originating and distributing underwritings, and market-making power in all kinds of trading.

Institutional investors of all sizes and varieties share a common denominator: central interest in producing "better than market" investment performances. They look to Wall Street[5] for many kinds of investment research. Table 6.3 lists the research services investors have considered most important in our annual studies—led by detailed studies of individual companies and of major industries.

In our consulting with stockbroker clients, we recommend each firm develop and define and commit consistently to a research "product positioning" based on one of these three approaches:

1. *Top-Down Strategy*. With a core commitment to excellence in portfolio strategy, usually based on strong economic analysis that leads directly into industry and company weightings in the portfolio.
2. *Maintenance*. With a broad-based and in-depth commitment to continuous coverage of all major sectors and industries, so the firm's research on specific companies is "must have."

TABLE 6.3   Most Important Research Services

	1999
Detailed studies of individual companies	78%
Detailed studies of major industries	56
Development of creative investment ideas	33
Access to brokers' analysts	31
Accurate EPS estimates	27
Portfolio strategy and asset allocation	25
Overall "maintenance" research	24
Research seminars and conferences	24
Overall economic analysis and interest-rate forecasts	22
Internet access to research	16
Specific buy and sell recommendations	15
Quantitative research	15

3. *Creative Ideas.* With a clear priority of generating compelling new ideas for bold investment in particular companies or industries.

While any stockbrokerage firm would quite naturally be delighted to be a "triple threat" winner with excellence on all three vectors, such omniscience is unrealistic. The culture and the priorities necessary for a "creative ideas" product strategy are very different from the culture and priorities needed for a "maintenance" product strategy, so trying to do *both* is seldom feasible.

More importantly, the objective in selecting a core competence in research is to be so very good at whatever you commit to doing that the institutions your firm most wants to serve will be sure they really want your firm as one of their very few *most important* research providers.

Since only two or three firms of each basic type of research provider—Top-Down Strategy *or* Creative Ideas *or* Maintenance—can become one of an institution's favored few *most important* research providers, the most effective strategy is to choose the type of research your firm can and will be best at and make certain that you become your very best at it. This is the surest way to become "best of breed" for the institutions you intend to serve as one of their *very important* research stockbrokers—always remembering that being very important is key to getting into and staying in the sweet spot of the stockbrokerage business: being very important to the very important institutional investors.

The secret to success as a Top-Down Strategist is to be listened to and read instead of somebody else receiving that attention. In this intensely competitive arena, each triumphant strategist must make a brilliant combination of:

- Ideas and insights that are provocative enough to capture attention and stimulating enough to generate thoughtful rethinking by hundreds, even thousands of bright, busy portfolio managers who are literally bombarded by ideas and information that compete all day every day for their time and attention.
- Great skills of communicating in writing and in speaking, one-on-one and to groups—all too often at breakfast, lunch, and dinner and with several other meetings scheduled during the morning and afternoon—day after day on the same topic. And each session should be sparkling with the enthusiasm of originality and commitment.

  Like a political candidate out on the hustings, the strategist is making contact, striving to build an eternal consistency of adherents among institutional investors. And simultaneously, the strategist is working internally to network with the firm's analysts and the sales force who will represent and merchandise the strategist's ideas and help create the consistency of adherents or audience.

A research product strategy based on creative ideas is high return—and high risk. This product strategy can be effective if a firm's analysts can repetitively develop and articulate original and compelling ideas for investment, sometimes for individual companies of large size and influence (such as General Motors, IBM, or AOL), but most often for whole sectors (such as oils, banks, or Internet stocks). A creative idea strategy is most often undertaken by smaller firms with articulate senior analysts, often with a focus on one or two sectors.

A broad-based maintenance research strategy is usually chosen by a larger firm, particularly one with a large retail business that needs research coverage to meet the disparate needs of a large group of customers who will own and be interested in stocks in all sorts of industries and/or a large and diversified investment banking business.

In managing a large research department, be both bold and careful in constructing "industry coverage" portfolios. The most productive research departments have boldness in the skills of their analysts—and visibility. The "be careful" part is at least as important. "Okay" analysts are *not* okay; they are dangerous because they are nearly as expensive as the real winners and will never achieve the all-star status that enables their firm to generate strong revenues.

We also recommend concentrating your portfolio of analysts on the industries that are really important to your institutional investor clients, either because they are changing rapidly (like Internet stocks and drug stocks today) or because they are widely owned. In either case, stockbrokerage firms need to match their investments in analysts with the focus of attention—and therefore, the buying and selling—of their institutional investor customers. As Willy Sutton said about why he robbed banks, "That's where the money is!"

The hero in research is the analyst who can create proprietary understanding from nonproprietary data and information by gathering more and better information, and interpreting it more astutely and effectively than his or her competitors. Such analysts can communicate that understanding clearly and convincingly to their own firm's sales force and to the hundreds of institutional analysts and portfolio managers who are the firm's largest, smartest, and most demanding customers.

An analyst's work is intellectually difficult because he or she is always striving to figure out the value of a company's stock more quickly and more accurately than can the dozens and dozens of other smart, resourceful, and creative analysts who are all striving to reach the same goal.

The work is physically difficult, too: long hours of work, lots of rush-rush travel, many nights of little sleep in unfamiliar places—under tremendous competitive pressure, both internal and external.

Finally, the work is emotionally difficult because being wrong hurts. Analysts must make public commitments to which investors direct millions of dollars based on their estimates of a future that is full of complex uncertainties. Analysts carry an awesome, lonely burden of responsibility for making correct judgments in an always changing world of incomplete information and estimates.

Researchers—whether industry analysts, economists, portfolio strategists, stock pickers, Washington observers, technical analysts, or demographers—all tend to suffer from the same misunderstanding: They tend to assume that "Being right is *it!*" Not true. Sure, being wrong is *wrong*. But being right on your facts or right on your recommendation is only part—even a minority part—of being important. It's vital to be relevant and *used*. And to be relevant and used, you have to be read and heard.

Research Communication

Communication, as Peter Drucker so wisely says, is controlled by the receiver, not by the sender. If I stop listening to you or stop reading your writing, you can write and say all you like: There's no communication. That's why you need to master the art of communication—the art of being listened to and heard and read.

As we recommend to all the brilliant and well-informed analysts at our clients, your editor is your friend, your very tough editor is your very good friend. We all know the KISS concept: Keep It Simple, Sweetheart! Brevity *is* the soul of wit.[6] Yes, it takes longer to write a clear, concise, and convincing report. But when you send a research report recommending a decision you care about to thousands of busy people who will either read it—or *not* read it—extra time invested in making your report *readable* is time well spent. If it took you a year to produce your report and reading it would take each of them one hour, you'd be ahead—not just because one hour times 2,000 equals a working year, but because the reader's decision is whether to stay focused on your report or to toss it away. It's all too easy to toss aside a dull or tedious report, in which case you might just as well have never written it at all.

We urge our clients: Don't be confused. It's even more important to be *read* than to be "*right*."

Institutional investors live and die by their investment performance. That's the bottom line in the work they do as professionals. So, they are going to make all the final decisions. Much as institutional investors admire and rely on stockbrokers' research, they are not interested in being "told what to do."

The tests of good design are two: First, do your target readers want to reach out and pick your report out of the large pile they receive each day; and second, do they keep it and reread it because the design is the best for regular and repetitive use? Strive for harmony and consistency of writing style, report content, and visual appearance because consistency encourages confidence. Everybody's busy—and getting busier all the time—so the competition is on for time and attention on the equivalent of "shelf space" in the congested day of a portfolio manager.

Best Practices

Since industry and company analysts are so very important for success in the institutional stockbrokerage business, let's examine some of the Best Practices followed by the repetitively leading analysts. Here's what we advise young analysts to do in developing their own "professional franchise."

Pick an Industry or Sector You Really Like   Choose one you find truly fascinating. If your family business is retail and you have a feel for and a love of the business, go for it. If you're particularly numerate and love financial analysis, consider insurance or banking. If you're a geek, go for technology. A career analyst should select with great care the industry or sector on which he or she will devote many long years of study striving to be sure the analyst's skills and personality are in harmony with the nature of that industry and its people.

The economic nature of an industry as well as its character, culture, and ethics differ from that of other industries. Oilmen are not retailers; utility executives don't do Internet; and steelmen can't do entertainment, or vice versa. The importance of scientific discovery in pharmaceuticals is utterly different from the importance of low-cost distribution in retailing or pricing in airlines or advertising and promotion in beverages.

We urge analysts to find the industry where they belong because they'll be working there "forever," and their efforts will be really wasteful if it isn't a "good marriage." You'll be devoting an outrageous amount of time and energy to whatever you choose—and for a long, long, time—so decide carefully and go with your passion.

Know Yourself   What are you best at: interesting reporting of insightful management interviews; sophisticated financial analysis; conceptualizing business strategy; analysis of industry data; making astute new product appraisals; understanding conceptual or technology breakthroughs? Do what you do best.

Immerse Yourself in Your Chosen Industry   Wise analysts will focus totally on learning all about that industry by working the numbers in the accounting of each company, studying trade press "all the way back," and reading all sorts of company reports and histories. They will go to all sorts of meetings, join and actively participate in industry splinter groups of like-minded analysts, and reach out to all the best analysts at the institutions—*and* at competitor firms—to maximize the information flow and the idea flow. Analysts should also visit with and become useful "information exchangers" with industry economists and journalists. They need to know and understand the industry's major suppliers and customers, regulators, and anyone else who can add information, insight, or perspective to that great "stew of expertise" that is the foundation for building a professional reputation or franchise as a recognized industry expert.

Know Your Competition   Be realistic in appraising what each competitor does very well, and not so well. Look for openings—research needs not being met by the others—where your special skills match up with a distinct need and where you can establish yourself as the "king of the mountain." Analysts should pick out an area within their chosen industry in which they can become known as the very best source of information, insight, and understanding—the expert to go to for knowledge and judgment.

For some analysts, the chosen niche or specialty will be industry statistics; for others, financial analysis and accounting; for others, market demand, pricing, and market shares; for others, international competition or overseas markets or both; for some, production; and for others, regulation. Being known as the best in your chosen research specialty really matters because in the fast and free market for ideas and information, only one or two analysts will get the call; and the more calls you get, the more your knowledge and understanding will build.

Several analysts working together in teams can have real expertise in several areas and "play off each other" in serving institutional investor clients.

Start Big   Every analyst begins his or her career as a stranger and an outsider. Nobody needs you or wants you—at least not yet. If it takes a long time to do something special, fine. The world can wait. So make your first research report a true "must-read" major report on an important subject.

Share of Mind Is Crucial   When you enter the business every one is already working full time *without you*. So, to make time for you, they'll have to cut back on others. And they'll have to want to do this *voluntarily* because they see making time for you as in their best interest. Everyone does most of everything with a few suppliers. If you intend to become one of the favored few, you must earn it. Winning a position as a primary analyst—against all the capable and committed analysts who are already established—takes lots of time and concentration.

The secret to success in researching and writing a major report is clear: Is it read, and believed, by many investors? If so, it will be a winner. But, as Bishop Berkeley shrewdly opined over 300 years ago, the tree falling in the forest with nobody listening has not really made a sound. And the research report not read is useless. Because being read carefully and thoroughly is so vital to a research report having impact, we urge our clients' analysts to be *sure* always to "write reading." And because few of us are natural, great authors, we urge all analysts to "love your editor" and work with the writing taskmaster who can and will help you convert your draft report into writing that will be really good *reading*.

Produce One or Two, or at Most Three, Major Reports Each Year   Make each report a Very Big Deal, devoting at least a month to a concerted campaign of selling and persuading; visit all the major institutions and all the other institutions that have a major interest in what you are recommending, not just once, but as many times as you can, always striving to help each one take *action*.

Even as the Internet and access to analytical models are changing the ways in which information flows, the preferred means of communicating and documenting investment ideas is the traditional research report, which should have all or almost all these characteristics:

- One-page summary of the investment recommendation.
- Clear articulation of the evidence that supports a different way of evaluating the company or industry group. If you don't have a different thing to say, you'll really have nothing to say.
- Lucid and insightful review and future projection of the company's strategic development, its strengths and weaknesses, threats and opportunities, resources and management, and so on.
- Full review of all relevant financial data.
- Historical perspective on the stock and its valuation.

■ Candid review of understanding—what could go *wrong* with this investment and how to see trouble coming; and what could go *better than expected* with this investment, why it might happen, and how to recognize the good news as it first develops.

Follow Up, Follow Up, Follow Up   Use the Internet, call, fax, write, e-mail, and call again after each visit to be sure the transfer of information, insight, and conviction from your mind to your customer's mind is as full and rich as possible.

Work on Two Levels   Communicate with both analysts and portfolio managers because at larger institutions, having the in-house analysts support your recommendation is "one hand clapping," while the "other hand" is having the portfolio manager agree to make the investment.

Follow Through, Follow Through, Follow Through   When an institutional portfolio manager decides to invest in the stock you're recommending, that's not the end of the trail for the professional investor; it's the beginning. You'll have lots of opportunity to add value and gain recognition for your added value by keeping the analysts and portfolio managers well informed of any developments that affect that stock.

With a one-page list of interested institutions (with their phone numbers and your own notes on the size of their holding and their most recent views), a shrewd analyst striving to maximize the productivity of his or her time will go into an office, close the door, and go down the list calling one key contact after another with a short, well-rehearsed update report on each important development.[7] In two hours, the disciplined analyst can complete what would take most analysts two days—and probably never get completed.

SELLING RESEARCH

Each analyst is a "Value Center," and establishing a professional franchise is a lot like building a brand, you are building a concept in the minds of others.

Recommendations for Becoming a Value Center

Win Friends to Influence People   An analyst's true friends are the salespeople in his or her own firm. The sales organization is particularly important because these persuasive professionals are in constant contact with the individual analysts and fund mangers at hundreds and hundreds of investing institutions.

The typical institutional sales force of 50 salespeople can make or break any analyst. Wise analysts get to know and understand every salesperson and how best to work with each one. We advise analysts to devote particular attention to the "idea leaders" in their firm—the salespeople that others tend to look up to and follow when deciding which new ideas to recommend. And wise analysts make themselves truly helpful to the sales force. As an expression from the 1960s put it: "If you're not part of the solution, you *are* part of the problem" for a busy salesperson.

Analysts and their firm's salespeople will want to coordinate their account-by-account microstrategies. At each important institution, they'll decide together who will call whom and when. Often, a two-channel effort will be best—one channel centered on in-depth analyst-to-analyst communication to develop the requisite foundation of knowledge and understanding, with a second channel centered on the specific buy or sell decision by the portfolio manager.

Achieving Maximum Results   Each investment recommendation needs an appropriate campaign. The research report can be a vital component in an effective campaign strategy, but it will need the whole strategy to be really effective. Avoid the all-too-natural impulse to "rush into print." Instead, carefully plan a strategy and process that can and will achieve the maximum benefits for clients' portfolios, for the analysts' professional reputation and franchises, and for the stockbrokerage firm's business.

An effective securities selling campaign will coordinate how these organizational resources are deployed and used:

- The sales force is well briefed on the investment recommendation, and key sales tips are outlined on a "cheat sheet" for effective sales calls.
- One-on-one meetings are held with each salesperson to plan the sales campaign on a city-by-city and an account-by-account basis, focusing on those institutions that will find this particular recommendation fits well with their investment convictions and their current portfolio strategies—especially those that have large holdings in the stock being recommended or have previously indicated particular interest. As always, attention should center on those who manage large funds and are known to be quick to take action.
- Research reports can be sent to all appropriate portfolio managers and analysts at the institutions the firm works with. Often, it pays off to send extra copies of the report, with key sections highlighted, to analysts and

portfolio managers who work particularly closely with the author analyst to be sure they get the message promptly and receive the full attention they may expect.

Go Where the Money Is Most of institutional investing in America is concentrated in six small areas: downtown New York City, midtown New York City, Boston, Los Angeles, and "Fairchester."[8] A well-organized person can complete five or more good visits in a single day in each of these "target-rich environments."

Concentrate on cities with lots and lots of institutions where three or four days of multiple productive visits can be easily organized. Our consultants continue to wonder at the tendency of analysts to get out on the road and travel to faraway cities with only a few institutions. You know it is hard work to cover "two or three account" cities like Portland, Atlanta, Dallas, Houston, Detroit, Pittsburgh, Denver, San Diego, and Charlotte, but if time and energy are your strategic limited resources, do you get paid by the frequent flyer miles *or* do you get paid by the hours you spend face-to-face with clients? So go where you'll see the most clients as you use your critically limited resource: your time.

When scheduling a sales campaign trip, the common error is to over-schedule, in an understandable effort to maximize the number of sales visits. This can be "penny wise and pound foolish." It's almost always best to allow time and space for those extra efforts that can so often make the vital difference between "not quite" and "definitely" moving forward on the step-by-step process of making an important investment decision.

Creating a Disciplined Environment Develop an explicit winning strategy and use self-discipline in following through on that plan. It's easy to get distracted and to run out of time to do what you'd originally intended, so we advise our clients' analysts to devote one hour—the first hour of every day—for taking those actions they know are particularly important to achieving their one-year plan.

Research Department Managers have the challenge of coordinating the work of many very different, very self-reliant *individual* analysts. Most of the best analysts are prima donnas. Here are some of the governing principles that work best for firmwide success:

- Consistency across the whole firm is valuable. It's hard to harmonize a group of brilliant individualists into a coordinated team, but it can be done—and the payoff is large because consistent output makes it so much easier for the receivers at the institutions.

A consistent look, tone, and content across the many reports a major firm produces about companies in many different industries can create a total greater than the sum of the parts. *Consistency,* which encourages feelings of familiarity and confidence, should be a priority in graphic design and in editorial style. If the visual look and the writing style are familiar—and so feel friendly—clients will know what to expect in content and will welcome more of what they already like and respect because that's what works for them. Good graphics help a lot. So does the quality of reproduction. We recommend hiring a professional designer to develop a template with an attractive and distinctive look for all your research reports. This will help them stand out among the plethora of research reports and other documents that pile into the in-boxes of thousands of institutional analysts and portfolio managers every day, *all* hoping to be read, *all* competing for "shelf-space" time in the busy days of the professional investors to whom they are sent—and who will each decide which to skip, which to skim, and which to study.

- Encourage concentration, by all analysts, on the firm's most important institutional clients. Sure, each analyst will have a few special analytical friends at major institutions with whom it's good to exchange information and ideas that are not on the firm's priority list. But most of the time, most of the analysts should be devoted to the *firm's* chosen primary customers.

- Coordination with the firm's Investment Banking Division will be important. At most major firms, the Investment Banking Division picks up the tab for at least half of the Research Department, and high profile industry analysts are often the *sine qua non* for a firm's breaking into major corporate investment banking relationships. So on both cost and value, research will want to coordinate with investment banking.

- Coordination with other "Value Centers"—analysts in related industries, economists, and the portfolio strategist—is also important because to the customer, it is always easier to understand the work of an individual analyst in the context of the firm's total research product.

- Celebrate the strengths of the firm's research commitment. Different firms do different things: Some do handsome Annual Reports. Some have weekly "what's current" newsletters that comment on individual analysts and what they're thinking—including "interesting disagreements." Many have Sector conferences at which they feature several industry analysts together. Some take a theme, such as the impact of the Internet, and have insightful reports from all the firm's analysts on how that theme applies to their particular industries.

Research Managers have lots of choices on how they will build their departments and their departmental franchise with each of their several constituencies: institutional investors, retail investors, salespeople, investment banking, and investment management. The key to success in the stockbrokerage business is to think through the strategic alternatives available to your firm very carefully and decide on and commit to the research plan that's best for the firm as a whole to achieve its overall strategic objectives.

INSTITUTIONAL SALES

Sales professionals at institutional stockbrokerage firms are the "team-leader playmakers" (or "beach masters") managing the extraordinarily complex organization-to-organization relationships that are so important for win-win *mutually* successful working relationships between a major stockbrokerage firm and a major investing institution. There may be 50 to 100 key participants at the institution *and* 50 to 100 key participants at the stockbrokerage firm working on a real-time basis with ever-changing markets, prices, "fundamentals," and a complex mixture of *research, sales,* and *trading.*

Portfolio managers at large institutions are clear about their four most important service needs:

1. Make good use of time during visits and calls.
2. Know and communicate clearly the critical factors in research recommendations.
3. Follow up promptly and effectively on information requests.
4. Understand the institution's investment strategy and decision-making process.

Table 6.4 shows how portfolio managers rate the qualities they need to be effective sales professionals. The best salespeople effectively represent both their clients' needs and priorities and their own firm's skills and capabilities in research, across dozens of industries, and in executions. This complex task requires understanding of the ever-changing aspects of both parties at interest.

Avoid disruptive changes in sales assignments and, particularly, avoid disruptive turnover in the sales force. Nothing diminishes a stockbrokerage firm's relationships so quickly or as gravely as turnover because despite the complexity and multiplicity of relationships and all the technology involved on "both sides of the Street" as well as the enormous capital values involved, institutional stockbrokerage remains a "people business."

TABLE 6.4 Attributes of Effective Sales Professionals

	Most Important
Make good use of time during visits and telephone calls	67%
Know and clearly communicate critical factors in research recommendations	61
Follow up promptly and effectively on information requests	50
Understand institution's investment strategy and decision-making process	46
Suggest helpful buy and sell recommendations	28
Keep firm's analysts in close contact	28
Keep up-to-date on changes in the fundamentals of past recommendations	26
Have good market judgment and sense of timing	17
Make frequent visits and calls	15
Use voice mail or e-mail effectively	15
Provide best backup coverage	7

In managing—and in upgrading—major relationships, a key strategy is to conduct rigorous "relationship progress reviews" at least annually. These reviews should focus on those important aspects of the relationship that are working well and should be made to continue working well, *and* on those aspects where improvements are wanted and would be most beneficial.

Knowing from our research how important these top-level relationship reviews can be, we urge you to make them a top management priority and to make effective follow-through a top management imperative. Candidly, the real value of relationship reviews is the difference between what was *promised* at the review and what was *delivered* thereafter: Any negative is a big negative.

EXECUTIONS

Execution of orders continues to become more and more important, year after year—particularly for those 100 largest institutions that execute a clear majority of all the trading done each day. These gigantic institutions—many of them doing over $100 billion in transactions, and some of them generating over $1 billion in annual commissions—have two kinds of needs for service by institutional stockbrokers:

- Low-cost *agency* executions, where efficiency is imperative if a firm is to earn a profit on commissions of 3 or 4 cents per share.
- Effective *principal* trading, where dealers risk their firm's capital by "inventorying"[9] blocks of stock until they are able to "find the other side."

Institutional stockbrokerage firms all compete for agency business, but only the larger firms compete for principal business because only a major firm has working relationships with enough major institutions to have the "order-flow" liquidity necessary to take positions without absorbing unacceptable risks of "getting stuck" with an inventory loss.

The position trader's grueling job is to buy large blocks of stock—$10 or 20 million at a time—that very smart investors want urgently to sell or vice versa. It's not nice work.

Position traders know they are doomed to take losses, day after day. After all, they are always buying shares that other people are determined and often highly motivated to sell. The need to sell may be due to a major restructuring of the fund manager's portfolio, but it may be driven by an astute analyst's sudden recognition that a popular company's fundamentals have gone badly wrong and the stock is soon going to "crater." With the right relationship, the senior trader at the institution will inform the stockbroker's position trader which type of trade is in the offing.

The secret to success in position trading is to take fewer and smaller losses than position traders are taking at competitor firms, and to increase the recognized importance of their firm at each of the institutions whose problems they help solve by positioning unwanted blocks of stock. We advise our clients to concentrate their position bidding and take their losses with those institutions that have shown they will take the time and make the commitment to work with their position traders through many trades over the long term. Being a "hero trader" is not being truly professional.

Everyone knows that position traders will be taking losses day after day, but the losses should be loss leaders. The wise position trader will take the *necessary* losses, but *not* the unnecessary losses. As we remind our clients' position traders, "There are old pilots and there are bold pilots, but there are no old, bold pilots."

Hard as it may at first seem, position traders have learned to budget their losses, usually at an average of 10 to 20 percent of annual commissions, and to manage their loss-taking so it is close to being an investment in developing relationships. They concentrate their investment in losses where they will, over time, do the most good for their firms.

Customers say the most important factors in position traders are the abilities to:

TABLE 6.5 Important Factors in Executions

	Most Important
Demonstrate sales trading capability	67%
Handle sensitive orders discreetly	49
Have best market judgment and sense of timing	49
Execute large trades skillfully	48
Have effective floor trading capability	39
Make good bids promptly	26
Have prompt and accurate settlements	22
Will position difficult blocks	18
Make best research calls	18
Commit capital consistently to facilitate trades	15

- Execute large trades skillfully.
- Make good bids promptly.
- Position difficult trades.
- Commit capital consistently to facilitate trades.

Senior traders at the larger institutions know from experience what they most want from position traders—the "combat commanders" who stand ready all through the trading day to take the calls from the senior traders at their largest and most important clients when they have a "need to sell."

Institutional traders also know what they want from a sales trader—those experts on agency executions who manage the trade-by-trade execution of large "working orders" over several days or even weeks. These traders should:

- Demonstrate overall capability.
- Handle sensitive orders discreetly.
- Have best market judgment and sense of timing.

Table 6.5 lists these and other important factors.

Stockbrokerage in Europe

Big Bang—the wholesale restructuring of the securities industry—struck the London stock market with the force and effect of a major plate-tectonic earthquake. It transformed a deliberately segregated and tightly regulated industry structure into a free and competitive market paragon that would soon become the model for the subsequent changes in the national markets across the Continent. Eventually, it would lead to the restructuring of all the stock markets of Europe.

The changes brought to Europe's stock markets can be described in several ways—starting with a "then versus now" comparison of the leading firms. Table 6.6 shows the leaders in order of the number of institutional investors they counted as important customers in 1989 versus 2000 in the United Kingdom.

Not only are the names greatly changed; the whole business has been changed:

- Separation of jobbers from brokers is no more; they are combined.
- Institutional investors are no longer co-underwriters of securities offerings.
- Fixed rates of commission have been abolished.
- Information technology prevails.
- Market-makers dominate what once was a broker's market.
- Capital requirements to be competitive are enormous.
- Spreads are narrow.
- Trading volumes have increased 10-fold in a decade.

TABLE 6.6　United Kingdom Stockbrokers

	1989		2000
James Capel	87%	HSBC Securities	88%
Warburg Securities	80	UBS Warburg	88
Barclays de Zoete Wedd	79	Merrill Lynch	86
Hoare Govett	78	Credit Suisse First Boston	83
Country NatWest Wood Mac	77	Deutsche Bank	82
Citicorp Scrimgeour Vickers	74	ABN AMRO	75
Phillips & Drew	71	Dresdner Kleinwort Benson	71
Kleinwort Benson	56	Cazenove	58
Smith New Court	45	Salomon Smith Barney	55
Cazenove	42	Morgan Stanley Dean Witter	52
CL—Alexanders Laing	39	Schroders	45
Kitcat & Aitken	31	Charterhouse Securities	42
Panmure Gordon	18	Goldman Sachs	41
Goldman Sachs	13	WestLB Panmure	38
Morgan Stanley	12	Commerzbank	30
Robert Fleming	8	Lehman Brothers	23

■ London does not deal exclusively or primarily in British equities. London makes the dominant markets in the equities of a dozen different countries—including Japanese warrants.

Visual changes are impressive. Gone are the quaint, drab, shabby offices of penny-wise brokers in small buildings—piled high with stacks of paper and populated by genial gentlemen in rumpled suits. Today, smartly dressed salespeople and dealers shout across the din of constant activity in cavernous, modern trading rooms, filled with row after row of colorful computer screens and multibutton telephone systems and other icons of the sophisticated communications centers that coordinate and control the movement of billions.

And no longer is the stock market a separate realm. Stockbroking is necessarily integrated with the businesses of bond dealing and, particularly, to investment banking.

The impact of investment banking is stunning. As institutional investors have become dominant participants in the stock market, trading volumes, market depth, and resilience have become larger and larger; and market spreads have become smaller and smaller encouraging more and more institutional selling and buying. This, in turn, has enabled dealers to transform the stock market from "brokered" to "dealt" (and from small volume to large). It has changed the process of new issue underwriting from a slow, careful, cooperative process taking several weeks of patient constituency development into a fast, transactional process completed within a few days or even hours.

To manage the risks inherent in equity underwriting and to compete successfully for the business and for lucrative mandates as M&A advisers—both of which depend on having developed primary working relationships with senior corporate executives—investment banks need to have demonstrable leadership in both capital markets (distribution, trading, and institutional access) and research (company and industry expertise).

The importance of research to investment bankers is particularly great in international industries—pharmaceuticals, telecomms, oil and gas, airlines, and computers—whose companies compete continuously without regard for national boundaries, because serving the needs of international corporations is the territory in which the strongest *international* investment banks compete most aggressively. To assure their strengths in research in the major international industries, the major investment banks have acquired individual analysts and research teams and even whole research firms. The analyst compensation and the support organization of a competitive research operation have increased greatly.

For institutional stockbrokers, the strategic consequences have been profound: Being part of a major investment bank has become an imperative.

Without the substantial profitability of investment banking, except for small "specialist" boutiques, the high cost structure of a contemporary investment research and market-making securities organization cannot be managed profitably.

In the United Kingdom, fund managers place strong priority on detailed studies of individual companies, as shown in Table 6.7. This reflects the strong analytical culture among British investors and the research focus of the City brokers. Other important research services include:

■ Industry studies.
■ Portfolio strategy.
■ Access to analysts.

In the United Kingdom, fund managers' priorities, when evaluating sales professionals, emphasize:

■ Market judgment.
■ Clear communication of research recommendations.
■ Helpful buy and sell recommendations.
■ Good use of time during visits and calls.

These and other important qualities are shown in Table 6.8

When evaluating sales professionals representing their most important stockbrokers, Continental professional investors are somewhat different. They are looking for help in fulfilling their responsibilities as portfolio managers. Table 6.9 lists the qualities they care *most* about in salespeople.

TABLE 6.7 Importance of Research Services in the United Kingdom

	Most Important		
Factor	1998	1999	2000
Detailed studies of individual companies	82%	83%	79%
Detailed studies of major industries	48	52	44
Portfolio strategy	35	38	43
Access to brokers' analysts	47	46	42
Access to companies' management	—	29	34
Development of creative investment ideas	49	46	32
Research seminars and conferences	13	15	30
Specific buy and sell recommendations	25	19	29
Overall economic analysis or interest rate forecasts	24	24	19

TABLE 6.8   Importance of Sales Professional Characteristics in the United Kingdom

	Most Important		
Characteristic	1998	1999	2000
Show good judgment and sense of timing	38%	50%	54%
Know and clearly communicate critical factors in research recommendations	65	73	54
Keep firm's analysts in close contact with you and your institution	39	41	42
Suggest helpful buy and sell recommendations	30	35	39
Make good use of time during visits and telephone calls	45	35	30
Understand your institution's current investment strategy	47	38	29
Follow up promptly and effectively on information requests	35	35	28
Keep you up-to-date on changes in the fundamentals of past recommendations	26	15	27

In the United Kingdom, institutional investors concentrate an important proportion of their total commissions with their most important stockbrokers—21 percent with their single most important stockbroker, 15 percent with the second most important, and nearly 70 percent with the five firms they use most. While commission allocations to particular stockbrokers by the larger institutions are somewhat less concentrated and the allocations of

TABLE 6.9   Importance of Sales Professional Characteristics on the Continent

	Most Important		
Characteristic	1998	1999	2000
Have good market judgment and sense of timing	36%	41%	48%
Follow up promptly and effectively on information requests	50	53	41
Suggest helpful buy and sell recommendations	34	37	39
Know and clearly communicate critical factors in research recommendations	40	50	37
Make good use of time during visits and telephone calls	34	29	35
Keep up-to-date on changes in fundamentals of past recommendations	44	42	35

TABLE 6.10 Importance of Execution Factors on the Continent

	Most Important		
Factor	1998	1999	2000
Prompt and accurate settlements	66%	68%	46%
Market judgment and sense of timing	60	46	43
Make good bids promptly	32	38	42
Handle sensitive orders discreetly	31	38	27
Capable generalist sales traders covering all European markets	21	36	24

smaller institutions are more concentrated, the structure of commission allocations is remarkably consistent over the years. We urge our clients to concentrate on the sweet spot of the business—being a very important broker to the very important institutions. The familiar 80/20 Rule clearly applies: Less than 20 percent of the institutions generate over 80 percent of the total institutional business.

In evaluating executions, Continental investors care most about the five factors—shown in Table 6.10.

Settlements continue to be a nettlesome problem on the Continent and are given far more emphasis than in other major stock markets, where settlements are automated and error-free executions are common.

In the United Kingdom, where in-house dealers have become dominant at more and more major institutions, the priorities are quite different, as shown in Table 6.11. "Prompt and accurate settlements" are seldom cited as important.

TABLE 6.11 Importance of Execution Factors in the United Kingdom

	Most Important		
Factor	1998	1999	2000
Handle sensitive orders discreetly	63%	56%	55%
Able to execute difficult trades most skillfully	78	68	55
Consistency in capital commitment	51	68	52
Will position difficult blocks	37	32	33

Over and over again, the pattern of major change is fundamentally the same. The stockbrokers that institutional investors on the Continent choose for making investment decisions in the shares of one country after another are less often brokers specializing in their home-country's companies; more often they are the large international brokers that provide Pan European sector research and execution services, concentrating on the major international industries and companies that are so important to their business in investment banking. The same earthquake that compelled the transformation of the London stock market has been repeating its impact in each of Europe's major stock markets, as shown in Tables 6.12 to 6.18.

Anticipating great change—not just change in degree, but change in kind—can be very difficult. So, too, is rational response, particularly when a way of life or a way of doing business is being transformed by changes that are not comfortable or familiar to the various firms' leaders. We urge our clients to imagine themselves being as far out in the future as possible, and then imagine looking back toward today. In that way, they can anticipate the most likely changes in the structure of the overall industry and what this global expectation can mean for the stockbrokerage firms in their own country, and for themselves.

TABLE 6.12   Leading Brokers in French Shares

	1989		2000
Credit Commercial de France	36%	EXANE	34%
Cheuvreux/Banque Indosuez	24	CAI Cheuvreux	32
De Cholet/Crédit Lyonnais	23	Morgan Stanley Dean Witter	27
Banque Paribas/Courcoux	21	BNP Paribas	26
Bertrand Michel/Credit Agricole	15	Merrill Lynch	24
Banque de Neuflize	12	SG Securities	24
Delahaye/Societe Generale	12	UBS Warburg	19
Du Bouzet/BNP	11	Goldman Sachs	19
Sellíer SA	11	CCF Securities	17
Louis Dreyfus & Co.	7	Deutsche Bank	16
Meeschaert-Rousselle	6	ABN AMRO	12
Warburg Securíties/Bacot Allain	6	Oddo/Pinatton	11
DLP James Capel	5	Crédit Lyonnais	11
Legrand, Legrand & Cie	4	Credit Suisse First Boston	10
Ferri, Ferri et Germe	4	Dresdner Kleinwort Benson	8

TABLE 6.13 Leading Brokers in Swiss Shares

	1989		2000
Union Bank of Switzerland	42%	UBS Warburg	35%
J. Vontobel	39	Credit Suisse First Boston	26
Julius Baer	37	Deutsche Bank	25
Swiss Bank/Ducatel Duval	32	Morgan Stanley Dean Witter	25
Lombard, Odier	28	Merrill Lynch	21
Pictet	24	Bank Julius Baer	20
Credit Suisse	23	Goldman Sachs	19
A. Sarasin	21	Bank J. Vontobel	16
Bank Leu	11	Pictet	14
DG Bank	3	Lombard, Odier	13
Sal Oppenheim Jr. & Cie	3	Dresdner Kleinwort Benson	8
SBC Stockbroking	2	Bank Sarasin	6
Banque Paribas/Courcoux	2	ABN AMRO	6
Cheuvreux/Banque Indosuez	2	HSBC Securities	5
Morgan Stanley	2	Lehman Brothers	4

TABLE 6.14 Leading Brokers in Dutch Shares

	1989		2000
AMRO Bank	44%	ABN AMRO	55%
Pierson, Helding & Pierson	32	Morgan Stanley Dean Witter	29
ABN Securities	31	ING Barings	24
Bank Mees & Hope	31	Merrill Lynch	21
Van Hafren & Co.	12	MeesPierson	18
Kempen & Co.	10	Goldman Sachs	17
Van Meer James Capel	6	Deutsche Bank	15
Banque Paribas/Courcoux	5	UBS Warburg	14
First Boston	3	HSBC Securities	12
Banque Bruxelles Lambert	2	Kempen	10
Morgan Stanley	2	Credit Suisse First Boston	6
BZW/Puget	2	Dresdner Kleinwort Benson	6
Enskilda Securities	2	Theodoor Gilissen	5
SBC Stockbroking	1	Salomon Smith Barney	5
Swiss Bank/Ducatel Duval	1	Commerzbank	3

TABLE 6.15 Penetration in Nordic Shares

	1989		2000
Enskilda Securities	61%	Enskilda Securities	30%
Svenska Handelsbanken	39	ABN AMRO	30
Carnegie Fondkommission	24	Morgan Stanley Dean Witter	23
Alfred Berg Fondkommission	7	Carnegie	22
James Capel	4	Goldman Sachs	16
Morgan Stanley	3	Den Danske Bank	15
Kleinwort Benson	2	Merrill Lynch	13
SBC Stockbroking	2	UBS Warburg	12
ABN Securities	2	Deutsche Bank	10
Bank Mees & Hope	2	CAI Cheuvreux	9

TABLE 6.16 Leading Brokers in Spanish Shares

	1989		2000
Banco Santander de Negocios	29%	BSCH Investment	26%
Asesores Bursatiles	28	Morgan Stanley Dean Witter	25
Morgan Stanley	3	Merrill Lynch	23
ARK Securities	2	BBV Argentaria	21
Carnegie Fondkommission	2	UBS Warburg	18
Cheuvreux/Banque Indosuez	2	Goldman Sachs	15
Kleinwort Benson	2	Deutsche Bank	14
BZW/Puget	1	CAI Cheuvreux	11
Banque Paribas/Couseaux	1	ABN AMRO	7
James Capel	1	Credit Suisse First Boston	7

TABLE 6.17 Leading Brokers in German Shares

	1989		2000
Deutsche Bank	68%	Deutsche Bank	54%
Commerzbank	28	Dresdner Kleinwort Benson	31
Dresdner Bank	22	Goldman Sachs	26
Schroder Munchmeyer Hengst	22	Morgan Stanley Dean Witter	26
BHF Bank	21	Merrill Lynch	23
Sal. Oppenheim Jr. & Co.	19	UBS Warburg	23
Bayerische Vereinsbank	16	Commerzbank	20
Baycrische HYPO Bank	15	Credit Suisse First Boston	14
MM Warburg-Brinckmann	14	HypoVereinsbank	13
Merck, Fink & Co.	14	WestLB Panmure	10
Trinkaus & Burkhardt	13	ABN AMRO	9
Bank in Liechtenstein	12	Bank Julius Baer	9
B. Metzler	10	Salomon Smith Barney	7
DG Bank	9	BHF Bank	5
Westdeutsche Landesbank	4	HSBC Securities/HSBC Trinkaus	5

TABLE 6.18 Leading Brokers in Italian Shares

	1989		2000
Banca Nazionale del Lavoro	20%	Morgan Stanley Dean Witter	22%
Euromobiliare	18	Merrill Lynch	21
SIGECO	16	Euromobiliare	19
IMI Capital Markets	6	Goldman Sachs	18
Cheuvreux/Banque Indosuez	5	UBS Warburg	17
Morgan Stanley	5	Deutsche Bank	16
Carnegie Fondkommission	3	Intermobiliare	13
Kleinwort Benson	2	Credit Suisse First Boston	11
Banque Paribas/Courcoux	1	CAI Cheuvreux	10
Citicorp Scrimgeour Vickers	1	SG Securities	9

Stockbrokers in Canada

The Canadian institutional stockbrokerage business is relatively small and highly concentrated. Total Canadian institutional commissions are less than C$400 million, and just the 10 largest institutions represent fully half of the total and the 30 largest represent three-quarters.

Commission allocations to brokers are also concentrated—one-fourth to one-third of all commissions are typically allocated to an institution's first and second brokers (and another 10% to 15% are allocated to "soft-dollar" arrangements).

With commissions from both principal trades, which are steadily increasing, and new issue credits expanding, agency commissions account for more than 75 percent of all commissions flows in Canada. Agency commissions continue to decline and are expected to drop to 4½ cents per share by 2001.

While allocations for research continue to dominate (they are currently twice the allocations for liquidity), allocations for liquidity are increasing.

When evaluating dealers' research services, as shown in Table 6.19, the most important factors to institutional portfolio managers are:

- Company studies.
- Industry studies.
- Creative investment ideas.

TABLE 6.19   Most Important Research Services

	Most Important		
	1997	1998	1999
Detailed studies of individual companies	84%	83%	86%
Detailed studies of major industries	41	61	50
Developing creative investment ideas	54	39	46
Research seminars and conferences	35	31	36
Access to brokers' analysts	35	36	32
Overall economic analysis and interest rate forecasts	11	14	29
Specific buy and sell recommendations	30	11	21
Overall maintenance research	11	8	21
Portfolio strategy and asset allocation	11	22	14
Accurate EPS estimates	5	19	14
Quantitative research	—	17	14
Follow-up reports on past recommendations	24	17	11
Electronic distribution of research	0	8	7

TABLE 6.20   Effective Sales Professionals

	Most Important		
	1997	1998	1999
Know and clearly communicate critical factors in research recommendations	52%	54%	60%
Make good use of time during visits and telephone calls	52	57	57
Follow up promptly and effectively on information requests	52	43	57
Understand your institution's strategy and decision-making process	62	62	37
Have good market judgment and sense of timing	19	22	33
Keep you up to date on changes in the fundamentals of past recommendations	42	27	30
Use voice mail or e-mail effectively	—	—	27
Keep firm's analysts in close contact with you and your institution	23	27	23
Suggest helpful buy and sell recommendations	48	27	17

The most important criteria that institutional portfolio managers use to evaluate sales representatives are:

- Communicate research clearly.
- Make good use of time.
- Follow up promptly on requests for information.

Table 6.20 shows these and other criteria. In evaluating dealers' execution services, senior traders at Canadian institutions give particular emphasis to three factors:

1. Capability of sales trader.
2. Ability to handle sensitive orders discreetly.
3. Good market judgment.

Two other factors are also important:

4. Ability to execute large trades skillfully.
5. Promptness in making good bids and offers.

Table 6.21 lists additional desirable factors.

TABLE 6.21   Effective Trading Services

	Most Important	
	1998	1999
Capability of sales trader	53%	64%
Discrete handling of sensitive orders	64	59
Best market judgment and sense of timing	52	59
Skillful execution of large agency trades	48	41
Promptness in making bids and offers	45	39
Ability to position difficult blocks	36	18
Ability to make best research calls	14	18
Consistency of capital commitments to facilitate trades	11	11
Prompt and accurate settlements	20	5
Ability to execute basket or portfolio trades	5	5
Best allocation from new issue syndicates	8	5
Willingness to soft or rebate business	6	2

The trading side of the institutional business continues to change:

- Positioning difficult blocks has fallen off in importance.
- Portfolio trading is being used by one out of three institutions generating over C$1 million in annual commissions.
- Over half of all Canadian institutions (and three quarters of large institutions) now use alternative trading systems—up from 41 percent a

TABLE 6.22   Penetration in Research and Executions in 1988

	Important in Research		Important in Executions
Burns Fry	96%	Burns Fry	92%
Nesbitt Thompson	85	Nesbitt Thompson	81
RBC Dominion Securities	78	RBC Dominion Securities	77
Wood Gundy	74	Merrill Lynch	76
Alfred Bunting	73	Wood Gundy	74
Scotia McLeod	73	Gordon Capital	69
Merrill Lynch	67	Scotia McLeod	69
Richardson Greenshields	59	Alfred Bunting	52
Loewen, Ondaatje, McCutcheon	53	Richardson Greenshields	50
Brown, Baldwin, Nisker	45	Loewen, Ondaatje, McCutcheon	46

TABLE 6.23   Penetration in Research and Executions in 1999

	Important in Research		Important in Executions
Nesbitt Burns	98%	Nesbitt Burns	96%
TD Securities	92	CIBC World Markets	90
RBC Dominion Securities	90	RBC Dominion Securities	89
Scotia Capital Markets	90	Scotia Capital Markets	89
CIBC World Markets	89	TD Securities	84
Merrill Lynch	87	Merrill Lynch	83
National Bank Financial	74	National Bank Financial	78
Newcrest Capital	69	Newcrest Capital	73
Bunting Warburg Dillon Read	63	Bunting Warburg Dillon Read	70
HSBC Securities	58	HSBC Securities	69

year ago and the proportion of trading done is expected to increase from 8 percent in 1999 to 13 percent in 2000. The institutions' reasons for using alternative trading systems include anonymity, quality of executions, and speed of completion.

With all the change dynamics in the Canadian institutional market, another major change has had great impact: Many of the largest dealers have been acquired by Canada's major commercial banks as an essential element in their strategic drive to make themselves effective competitors in investment banking.

The consequences of all these changes is evident in a comparison of the leading competitors in 1988 (when we began our research and consulting in Canada) versus current competitive positions. As shown in Tables 6.22 and 6.23 fully half of the leading competitors in 1988 are no longer both independent and in business.

Japanese Stockbrokerage: Responding to Hyperchange

A veritable *tsunami* has forced its way through the Japanese stockmarket, wreaking havoc with an established structure that appeared just 10 years ago to be virtually certain to continue forever as the proverbial Big Four—Nomura, Daiwa, Yamaichi, and Nikko—held effective control over their market.

In a society that deeply respects the "right order of things," stockbrokerage firms became highly skilled at maintaining correct protocols, respecting rank and authority that kept the different firms in predetermined order. The Tokyo Stock Exchange and the Japanese stockbrokerage industry were separated by more than geography from the West's adaptive discipline of an open, competitive, free market that requires intermediaries to adapt responsively to changing customers and changing customer needs. In Japan, a labyrinthian, tightly regulated, closely managed, multilayered system developed. It was based on carefully controlled long-term interlocking or reciprocal relationships, elaborate entertainment, and shared insider information about which stocks were going to move up.

The Tokyo Stock Exchange system worked for many years with these characteristics:

- Only Japanese firms could be members of the Tokyo Stock Exchange.[10]
- Commissions were fixed. The Ministry of Finance set commission rates (and the MOF had very close ties with the major brokers).
- Block trading was forbidden, and brokers were not permitted to risk their own capital to "position" blocks of stock for institutional investors who might want to sell large holdings.
- In-depth research on companies, industries, and the economy was the exception in Japan, while such research—costly to produce—was the norm in the United Kingdom, Canada, Australia, and the United States.
- Well over half of all commission business was "locked up" in formal reciprocal relationships and transactions—compensating for bank balances, insurance contracts, and so on.
- Data on all transactions by all brokers were "available" daily to member firms. This enabled the major brokers to know who was doing what on a timely basis—key to controlling the structure of the system and the participating firms.

The big stockbrokerage business in Japan was, and had always been, *retail* stockbrokerage. And the stockbrokerage firms were organized to conduct a highly profitable retail stockbrokerage business, epitomized by the notorious armies of part-time workers—housewives who dutifully and untiringly sold, door to door, the brokers' current recommendations of specific stocks and broker-sponsored mutual funds.

As shares rose in price on the Tokyo Stock Exchange, the apparent beneficiaries included the small investors, whose phenomenal savings were channeled into investments in the nation's famous companies, which were prospering in the Japanese "economic miracle." Investors felt they were doing well *and* doing good, while participating in their own modest way in the restoration of Japan to industrial greatness. They were not entirely wrong, but they were far from entirely right.

Highly profitable, rigid systems tend to become corrupt. But even very corrupt systems, if their discipline is effective, can and will "work." Whether they work *well*, and for whom they work, is a different matter. The stockbrokerage industry in Japan worked well for the stockbrokers.

With fixed-rate commissions, as trading volume increased, the stockbrokerage business became highly profitable for the stockbrokers. In 1988, the profits of Toyota—the giant world-class automobile manufacturer— were actually exceeded by a stockbroker: Nomura. More importantly, the stockbrokerage industry was not working well for the investors: The costs of the brokers' services (commissions in particular) were high by global standards and the value delivered low (particularly investment research).

Alas, for the stockbrokers, this extraordinarily favorable set of business conditions would not last. As so often happens, change would come from an unexpected quarter. And the great strength of the stockbrokers would become an important weakness: The remarkably efficient organizational structure that was so effectively designed to control a centrally disciplined sales organization that would push product and generate the maximum profitability may have been perfected for a retail stockbrokerage business, but it was far from perfect for a very different kind of business: *institutional* stockbrokerage.

The particular needs and interests of institutional investors—for thorough research on companies and industries and the economy; for professional service by well-informed research salespeople; and for liquidity through block trading—were largely unmet as the major stockbrokers concentrated on their retail business.

Until recently, Japanese institutional investors contributed to the "no need to change" consensus when they accepted and affirmed the curious belief that the Tokyo market was determined by two forces: the *objective* or factual force (which would include Earnings-per-Share analyses, and all the other rational aspects of Western-style investment research) and the *subjective* or spiritual force (which was considered by many Japanese to be unique to Japan and so quite understandably beyond the comprehension of most Western investors).

The spiritual or subjective factor relates to the capacity of the market to develop an enthusiasm for the shares of a particular company or an industry and cause their prices to rise without apparent reason to Western investors whose understanding is limited to objective factors. Skeptics would say the price escalation was a direct result of the ability of major stockbrokers to pick a stock, organize substantial buying by "cooperating" institutional investors, and then announce to a wider and wider group of potential investors that it was going up in price—and then "make it happen" by organizing increasingly urgent retail buying. (All this is reminiscent of the notorious "pools" of the 1920s in New York.) Of course, it was best to be in on the ramp-up *before* retail investors were brought in. Information on what would soon be happening would be passed to favored institutions during elaborate and elegant luncheons or dinners. And, the most favored institutions were those that directed most of their business to the informing stockbrokers.

Equally important was the lack of emphasis by Japanese institutional investors on the objective factors. Securities analysis was not recognized as an honored profession, but was considered just a brief prerequisite for promotion into service as a junior fund manager—and the opportunity to be included in the luncheons and dinners where those "in the know" identified which stocks would now be going up.

Significant for understanding what could and would occur in Japan is recognition that while there were well over a hundred large institutional investors and several hundred smaller institutional investors in this great nation's financial system, they were remarkably docile and very undemanding of the stockbrokers. They went along with the system.

This passivity by Japan's institutional investors (while British and American institutional investors were so active that they would be called "aggressive" in their dealings with brokers) is understandable when considered in the Japanese context. Insurance companies, for example, were long accustomed to agreeing within the industry on the rate of return on investments that would be used to determine insurance rates to charge customers. This process of collective agreement on investment returns was extended systematically into the pension system, which the insurance companies dominated.

With investment returns "fixed" in advance, why would anyone strive to "do better"? No one would. So the top jobs in the investment departments of Japan's major institutions became quiet sinecures for senior executives who had spent their careers in insurance sales. And the most able and committed young people in Japan avoided or gave short shrift to the dull investment departments because they would be poor places to develop a career.

Meanwhile, the unusually talented and ambitious young people in Western nations were being attracted in increasing numbers into investment management. They were learning how to analyze securities and construct efficient portfolios; studying to pass the three-exam sequence to become Chartered Financial Analysts (CFAs); attending seminars, conferences, and workshops; devoting long days to studying and comparing brokers' research reports on companies and industries; meeting with corporate managements; and competing in the stockmarket for investment performance. The understandable result: Western institutional investors and the stockbrokers that served them were gaining steadily increasing proficiency in the disciplines of modern institutional investing, but most of the Japanese were not.

With a few important exceptions, the Japanese stockbrokerage firms were not interested in providing the sorts of services these *gaijin* institutions wanted; and the reasons were clear to students of the conflict between business *strategy* and business *structure*.[11] In contrast to the usual expectation, structure is not the obedient "implementing means" to achieve the corporate objectives laid out in the organization's explicit strategy. Quite the contrary. Structure has an agenda and a will of its own. And unless deliberately controlled, structure will actually dominate strategy by imposing behavior on the organization that primarily preserves and protects the structure rather than aligning the organization's resources to serve the external market through astute strategy.

The emergence of institutional investors as the increasingly dominant customer caused a profound rearrangement of stockmarket after stockmarket in one nation after another. Stockbroker intermediaries were compelled to convert their research and execution services, their pricing and compensation, their organizational structures and staffing from an intermediation that worked for retail investor markets into alternatives that would work for institutional investor markets. In America, the process of transformation developed over 30 years; in Britain, it developed over 20 years. In Japan, it would come in less than 10 years. In this compressed time period, the change was not an evolution, but a revolution.

In every major economy, as institutional investors grew in asset size and volume of trading activity to dominance in the stockmarket, the stockbrokers, as intermediaries, were obliged to change. Typically, the major stockbrokerage firms at the start of the transformation would refuse to change, primarily because they were well organized for the passing retail business and were led by individuals who had climbed up their firms' organizational hierarchy because they were skilled at the retail business. In addition, these executives felt loyal to the informal as well as the formal organizations that had been perfected as economic creatures to match the challenges and opportunities of the retail business.

Institutional stockbrokerage is very different from retail stockbrokerage. Research analysts in their 30s are centers of great influence because of *what* they know about companies, products, and industries. Traders in their 30s and 40s are centers of business because of *whom* they know—the important traders at major institutions. Salespeople who create business are important because of *how* they generate revenues. For a hierarchical, power-concentrated command organization like a Big Four retail stockbroker, these myriad individuals would be very hard to deal with and the dynamic, open, entrepreneurial structure these individuals prefer would be very hard for senior management to accept.

In most national markets, the process of change from retail to institutional dominance developed from within. Some major firms changed with the times (although most did not and so would become obsolete), while newly organized "specialist" firms that focused on institutional investors grew larger and larger with the growth of their institutional business.

In Japan, just as 150 years ago Commodore Perry arrived with gunpowder and provoked a socioeconomic revolution; likewise, outsiders brought about a revolution to the stockbrokerage business. Here is the bare outline of the history:

- British investing institutions, long experienced in international investing, became increasingly active investors in Japan in the 1960s.
- American institutions—mutual funds and managers of pension funds—got increasingly active in Japan in the 1970s and 1980s.
- Japanese stockbrokers—primarily the Big Four—expanded to keep pace with this new business from investors located in the United Kingdom, the United States, and Europe by opening branch offices in various Western cities.
- In the 1980s, as institutional investors grew substantially in assets and in activity, particularly in America where a few dozen institutions became especially large and active, several large British and American stockbrokers that were well-experienced in institutional stockbrokerage decided to build up their capabilities in Japan. These buildups were part of an overall strategic drive to deal in the stocks and bonds of *all* the major economies of the world and to develop the company and industry research expertise to compete in the increasingly globalized investment banking business.
- With the boom year profits of the late 1980s and with the steady buildup of international investing at more and more American institutions, the American stockbrokerage firms expanded their commitment in Japanese economic, industry, and company research *and* in sales *and* in trading Japanese stocks, warrants, and convertibles. (The Japanese Big Four were reluctant followers in developing institutional research, with the impressive exception of Nomura, which had established and strongly supported a semi-independent research institute that would continue to be the recognized leader in company, industry, and economic research.)
- In the later 1990s—with powerful capabilities in derivatives and in international block trading—several American firms would move to leadership

positions and one of the Big Four Japanese firms would be closed while another would be effectively taken over by an American firm.

- In the late 1990s, as more and more Japanese institutional investors established in-house dealing desks to centralize trading in Japanese shares, the Western firms' skills in trading would give them yet another opportunity to gain market share.

The dramatic changes in the structure of the stockbrokerage industry in Japan is shown in Table 6.24. The column on the left shows the 15 stockbrokers that were most important to the major Japanese institutions in 1988 when Greenwich Associates first began consulting with the stockbrokers in Japan. Only two Western stockbrokers made the list in 1988—and none made it into the "Top 10."

By 1998, just 10 years later, the competitive situation was startlingly different: Five of the six most important firms were not Japanese—they were American. To add to their pain, the two strongest Japanese firms, caught in an ugly scandal involving secret dealings with organized criminals, were barred from important aspects of the institutional business.

TABLE 6.24 Penetration in Japanese Shares—Large Institutions in Japan

	1988		2000
Nikko Securities	75%	Merrill Lynch	100%
Nomura Securities	71	Morgan Stanley Dean Witter	100
Yamaichi Securities	68	Nikko Salomon Smith Barney	100
Daiwa Securities	75	Nomura	100
New Japan Securities	36	Daiwa SBCM	97
Okasan International	29	Goldman Sachs	97
Wako Securities	39	Deutsche Securities	86
Kokusai Securities	39	UBS Warburg	86
Sanyo Securities	36	Jardine Fleming	71
Nippon Kangyo Kakumaru	18	HSBC Securities	71
Cosmo Securities	25	IBJ Securities	71
Universal Securities	25	BNP Paribas	57
Dai Ichi Securities	21	Shinko Securities	57
Salomon Brothers	14	Kokusai	51
James Capel	11	ABN AMRO	49

Note: The stockbrokers with the largest commission income from institutions in 2000 were Morgan Stanley Dean Witter, Daiwa SBCM, Nomura, Nikko Salomon Smith Barney, and Goldman Sachs.

This dramatic change may have been a "sudden surprise" to the senior executives at the large Japanese stockbrokers, but its coming was clearly signaled by prior developments in the United Kingdom and the United States. In London and New York, the Japanese firms hurt themselves badly with self-imposed turnover among their sales representatives, typically sending their salesmen back to Tokyo after only three-year tours of duty. As we urged our Japanese clients, such turnover virtually guaranteed that their salespeople would be unable to develop the person-to-person trust and mutual understanding that are so vital for "very important" relationships with the leading portfolio managers and analysts at investing institutions. Of course, the "push-push" selling techniques learned and perfected for a retail business and the well-known difficulty many Japanese would have with the English language were also important negatives.

Meanwhile in both the United States and the United Kingdom, leading firms and individual analysts and salespeople were developing proficiency in Japanese stockbroking, and were gaining market share in their respective home markets. Tables 6.25 and 6.26 shows the leading competitors almost 10 years ago and currently. In the United States, in 1990, 3 of the 5 largest and 4 of the 10 largest brokers of Japanese shares to large institutions in America were Japanese. By the end of the decade, only 1 Japanese firm made the list of the 10 largest brokers.

In the United Kingdom, the same sort of phenomenon occurred: Among the 10 leading stockbrokers serving the largest institutional investors active in Japanese stocks, four were Japanese in 1990. Less than a decade later, only 1 in 10 was Japanese.

TABLE 6.25 Research Penetration in Japanese Shares—Large Institutions in the United States

	1990		1999
Nomura Securities	80%	Morgan Stanley Dean Witter	95%
Salomon Brothers	50	Goldman Sachs	86
Daiwa Securities	43	Merrill Lynch	81
Nikko Securities	43	Salomon Smith Barney	81
Baring Securities	37	Nomura Securities	71
Yamaichi Securities	37	HSBC Securities	62
Warburg Securities	37	UBS Warburg	57
Morgan Stanley	33	Jardine Fleming	52
Robert Fleming	33	Credit Suisse First Boston	48
James Capel	30	ING Barings	38

TABLE 6.26 Penetration in Japanese Shares—Large Institutions in the United Kingdom

	1990		2000
Baring Securities	74%	Nomura Securities	94%
Nomura International	68	Salomon Smith Barney	87
Salomon Brothers	68	HSBC Securities	87
James Capel	64	Morgan Stanley Dean Witter	81
Robert Fleming	58	Merrill Lynch	77
Daiwa Europe	57	Flemings	77
Nikko Securities	55	Goldman Sachs	74
Barclays de Zoete Wedd	47	UBS Warburg	71
Yamaichi International	45	ING Barings	55
W.I. Carr	42	Dresdner Kleinwort Benson	55

As Japanese institutional investors adapted to the increasing importance of superior performance in investment management, our research documented that Japanese institutional investors wanted virtually the same kinds of service from salespeople that were wanted by institutional investors in other countries—and they are frustrated by the same shortfalls, as documented in Table 6.27.

And in research, Japanese institutional investors have many of the same wants and needs as do their counterparts in each of the other major markets, as shown in Table 6.28.

Other shifts in importance show how strong are the change-forces in Japan:

- The proportion of commission business done with non-Japanese stockbrokers has gone in just two years from 37 percent to 58 percent—increasing the business done with Western brokers by more than 50 percent.
- The proportion of commission preallocated to reciprocal relationships dropped by one third in just two years—from 45 percent to 30 percent.

Even as the structure of the institutional stockbrokerage industry in Japan went through a major transformation, with Western firms displacing most of the traditional competitors, the individual people working as research analysts, salespeople, traders, and managers were and are almost entirely *Japanese* people. When Western firms that were organizationally experienced in meeting the requirements of institutional investors in other

TABLE 6.27   Most Important Sales Professional Factors

Factors	Japanese Institutions	British Institutions	American Institutions
Follow up promptly and effectively on information requests	80%	38%	57%
Know and clearly communicate critical factors in research recommendations	57	62	53
Keep firm's analysts in close contact with you and your institution	42	33	30
Have good market judgment and sense of timing	37	43	20
Keep you up-to-date on changes in the funda entals of past recommendations	34	43	27
Make good use of time during visits and elephone calls	28	29	47
Suggest helpful buy and sell recommendations	19	62	27
Understand your institution's current investment strategy	18	29	53
Provide best backup coverage		5	7
Make frequent calls and visits	8	5	10

nations' stockmarkets opened offices and expanded in Tokyo, they hired able and committed Japanese people. The most effective firms rapidly developed into the market leaders in Japan.

Within these Western organizational structures that required and rewarded individual contributors, celebrated unusual skill in research, encouraged long-term personal-professional relationships in sales, risked capital in making markets, and sought to push an intensively delivered "demand pull"

TABLE 6.28   Most Important Research Services

Factors	Japanese Institutions	British Institutions	American Institutions
Detailed studies of individual companies	82%	90%	79%
Detailed studies of major industries	64	25	52
Overall economic analysis or interest rate forecasts	36	35	7
Access to brokers' analysts	31	50	45
Research seminars and conferences	26	5	17
Portfolio strategy	22	40	21
Developing creative investment ideas	22	45	38
Specific buy and sell recommendations	16	40	24

service—Japanese workers provided to their countrymen the service institutional investors want and need everywhere in the world.

The change in industry leadership was not due to nationality. Far from it. The change was due to the simple, dominating reality that the strongest Western stockbrokers were organized to serve the particular needs of institutional investors.[12] Specifically, it was not that they were "Western" firms, but that they were "institutional" firms.

CHAPTER 7

Institutional Investment Management in the United States

Charles D. Ellis, Devereaux A. Clifford, and Rodger F. Smith

Institutional Investment Management

The business environment of institutional investment management for pensions and endowments has undergone profound and dynamic change over the past 25 years:

- While banks and insurance companies were the dominant providers, very few remain viable competitors today. Investment counselors were few in number a quarter century ago, but they dominate the industry today.
- Assets are up 400 percent—due to accumulation and market appreciation.
- Fee *rates* have tripled—with assets also up strongly, actual fees paid are up more than tenfold.
- Portfolio turnover has increased four or five times.
- International investing, "value" investing, mortgage-backed securities, high-yield bonds, and Guaranteed Investment Contracts and all sort of derivatives are all new.
- Performance measurement, master trusts, and passive investing are all new.

Charles D. Ellis and Devereaux A. Clifford wrote "Institutional Investment Management" and Devereaux A. Clifford and Rodger F. Smith wrote "Defined Contribution Plans: The 401(k) Revolution."

- In regulation, ERISA and the government's Pension Benefit Guarantee Corporation are new.
- Asset consultants are now major factors in the selection of investment managers.
- Defined Contribution plan assets—particularly 401(k) plans—are catching up with traditional Defined Benefit pension plans and in a decade may surpass the assets of Defined Benefit plans for employee retirement.

Table 7.1 shows the structure of the employee benefit market. Table 7.2 shows the overall asset mix. The leading investment managers have changed greatly. In order of their competitive position as investment managers of employee benefit funds, here are the 20 leaders of 1972 and 1997. Names appearing on *both* lists are highlighted. Most names are different.

Over a decade, almost every investment manager has at least one period of "poor" performance and one period of "superior" performance. While clients might aspire to hire and fire investment managers based on objective and rational evaluations of the data on the managers' investment performance, they find it very hard to use past results to predict future results. The past is not prologue in investing. That's why those investment managers with the best client relationships get more assets added during good performance years and lose less during their poor performance years. They ratchet up more and ratchet down less. Over time, the compounding effect on total assets managed and profitability can be truly splendid.

Investment managers would be wise to rename their business the *investor services business* because, while everybody always talks about "performance" (and very poor investment performance will hurt badly) and only the managers with "good" performance are invited to selection finals

TABLE 7.1   Employee Benefit Market

	Total		Corporate		Public		Endowments	
	Funds	Assets	Funds	Assets	Funds	Assets	Funds	Assets
Over $5 billion	169	$4,533	88	$1,661	66	$2,652	15	$220
$1–$5 billion	349	1,102	222	722	86	235	41	145
$501–$1,000 million	266	303	150	182	46	43	70	78
$251–$500 million	278	194	147	117	60	32	71	45
$100–$250 million	312	138	176	87	62	18	74	33

Note: Assets in billions.

TABLE 7.2   Overall Asset Mix

Leading Managers in 1972	Leading Managers in 1999
Morgan Guaranty	Fidelity
First National City	The Vanguard Group
T. Rowe Price	Barclays Global Investors
Bankers Trust	State Street Global Advisors
Prudential Life	Alliance Capital Management
DLJ	INVESCO
Bank of America	*J.P. Morgan Investment*
Continental Illinois	UBS Asset Management
Metropolitan	Sanford C. Bernstein
Lehman Brothers	Deutsche Asset Management
Northern Trust	Putnam Investments
Oppenheimer	Morgan Stanley Dean Witter
The Boston Company	Fayez Sarofim
Wells Fargo	Mellon
IDS Advisory	Nicholas-Applegate
Jennison Associates	*Oppenheimer Capital*
Thorndike, Doran, Paine & Lewis	Capital Guardian Trust
Keystone	Delaware Investment Advisers
United Bank of Denver	Independence Investment
William D. Witter	Ark Asset Management

when new managers are chosen, relationships based on good service matter even more than investment performance so long as that performance is within range.

Sustained superior service and the trust and confidence this develops in each client relationship matter more and more as the years go by because investment performance comes and goes. Over the long run, the decisive differentiation in building a larger and profitable business between very successful investment firms and fairly successful firms can almost always be traced to the consistently superior investor service delivered to clients—not to their respective investment performance.

The most successful firms recognize that really good working relationships are highly valued by clients and are crucial to client satisfaction and client loyalty. This is particularly true when the client organization faces such action decisions as whether to terminate the manager or "give them another year" to improve performance, or when the fund executive is considering which manager to give additional funds to, or whether to add another asset class to the present mandate.

Clients seek and reward relationships in which they work with managers they can trust and with whom they can develop comfortable relationships with confidence.

The core of an effective program of investor service is the manager's investment *product,* particularly when it is clearly defined and consistently delivered in harmony with client expectations. Two parts of the *reliable* product definition are crucial. The first is the investment manager's overarching, enduring concept or *investment philosophy*—the proverbial big idea, or the *what* aspect of investing. The second is the specific investment decision-making process by which this philosophy is translated into real portfolios in different markets over many months and years—the *how* aspect of investing. The manager's investment philosophy and its implementation through specific investment decisions are complementary and naturally reinforcing.

A POWERFUL INVESTMENT PHILOSOPHY IS A KEY SALES TOOL

A well-conceived, compelling investment philosophy that is clearly and boldly articulated to both clients and prospects and is consistently implemented with positive, profitable results is a powerful strategic advantage for an investment management organization:

- Externally, it is consistently one of the most important criteria by which customers evaluate managers—whether hiring or terminating. (The only real rival in importance is outstanding investment performance, an increasingly difficult and unpredictably variable foundation on which to build a substantial business.) Managers who are recognized as having superior investment philosophies win more new accounts, and keep existing accounts longer and lose accounts less often.
- Internally, it provides a central vision around which individual professionals and the investment team will organize their work and their decisions.

Powerful investment philosophies begin with one or more important insights into and solid understanding of either major investment opportunities the manager can capitalize on and maximize or major investment problems the manager could minimize or control. Here are two conceptualizations that both lead to growth investing, but get there in virtually opposite ways.

In the first philosophy, growth investing addresses a *problem,* and the investment manager says something like this:

Inflation is the great investment problem because it constantly corrodes the investor's purchasing power. Therefore, the investor's dividends must grow faster than inflation corrodes purchasing power—so rapidly growing earnings are essential for success. That's why we invest in growth stocks.

In the second philosophy, the focus is turned 180 degrees to focus on *opportunity,* and managers working with this philosophy would say something like:

Growth stocks are a great opportunity—if you concentrate on true growth *companies that have proprietary products, increasing unit volume, control of pricing, no governmental intrusions, little competition, low labor costs, and so on. Be very self-disciplined, do thorough homework, take a long-term view, and you will be able to invest in great companies that will earn great returns for investors.*

In either case, the manager has a vision of *why* he or she can and will add value to clients' portfolios. Moreover, clients and prospects will be able to buy into that concept, because the manager enables them to understand and become convinced that it makes sense: The payoffs are both probable and significant, and the investment manager generates confidence that he or she knows what to do and how to do it.

A well-reasoned, vibrant investment philosophy statement presents the investment manager's most important and enduring professional convictions: It's not "packaging" and cannot be done by outsiders. It is really the public definition of the firm as a professional investment manager.

Strong investment philosophies crystallize a firm's deep beliefs about investing. They can be illustrated by numerous examples from past decisions that managers take pride in and use to teach young professionals "how we do things here" and "what we care most about doing well here." Strong investment philosophies are what the senior professionals really stand for, can be stated clearly because they are so clearly thought out, and are expected to continue to be true 5 and 10 years from now.

Another, and far more important, test is that the investment professionals would all feel comfortable that they could live with the firm's investment philosophy statement for 5 to 10 years, through good times and bad times.

IMPLEMENTING THE INVESTMENT PHILOSOPHY

Having defined and articulated their investment philosophy, the investment manager should turn from the "what" to the "how." All managers will want to have a straightforward description of the *decision-making process* by which they will implement their investment philosophy in managing portfolios. The managers will want persuasive clarity of process for their own internal use ("Plan your play and play your plan!" admonishes every great team's coach), and clients want a clearly defined process because they've learned that like the proverbial one hand clapping, an investment philosophy without a confirming decision-making process is useless and cannot and must not be trusted.

The process for making investment decisions identifies the decisions that will be made, the individuals or groups responsible for making these decisions, the criteria that will be used, the scale of decision or the decision boundaries or limits (i.e., no more than X% in any one security or Y% in any one type of security), the criteria by which a decision would be changed or reversed, and the process by which decisions will be reviewed. Often, it will help clarify the decision-making process to have a complementary description of the organization and the specification of individual and group responsibilities, and how they work together.

The test for a decision-making process is that it explains in a way clients can understand how competent, disciplined professionals can execute the process repetitively in differing market environments, with results that are predictable, expected, and reliable.

A second test: Each professional investor would be comfortably willing to have an able associate take his or her place in the process, knowing the associate's actions and decisions will be governed by an agreed-on procedure for making decisions. (A good process will not be dependent on the "artistic genius" of an individual practitioner.)

HIRING INVESTMENT MANAGERS

The hiring of investment managers—usually to replace managers who have been terminated—creates an active secondary market for investment management services. Most "new" accounts will actually be "second-hand" accounts, with prospective clients who are at least somewhat affected by their recent disappointing experiences.

Investment managers will be wise to recognize and appreciate the daunting difficulties fund executives face when selecting new managers. Consider these realities for the fund that has managers for domestic equities, bonds, international, and real estate—not to mention master trustees, asset consultants, and 401(k) administrators. The fund executive could give consideration to as many as 50 domestic equity managers, 25 fixed-income managers, 25 international investment managers, and 20 real estate managers. With more than 100 investment managers to take into consideration, the fund executive could be overwhelmed: Just to meet each manager once a year could involve two meetings every week.

Selecting investment managers is usually the responsibility of an investment committee—led by the executive who works full time on managing the managers, and his or her staff of professionals. (At very large funds, the staff may total more than 50.) For the prospective manager, this means a two-tier decision-making process—and therefore a two-tier selling process.

WHAT'S IMPORTANT—THEN AND NOW

The criteria used in selecting investment managers have been remarkably consistent over the years. The important selection criteria concentrate on *value*, not *price*. Here are the salient criteria, grouped by importance:

- *Very important:*
  Superior long-term investment performance.
  Clear and consistent investment philosophy.
  Understanding of fund's objectives and risk tolerance.
  Consistent performance over time.
  Well-defined decision-making process.
- *Important:*
  Superior portfolio manager.
  Capable research staff.
  Outstanding chief investment officer.
- *Unimportant:*
  Low fees.
  Market timing ability.

Pension funds and endowment funds are active in hiring new investment managers. As noted, this is mostly "secondary market" activity—hiring managers to replace those managers who have recently been terminated:

- 42 percent of funds over $50 million hire one or more managers every year.
- 55 percent of funds over $1 billion hire one or more managers every year.

Behind the 42 percent aggregate hiring, and allowing for double counting because some funds hire more than one manager in a year, the following proportion of funds hire each of the major types of managers:

- 21 percent for international stocks.
- 15 percent for "value" stocks.
- 15 percent for "growth" stocks.
- 6 percent for passive management of stocks.
- 12 percent for bonds.
- 8 percent for real estate.

More than 60 percent of the funds that hired investment managers in a particular year also fired one or more of their former investment managers. This means that keeping clients by building loyalty into each client relationship is essential for long-term success in building a major investment management business. Effective client service is critical.

Investment managers increasingly recognize that fund executives do not take accounts away: *The managers lose them.* Funds executives who recently terminated investment managers gave the following reasons for termination. The record is not complimentary to the investment managers:

- *Very important:*
    Loss of confidence in managers' decision-making process.
    Disappointing performance over past 3–5 years.
- *Important:*
    Loss of key people in recent past.
    Violation of specific investment restrictions.
    Lack of credibility with investment committee or trustees.
    Investment philosophy or style not clear or consistent.
    Not adapting investments to fund's specific goals and objectives.
    Inconsistent performance from year to year.
- *Unimportant:*
    Fees too high.
    Disappointing recent performance.

INTENSIVE SELLING: THE GOLDEN CHAIN

When an investment management firm is planning its new business strategy, a structured series of sales meetings that build sequentially toward a good working relationship can create a desirable "unfair" competitive advantage.

The approach we recommend is certainly unusual. Our experience is that investment managers are all too willing to "go anywhere, see anyone." They make lots of calls and meet lots of people, but they also get spread way too thin. Institutional selling is most effective when it is *intensive,* and is least effective when it is *extensive.*

Our approach is designed to meet and take advantage of the unique characteristics of the selling situation in the institutional investment market; it develops shared understanding and good professional relationships between the aspiring investment manager and the prospective client.

First, here are six special characteristics of the institutional fund market in America:

1. It is huge. With 3,000 funds over $50,000,000 and nearly $4 trillion in total assets, the market is realistically *too* big for any one firm to cover all of it thoroughly.
2. It is very competitive. From 100–150 possible candidates, the typical buyer keeps files on 40–60, is solicited by 25–50, and monitors 10–25 closely. When it's time for a selection, the investment consultant will consult his or her files for the records of 150–250 possible managers and carefully screen 20–40 managers. Of these, 15–25 will be asked to fill out questionnaires, half a dozen will be interviewed, and the fund executive and the consultant will select for final examination 3–6 managers who best match the desires of the particular organization. After a series of formal final presentations, the fund's investment committee will then award an account to just one or two of these finalists.
3. A manager can only win when selected as the best of all the top competitors in the judgment of the particular group of decision-makers at a specific fund.
4. *Winning is done one account at a time* because each fund makes it own decisions.
5. While managers sometimes win accounts solely "on the numbers"—because their recent investment performance seems so compelling to some prospects—most new accounts are won by managers with good records who have developed a significant comparative advantage based on professional-personal *relationships* with the key people at the particular fund. To build these superior relationships takes "deep selling."
6. Deep selling takes lots of time, particularly when selling to large structured organizations in which the standard practice is to put any new supplier "on hold"—often for several years—for observation. This period of observation also provides time for the development of an organization-to-organization relationship if the manager recognizes the opportunity.

FOCUS TO WIN

Focus is the key to success in industrial or institutional selling. And focus depends on astute market segmentation to isolate priority prospects for "total-immersion" selling, based on carefully constructed, intensively serviced *relationships*. Focus on those funds that want most to obtain the particular investment services your firm is best at producing. Investment managers should always look for the win-win situation.

The most common mistake among salespeople is to be too democratic in organizing their marketing strategies. Saying something like, "If any major fund wants to invite us to compete, we want to go!" may be courageous, but it isn't very smart. If the selection process is at all advanced, coming in late is almost always coming in way *too* late. At least some of the competitor managers will have an important relationship-based head start. (As they say in poker, if you don't know who the patsy is after half an hour's playing, *you* are the patsy.)

Winning requires deep selling. And deep selling—relationship building—takes *time*.

Time is the critically limited strategic resource of every investment manager. So the best strategy for selling will maximize returns on limited time. (Similarly, candy makers, during wartime sugar rationing, maximized profits per pound of sugar, not per dollar of sales.) It takes a lot of time to develop a superior relationship with each prospective client. So, just as corporate business strategies are best defined by what the corporation does *not* do and *will not* do, an investment manager's new business strategy can be defined by the invitations to selection "finals" the manager does not seek and will not accept. Here are some useful tips.

Concentrate on "three-day cities" where there are enough large funds to keep a good salesperson busy for three full days with a dozen good appointments. Experienced salespeople know it's harder to match calendars with prospects when they are in a city for only one day, but over three days almost every prospect is available. Plan on going to any target city at least six times a year so you can call on every prospect at least three times a year. You'll not only get to know—and enjoy—the city, you'll make it abundantly clear that you are committed to the city, and prospects will recognize you as "almost one of us." When you win a client, pass the word around town, and invite your new client to do the same thing. It's all part of astute "precinct marketing."

Avoid "one-day" cities where there are only a few prospects. You'll be spending too much of your valuable time in airplanes, airports, and taxis while your best competitors are spending their time in meetings with good prospects. Besides, your "hard-yards" logistics will wear you down, while your best competitors stay fresh and rested. Remember: If you do win a client in such a city, you'll be going back again and again. There really *are* competitions you can't afford to win! Also, avoid cities or people you don't really like. The work of institutional sales is hard enough when you really like what you're doing and the folks you're working with.

Astute sales executives know the crucial difference between "playing to play" and playing to *win*. Sure, you'll hear barroom stories of the sales that involved a "Hail, Mary"—and worked. But you hear about those wins because they are so rare. That's no way to build a professional business. If you don't have an unfair competitive advantage at the selection finals, at least one of your competitors *will* have it—to your serious disadvantage!

Don't advertise. More particularly, don't advertise in newspapers or magazines. It doesn't pay off when competing for institutional clients. If you have a message you want to communicate, identify your target audience and write individual letters to each and every targeted prospect. If you want many people to get your message, write lots of letters. They're cheap. And letters will get read and usually saved, particularly if you write well and have something interesting and useful to say.

Visit competitors. Get to know them. Help them know you. Tell them what you do best (ideally make a full formal presentation) so they'll know. What more could you ask for than to have your competitors know—and inevitably acknowledge to your prospects—what you do best?

Never ever promise—or imply—more than you know you can and will deliver. In a service business, it pays handsomely to overdeliver. It does real harm to overpromise.

One way an investment manager can strengthen a sales message is to develop a thoughtful and effective program of *institutionalized* client service and relationship management; he or she then carefully explains that program of prospective client service *and* its benefits during the "selling" process, ideally with examples of reports the client will receive and the number and content of meetings. We advise our clients to spell-out their client service strategy on two levels: what you should expect of us and what we will expect of you to have a great win-win relationship over many years.

DEEP SELLING: GOLDEN CHAINS PAY OFF

Meetings differ over time in the mutual courting process in which investment managers and prospective managers engage. (Both parties know what's going on; both are actively looking and both have numerous alternatives.)

A first meeting has only one purpose for the buyer: to look the manager over and decide whether to get serious. For the seller, the purpose of the first meeting is to decide whether this prospect is a likely winner and to arrange for a second *substantive* meeting. The key questions on the investment manager's agenda are: Will you be an active buyer? Will you be seeking what we do best? Will we have enough time between now and "decision time" to build a strong, winning relationship?

Once accepted as qualified, the investment manager's sales process should—block by block—build a strong foundation of mutual understanding and trust. Remember, just as men are more "transactional" and women are more "relationship minded," fund executives have a staff role and responsibility and are focused on *relationships,* while investment managers and salespeople are *transactional* in orientation.

The most successful relationship builders, deservedly, are the major long-term winners of new clients. They concentrate on developing superb *relationships,* through which desirable transactions can then be executed.

The following suggestions might be used to create a "golden chain" of sequential, linked meetings with prospects—the central substance of each meeting taking about 20 or 25 minutes. This reserves ample time for follow-on questions and answers that build real understanding *and* for particularization to the specific fund by thoughtful give-and-take with the fund executive.

Round One

- Send ahead an interesting, thoughtful letter, confirming date and briefly specifying the manager's main strengths in equity management.
- First meeting: Brief review of investment record and underpinning investment philosophy. Key topic: Are we the kind of managers you would seriously consider? If it's "no," not a good fit, be gracious but clear: Close it out early. If "yes," the manager will want to learn which specific investment capability would benefit the prospective client most, so future meetings can focus on that particular best opportunity.
- Follow-up letter on the manager's investment philosophy, focusing on the particular investment capability in which interest was shown.

Round Two

- Letter confirming appointment and the importance of explaining the investment philosophy for the particular type of investing in which interest was shown and illustrating that investment philosophy with real and interesting investment case histories.
- Second meeting: Careful exposition of investment philosophy for the type of investing chosen and how and why it was developed. Examples

of specific investment decisions showing what the manager does—and does not do—as a result of the investment philosophy.

▦ Follow-up letter with key examples as evidence of investment philosophy.

Round Three

▦ Letter confirming appointment and a brief summary of the manager's investment decision-making process.

▦ Third meeting: Careful, engaging review of three or four key investment decisions and how they were made, and how decision process confirms the investment philosophy.

▦ Follow-up letter on how decision-making process validates the firm's investment philosophy.

Round Four

▦ Letter confirming appointment and giving brief, interesting, and relevant profile sketches of key investment professionals.

▦ Fourth meeting: Features introduction of the prospective portfolio manager, who restates and confirms investment philosophy and decision-making process.

▦ Follow-up letter reaffirming the investment firm's policies on people, recruiting professionals, professional development, and so on.

Round Five

▦ Letter confirming appointment and key questions manager expects *prospect* to cover: investment strategy, risk tolerances, actuarial assumptions, past experiences with managers—most and least favorable—and role available for soliciting manager if all goes well.

▦ Fifth meeting: Prospect explains what he wants from a manager, and manager draws him out on specifics and how the fund's decisions on new managers are made, often best done over lunch or dinner.

▦ Follow-up letter shows manager paid attention and learned—and appreciates time given.

Round Six

▦ Letter confirming appointment and asserting the investment manager's commitment to developing and sustaining first-rate, two-way relationships with fund executive.

▦ Sixth meeting: Careful, step-by-step review of each component of manager's client service program, with examples of all documents, prepared as though prospect already is a client.

- ■ Follow-up letter urging prospect to contact other clients for further discussion of manager's service program, enclosing list of clients to call (with telephone numbers).

Round Seven

- ■ Letter confirming appointment and outlining investment manager's major business goals and business policies.
- ■ Seventh meeting: Review history of firm and its past, present, and future strategy as a business—and why this particular fund would, as a new client, be important to the manager's business strategy.
- ■ Follow-up letter on strengths of manager's organization and business.

The topics can be varied from this pattern. The important thing is to have a series of interesting and informative meetings with each prospect that will build sequentially into a strong, balanced case for being chosen as the fund's next manager.

MAKING THE MOST OF FUND MANAGERS' TIME

Fund executives are busy people with major responsibilities and must make good use of their seriously limited time. So when asked what they want most in a sales representative, their preferences are clear. They want marketers who:

- ■ Can explain their firm's investment philosophy clearly.
- ■ Can explain their firm's current investment strategy clearly.
- ■ Understands the fund's investment goals and objectives.
- ■ Knows their firm's investment decision-making process.
- ■ Follows up promptly on the fund's information requests.
- ■ Makes good use of the fund executive's time during meetings and telephone calls.

What we find disturbing is the following inventory of the most common mistakes made by salespeople representing investment managers. Fund executives complain that investment managers' sales representatives:

- ■ Telephone fund executives too often.
- ■ Do not make good use of the executive's time during meetings and telephone calls.
- ■ Do not understand the fund's specific needs.
- ■ Send too much written information.

- Do not understand how the fund's investment committee makes decisions.
- Have poor presentation materials.
- Do not understand their own firm's investment philosophy.
- Do not understand their firm's decision-making process.

Committee meetings are not like one-on-one meetings. Committees are very different, as litigation lawyers all know about juries making decisions. Investment managers going to a finals meeting should not expect a "fair hearing." Life itself is unfair. And so are committee decisions. Almost always, the competition for a particular piece of new business has been effectively won before the committee meets by the managers that were best aligned with the fund's objectives and have done the best deep selling, ideally with effective focus on the one or two most influential members of the decision-making committee. *Be sure that "lucky" manager is you.*

An effective finals presentation is less an advocacy or "case making" than it is an assuring affirmation and confirmation of the wisdom of the committee's well-nurtured nascent decision to hire the particular manager.

Fund executives have learned from past experience and disappointments that investment managers can disappoint. So they are understandably cautious—even skeptical. Experienced fund executives know, as cited earlier in this chapter, that investment performance data does not predict or foretell superior future performance. So they know to look elsewhere, at the qualitative strength of the organization and the strength of its investment philosophy and decision-making process.

Building a winning sales presentation starts with a focus on factors that plan sponsors consider most important in selecting a new manager.

The goal should be to develop clear, relevant, and compelling examples and proof statements for each key assertion. The strength of the presentation will depend directly on the number of *proved* assertions. Said another way, the more assertions that lack proof, the weaker the presentation will be.

The KISS concept ("Keep It Simple, Sweetheart") is a helpful proposition to remember and follow when articulating an investment philosophy or process. It pays to reread Strunk and White's *The Elements of Style* (Allyn & Bacon) or *The Economist*'s *Style Book* (John Wiley & Sons) before attempting a final draft.

We advise our clients: "Remember, everything you say *will* be summarized by others—when you are no longer present. The secret to success is to create the short summary you really want them to use—and then teach them to use it!" Most short summaries take five words or less; almost all take less than ten words. Note, for example, how we describe presidential candidates, restaurants, corporations, and even religions.

SELLING THROUGH CONSULTANTS

At a majority of funds, an independent *investment consultant* is used to inform and advise the fund executive and the committee. (As shown in Table 7.3, more than 60 percent of all large funds and nearly 80 percent of public pension funds now use asset consultants.)

In number of clients, these are the leading investment consultants in the United States:

Mercer	Merrill Lynch
Cambridge	Ennis, Knupp
Callan	Towers Perrin
Frank Russell	Capital Resources
BARRA RogersCasey	Consulting Group
Hewitt	New England Pension Consultants
Evaluation Associates	J.H. Ellwood
Watson Wyatt	Jeffrey Slocum
Wilshire Associates	LCG Associates
DeMarche Associates	Strategic Investment Solutions

There are two keys to selling through the consultants: First, engage the interest and assure the confidence of the consultants in the investment manager's *reliable* capability to do good work as an investment manager. And second, "make the consultant look good" by *being* very good as an investment manager in each of three different time periods:

1. The finals presentation.
2. The first year after getting the account.
3. Forever after.

Realistically, consultants have many managers from which to choose those few they will feature with their clients. So from the long list, they will sort out a short list of the managers they perceive to have superior capabil-

TABLE 7.3   Change in Use of Investment Consultants

	1992	1994	1996	1998	2000
Corporate Funds	59%	54%	59%	66%	67%
Public Funds	75	75	76	71	85
Endowments	54	63	70	69	72
Total Funds	62%	60%	65%	67%	72%

ity—and then select from the group of qualified suppliers the few that are easy for them to work with and that they trust will not let them down.

Most consultants are diligent in their searching examination of hopeful investment managers—some are even aggressive. However, their driving motivation is primarily *defensive:* They are properly protective of their clients (and, naturally, of their business relationships with those clients). They do not want to risk serious disappointment with a manager. In formal terms, they "satisfice" (by striving for the most "acceptable" recommendation) rather than *maximize* success (by striving for the "best") in their advice on which managers to select.

As a result, confidence winning—through careful relationship management and reliable informative service vis-à-vis the consultant—will be crucial for investment managers who want their steady support. Therefore, an investment firm should focus its resources on providing superior responsive service and support to those selected consultants who are most influential within the firm's chosen target markets.

Investment managers need to remember: To win the active support of an investment consultant, the new manager must displace an old and established manager, *with the consent of the consultant,* who decides the new manager is better for that consultant's clients and for that consultant's business.

The most effective business development strategy will be a deliberate blend of direct selling and consultant selling, with "both hands clapping."

SERVICE STRATEGY: RELATIONSHIP BUILDING

The purpose of a service strategy is to build strong, enduring, and mutually satisfying relationships with client organizations. The best way to build a bigger and better business is to build each relationship by increasing the assets managed in the present asset class, or adding another asset class to the original mandate. (Note: Any new investment product should always be introduced first to established clients, not taken on the road to get new clients.)

A good relationship is based on clear and explicit understanding. It avoids unnecessary difficulties due to misunderstandings about the manager's investment mission or the client's investment objectives. Such a relationship will, over time, increase the manager's share of each client's total business through above-average cash flows when results are good, and minimize loss of business during periods of unsatisfactory performance. The more fully clients understand what the manager is doing and why, the longer they can remain confident—and remain clients.

The service strategy should be responsive both to clients' long-term interests and to the manager's capacity to deliver service consistently and over time. Instead of committing to develop new information or new capabilities, look for opportunities to apply to your client service program the capabilities, information, and resources you already have. Using what you already know how to do well will greatly increase the chances of sustained successful delivery and client satisfaction.

The central portion of the investment manager's service strategy will be the quarterly investment review meetings with clients. If you cannot arrange four formal meetings each year (because most clients are extremely busy, most managers cannot) try to substitute an informal one-on-one session with their principal contact at the client organizations. Cover the same ground as in a formal meeting, including the follow-up letter procedure.

Investments in meetings build strong relationships. The institutional investment management business really is a personal-professional *relationship* business, so time, energy, and skill committed to developing strong relationships really pay off. Here are four useful guidelines for meetings:

1. The primary objective of meetings is to provide clients with the explicit assurance that their portfolio is being managed—and will be managed—competently and in accordance with their objectives. Investment *con*formance is more important than investment *per*formance.
2. Next, affirm that what the client wants is both realistic and well matched to the work the manager does best.
3. Demonstrate the manager's professional capabilities to achieve good results over and over again, in changing investment environments.
4. Finally, build solid personal-professional relationships between the several executives who are important at the typical large client organization and the several key professionals at the investment management organization. Major relationships are far too important to be left dependent on personal relationships between two individuals. Major relationships should be *organizational.*

To achieve these objectives, we recommend the following steps:

■ Call the fund executive two or three weeks ahead of each meeting to agree on the agenda, to identify who (particularly any new people) will attend the meeting, and to learn about any questions or issues that might warrant extra attention.
■ If possible, arrange to have half an hour with any new committee member prior to the group meeting to review your relationship and inform him or her about your organization, your investment philosophy, and so on, so he or she will be "sold" on you *before* the meeting. (Breakfast on the day of the meeting or dinner the night before can work well for this purpose.)

- Confirm the agenda in writing.
- Send ahead the documents that could properly be reviewed by the committee members before the meeting including biographical material on each person coming from your firm.
- Write a follow-up letter immediately after the meeting, emphasizing the key areas discussed and noting any action commitments you made. (It pays handsomely to have this letter actually drafted in advance of the meeting, so it can easily be revised right after the meeting and sent quickly to each participant, with a copy to anyone who missed the meeting.)
- Be as formal as you can be during the meeting: Stand up, speak slowly, use slides, and so on.
- No matter how strongly the client urges that you "skip the formal part" of the meeting and go into an informal discussion right away, insist, if you can, on at least an abbreviated formal initial section.

The ideal investment review meeting will have four parts; the two most important parts come first—and take the least time—usually only 5 to 10 minutes total:

1. The first part of an investment review meeting is a careful, explicit review of the investment objectives to which the manager is committed for this client, and the specific policy guidelines the investment manager has agreed to follow in pursuit of those agreed-on objectives.
2. Next comes a careful restatement of the manager's investment philosophy or concept and the manager's process for making investment decisions.

The combination of the client's objectives and policy constraints and the investment manager's professional commitments on philosophy and process make up the manager's mission statement. It should be realistic in relation to the market and within the manager's demonstrated competence. And it should be suited to the specific client.

Because it is difficult to get such mission statements in clear form, we urge our clients to work on defining and articulating an accurate mission statement with each client and to put the results in writing. The reaffirmation of that statement—the manager's core professional convictions and the client's goals—should be repeated at the beginning of every meeting with every client.

If the investment manager believes the mission statement should be modified in any way, he or she should advise the client in advance and explain the reason for recommending each modification. Clients should also be invited either to modify the mission statement if the specific characteristics of their internal situation have changed—or to reaffirm the established statement.

3. After the reaffirmation of both the manager's part and the client's part of the mission statement, the next portion of the meeting should be a brief review of how the manager has followed the client's guidelines in pursuit of the fund's objectives, by applying the manager's process to fulfill the manager's philosophy—how the manager has, in fact, fulfilled the investment mission during the period under review.
4. The fourth part of the meeting is an opportunity to demonstrate—at length and with care—the manager's professional competence by discussing, in a well-thought-out and well-documented manner, any *one* important investment topic. This should take 15–20 minutes—as much time as needed to be complete.

   The topic discussed should be important to the manager's work and relevant to the client as well as interesting and useful. A rigorous review of a major industry, or of a change in the economy, or of several key purchases or sales in the portfolio will be interesting and helpful to developing deep "shared understanding." The manager should make the same presentation in all client review meetings for that reporting period and therefore should invest substantial time and effort to be sure the presentation is first rate.

   A 2- to 4-page memorandum—beautifully written so it is worth reading again and saving—that reproduces the substance of the special presentation should be sent within a week of the meeting. Every member of the investment committee should receive a copy along with a cover letter affirming how important this particular client relationship is to the investment manager.

In addition to first-rate investment review meetings, the service strategy should have a disciplined program of account reports sent on time, with a cover letter on the highlights.

Finally, the service strategy should include prompt and reliable responses to inquiries and requests for information. Generally, this part of the service program is done best by a paraprofessional who cares greatly about people and enjoys good service relationships and has good self-discipline and self-motivation.

Some informal contact and communication can enhance a good professional relationship and is well worth considering. Clients usually prefer having a personal dimension to their most important professional relationships.

Always give extra attention when developing a new relationship: Exchange visits to get to know each other; specify investment objectives and guidelines or restrictions on investment objectives and quicklines or restrictions on investments; and learn how the new client prefers to work with managers.

And remember: When a new person becomes the primary fund executive, for that person, the relationship really is new. Pay special attention to a newly appointed fund executive, *every* time; recognize the opportunity to move up to a better relationship—particularly if a competitor is napping.

Here are some more helpful "tips from experience":

- Receivers—not senders—control all communication. *Hearing* is not the same as *listening* and truly *understanding*. Repetition is important and takes time, as does any form of active listening. Everyone likes to know they are understood. Time spent in active listening is time well spent.
- Most people cannot or will not concentrate on understanding you until after they are confident you truly understand them. Active listening is the best way to give your partners in communication that vital confidence and the best way to enlist their help in your attaining full and accurate understanding of their views and feelings. Most people really can't even start listening until they feel assured what they've been saying is well understood.
- Believing precedes acting. Good relationships come before good transactions particularly for staff agents whose first priority is defensive.
- Good relationships depend on trust—always a personal confidence that there is no risk in depending on the other person's understanding.
- Trust builds over time through successful interactions—usually involving useful information that is accurate and received promptly—that demonstrate sincere commitment to being trustworthy.
- Good performance in any service is a function of expectations being consistently fulfilled or exceeded.
- Managing expectations is as important to good investment performance as it is in managing the service delivery. Clients with realistic expectations can be satisfied well, repetitively.
- Nobody will tell you "the truth" unless you make it very, very easy by listening for and actively hearing the truth.
- Everybody is busy, usually too busy. So we all treasure our time. For a client to have a winning experience, the investment manager needs to deliver more value than the client's treasured time costs. The investment manager can do this with information and ideas the client finds useful. Churchill said it: "People like winning very much!" And all clients like winning relationships.

Investment managers should have one- and five-year growth plans for each client relationship, in writing. One page will do and will usually be far more than most investment managers project. Divide the page into thirds.

The top third of the page identifies the key fund executives and investment committee members, the asset consultant, other investment managers, and such facts as cash flow, actuarial assumptions, and so on.

The middle section describes the client's current views of the investment manager—pro and con—and the most important actions to take to improve the client's perception.

The bottom third identifies the actions the investment manager believes will contribute most to making this client relationship all it can be, with dates for completion and names of those responsible for taking each action.

The term *relationship manager* implies a courteous, affable custodian who would be glad to keep the business his or her firm already has. In consulting with our clients, we prefer the term *relationship builder* because we believe every account should be treated as a *growth* account. This means an imaginative, committed business builder is in charge of the investment manager's side of the relationship and is responsible for making it both better and bigger.

Still, clients do not like change, any more than the rest of us do, because they know what they are losing and don't know what the new person will do or be like. Clients typically feel they have invested a lot of time and emotional energy in developing their personal and business relationships with the specific individuals who have been representing their investment managers.

"People changes" are going on all the time and are to be expected. Transitions and change are inevitable. Key people get promoted or transferred or leave. So managing transitions—particularly when there's a change in the individual who is most important in managing a major client relationship—can play an important part in the growth of an investment management firm and in the professional and career growth of individuals within the firm. Doing it well truly matters to both the manager and to clients.

First, do all you can to minimize changes in the people managing relationships with clients. Hire relationship builders very carefully; develop challenging and satisfying career plans with each of them; be sure the job of relationship builder is important within the organization and is well rewarded, financially and nonfinancially; and treat relationship builders as the absolute equals of investment professionals.

Second, do all you can to develop relationships that are "firm-to-firm" and "organizational" and are not dependent on specific individuals. Excellent programmed meetings using first-rate and consistent materials, prepared for use by all relationship builders with all clients, make it much easier to change individual presenters. It is surprising how many investment firms allow each relationship manager to do his or her "own thing" in meetings and reports instead of concentrating on building a clear and consistent service that adds "brand" value to the relationship.

Sell the *firm* to both prospects and clients in presentations, with annual reports, with position papers, in informal conversations, in letters, in organized visits to your office or group dinners, and in the consistency with which everyone delivers the investment management and the relationship management performance.

Third, *plan* for transition. It pays to have a written relationship plan for each client, specifying when the current key contact will change and estimating who will be his or her successor. This plan will help the manager recognize the inevitability of change and implement it smoothly.

Fourth, consider the concept "*we* decide and our *client* chooses." In other words, the investment manager decides when a relationship manager is going to be changed—say, two years from now—and then arranges the contacts and communications with this client, so all their key people get to know, like, and respect the intended successor relationship manager well before the transition time. With planning, it's easy to find numerous opportunities for the intended successor to "look good and do good" for the particular client. The successor relationship builder can usually, with some extra initiative, provide more service and become a "better bet" for the client—as the client executives see it—so everybody wins when the change comes.

Fifth, we advise our clients: Make time your friend. Transition is particularly easy if the investment manager links change in relationship manager to the client's change in primary contact. The successor relationship builder then can get to know the successor client fund executive before the changeover so that they come in together. Anticipate or lead the change in executives by having the relationship builder's successor deliver extra service before a change is made. This is one way to ally with time. Continuing communications after the expected change has been made—if only in writing and informal "Joe sends his best" comments plus occasional visits or calls—can be a great help. The client will sensibly think, "He didn't forget; we *are* important."

The key to any successful transition is that the new people coming into the relationships are first rate and genuinely interested in and committed to working to achieve long-term success.

NEW PARADIGM MANAGERS

Returning now to the overall relationship between a major investment manager and a major investment client, we find evidence that a new paradigm is developing in the investment management industry, particularly in the United States, where the past 20 years have seen so much specialization among managers. The new organizational and "management-management" paradigm has the competitive strength to become the new norm in the business over the next decade or so and to dominate the investment management business and the practice of the investment profession.

The new paradigm is remarkably different from the paradigm that has, over the past quarter century, become the accepted and now dominant norm in the field. The presently dominant paradigm is a specialist manager with one investment product serving one market, usually pension funds. The developing *new* paradigm is a multimarket, multiproduct investment management organization.

Because the new multimarket, multiproduct organization (when properly led and managed) is more consistently capable of meeting the long-term needs of clients and the objectives of investment professionals, it will be increasingly accepted and will become the industry norm. In fact, the evidence suggests the Darwinian process of one species displacing another—because it is even better matched to the situation—is progressing fairly rapidly now.

The old paradigm is underperforming in part because it is overspecialized. Managers are classified according to an ever-expanding set of increasingly narrowly specified categories of investing. A manager is either a value manager or a growth manager, and within each of those categories, a large-capitalization or a small-capitalization manager. A manager is passive, quantitative, or active—and operates with or without technology. A global or international manager can concentrate on the Pacific Rim, on Europe or Latin America, or on the emerging markets globally, or on any specific part of the world—with or without currency overlays.

On the bond side of the business, a manager can specialize in portfolios of bonds that are immunized or dedicated, structured or indexed or index-plussed—and could have GICs or BICs or be in the high-yield sector, with or without credit limitations; deal with private placements or the extended market; avoid or concentrate in mortgages and asset-backed securities of all kinds. A bond manager could be international or global, with or without currency overrides; be involved in bank loan packaging or convertibles, sector switching, arbitrage, constant yield, constant duration, and so on.

From the investment manager's point of view, the world of possible markets to serve is not particularly simple either. The large, medium-size, and small corporate funds have fundamentally different characteristics. Public funds are different from corporate funds, and endowment funds are different from both. The 401(k) plans are growing rapidly and have fundamentally changed the terms of competition. Nuclear decommissioning could be an important market. Insurance companies are becoming interesting and, of course, there are many different kinds of offshore funds. The United Kingdom, Japan, Germany, and Canada—each an important market opportunity for U.S. managers—are very different from each other and from the American market.

All the complexity of investment management and of investment managers is beyond the capacity of most clients' fund executives to manage successfully and economically, and with assurance. Many fund executives have hoped or expected the consultants would work it all out. But the consultants are having disagreeable experiences as they try to keep up with product and manager proliferation and with the vagaries of performance by individual managers.

Investment managers need some new way of being organized with the capacity to deal in many different markets. It must be effective for the client, and it must be productive for the investment manager. It must be capable of dealing successfully with multiple products. And it must be a multimarket-capable organization, so it can access business from many sources.

The new form of organization must be reliable and sustainable, both for the client and for the manager. It must allow individuals of considerable talent and pools of capital of large size to make long-term commitments.

What we find emerging as the New Paradigm is the kind of structure shown in Table 7.4. The investment products in the first column represent specific investment management capabilities. Each is carefully and rigorously defined as to concept, specifications, and performance. They can be defined

TABLE 7.4 The New Paradigm

Investment Products	Large Corporate Funds	Midsize Corporate Funds	Public Funds	Endowments	Insurance Companies
Active core equity					
Value Stocks					
Large cap					
Small cap					
Growth Stocks					
Large cap					
Small cap					
Passive domestic equities					
Enhanced index					
International Equities					
Active Bonds					
Global					
Domestic					
International					
Balanced funds					
Equity real estate					
Private equity					
Etc.					
Etc.					

as "products." The *markets* shown in the column heads represent markets to which the organization could or does sell its products. The interior space between products and markets will be dominated by superior capabilities in relationship management and relationship development. This integrating and coordinating territory is an important opportunity for strong professional investment counseling and problem solving to serve the specific needs of specific clients.

The New Paradigm multimarket, multiproduct investment management organization meets several needs of major clients: product specification and product conformance; product innovation to meet new needs or exploit new opportunities; the confidence and convenience that go with long-term professional relationships; possibly lower costs; and relationships that are client-driven rather than product-driven. This organization can also better meet the needs of investment managers for professional growth and creativity and financial security at high pay levels, without betting their business careers as well as their professional reputations on a single way of investing in a single asset class (as has so often been true of the specialist management firms).

The successful New Paradigm investment management organizations can afford to invest in acquiring increasingly costly and essential information technology systems, developing new products, and developing new markets. And they will. As product specialization and market segmentation proliferate, we anticipate that an increasingly large share of new products and new markets will be developed by the organizations that master the new paradigm. In fact, New Paradigm organizations are already dominating new product and market development.

Three concluding observations seem important. First, the New Paradigm managers will not overwhelm all the investment boutiques. The best specialist firms will continue to prosper, but they will find it more and more important to be very, very good at their chosen specialty.

Second, not all of the multiproduct, multimarket organizations will be assured of success. Only those that produce consistent product quality and consistent service quality will succeed.

Finally, the New Paradigm is certainly not just a return to the old-style "balanced manager." The New Paradigm organization is profoundly different on every important variable: It has leading-edge investment innovation; devotion to product excellence in design and conformance in execution; strong business development; exceptionally rewarding careers for gifted, motivated professionals; and strong client-centered relationships—with business strength the foundation for professional excellence.

The old paradigm trust department or insured plan couldn't come close to competing with New Paradigm organizations that are truly committed to consistently high standards of investment management and faithfully follow their promised process to fulfill the intentions and aspirations of their investment philosophy.

Even more important, the effective New Paradigm managers will engage in the larger dimensioned, overarching profession of investment counseling—giving wise, documented advice on long-term investment policy and its rational implementation. Clients will find this broad, long-term investment counseling delivers important value and provides a strong foundation for major relationships that endure for the very long term.

While the *profession* of institutional investment management is extraordinarily difficult and sustained excellence is even more difficult, the *business* of institutional investment management is remarkably straightforward. The essential reality to keep always in focus is that superior *relationship* management is even more important than superior *investment* management. That's why managers of all types and sizes must recognize that this is the *investor services business,* not the "money management" business. Yes, a vital part of the service is a good investment product—delivered as promised and as expected—but this is only one part of a complex and multifaceted service relationship with large, informed clients.

Defined Contribution Plans: The 401(k) Revolution

The great transformation away from Defined Benefit plans over to Defined Contribution plans is changing profoundly the way retirement benefits are provided for employees in the United States, with 401(k) plans serving as the principal engine of change.[1] In Australia, the transformation is even more advanced; in Canada and the United Kingdom, it is "early days"; in Japan, it is not yet allowed.

Our research in the United States, which began in 1983 and has been continued annually ever since, documents that more than 90 percent of the nation's 1,000 largest corporations now use 401(k) plans. Fifteen years ago, our research documented that of the 40 percent of the 1,000 largest corporate plans that then had DC plans, half had established a new plan and half had converted an old "savings" plan over to the 401(k) format. Use of DC plans increased by nearly 50 percent the very next year to 60 percent overall—and is now over 90 percent.

As shown in Table 7.5, corporate executives expect the forceful changes of the past to continue into the future—with the "crossover" when DC assets exceed DB assets expected to occur in a few years.

TABLE 7.5 Percentage of Corporations Using Defined Contribution and Defined Benefit Plans

	Defined Contribution	Defined Benefit
1990	31%	69%
1995	36	64
2000	42	58
2005	60	40
2009	66	34

The confluence of several factors propel forward the major shift toward DC plans. These are some of the principal forces at work:

- For corporations that sponsor Defined Benefit retirement plans—with their very large, long-term benefit liabilities—the financial risks were certainly clarified in the 1980s when interest rates rose to record levels. Because the present value of benefit obligations is magnified by changes in interest rates, financial executives witnessed the adverse impact on a corporation's earnings per share (EPS) when benefit payments must be increased.

    Also, the balance sheet leverage of large, unfunded pension obligations could impact a corporation's credit rating adversely. For a corporation, the financial management advantages of a DC over a DB plan—particularly avoiding a large, long-term fixed obligation that can, for reasons beyond management's control, have a "surprise" impact on current EPS—are both clear and compelling. (Of course, it doesn't hurt that the norm with DC plans is that plan participants pay the management fees by deduction.)

- For employees—particularly after a phenomenal 25 years of favorable markets—the attractions of being empowered to "control your own destiny" are appealing. It's true that workers have different sets of financial circumstances, and investment preferences also differ. But home ownership, "do-it-yourself" craftsmanship, numerous small enterprises, and other aspects of self-reliance are all part of the American society. And many Americans are accustomed to investing through mutual funds.

- For investment managers—particularly those mutual fund managers with strong consumer name recognition and franchises; sophisticated computers designed to maintain investors' records and daily valuations accurately; experience in consumer marketing and communications; and the base of profitability and organizational resources with which to support a nationwide business development campaign—the creation of 401(k) plans truly "rang the gong" of major opportunity.

"Investments are *sold*—not bought" continues to be true. The most forceful force for change in 401(k) plans has been the strong competitive efforts of the leading mutual fund contenders for 401(k) Defined Contribution plans—Fidelity, Vanguard, T. Rowe Price, Putnam, and American Express—as they've sought to establish major "instividual" businesses.

One of the great characteristics of the 401(k) business is that once sold, sponsors *stay* sold. Consequently, the long-term economics of the 401(k) business can be very attractive provided the organization already has most or all of the required capabilities in investing, record keeping, and communications; a strong consumer franchise or reputation; *and* the capacity to absorb short-term losses.

One "secret" is in the accounting, just as it is in selling life insurance, drilling oil, or planting asparagus. The cost of selling a new relationship and the cost of establishing a new relationship are substantial. And 401(k) plans start out with very small initial assets, so the early years with each account can be "loss makers." Over time, however, these assets build up and the revenues rise steadily. The effective 401(k) manager will enjoy a long-term "growth annuity" in each client relationship it develops effectively. So, while the accounting may report losses, the astute manager knows this is misleading: He or she is establishing long-term growth annuities, so in a way, the more accounting "losses," the better!

Another secret has been the willingness of competitors from the mutual fund industry to offer both employee communications services and participant record keeping *without charge*. Because the incremental profitability of additional mutual fund assets is so lucrative, the mutual fund organizations can "give away" such support services as record keeping and communications to win the investment business.

For many corporate sponsors, the opportunity to obtain a fully integrated "one-stop" service has proven attractive. (While a few of the strongest firms of consulting actuaries have sought to respond by establishing fee-sharing "alliances" with investment managers to serve their long-standing clients, this strategic response does not appear to be successful.[2])

As technology allows and competitors develop the capability to provide new and better services, communications services rise to the fore. The substantive and visual quality of print communications continues to advance steadily, and new communications services are thrusting forward, particularly telephone and Internet.

The criteria by which corporate executives would select investment managers for 401(k) plans are shown in Table 7.6. The six most important criteria include three on investments:

1. Superior long-term performance.
2. Consistent investment performance.
3. Clear and consistent investment philosophy.

Two represent convenience for participants in exercising *choice:*

4. Range of products offered.
5. Daily valuations.

And one refers to overall *capabilities:*

6. Known and respected by employees.

Over the past 15 years, our annual research has shown a major increase in the importance of offering a full range of investment products (which plays to the advantage of mutual fund organizations that have many products already).[3]

With more and more corporations having established their 401(k) plans and with the major structural shift that has moved assets from banks and insurance companies over to mutual funds as their investment managers, the new manager hiring activity among larger funds has declined rapidly, as shown in Table 7.7. (Competition for new accounts and for "switch business" continues to be active among the middle market companies.)

Hiring has shifted also from primary manager hiring to the addition of supplemental or specialist managers. And as shown in Table 7.7, terminations of managers have also declined significantly.

TABLE 7.6 Investment Management Selection Criteria—
Total Corporations

Superior long-term investment performance	77
Range of quality of investment products offered	75
Consistent investment performance	73
Daily valuations	71
Clear and consistent investment philosophy	70
Known and respected by employees	54

TABLE 7.7 Past and Expected Hiring of
Investment Managers

	Hired an Investment Manager	Expect to Hire Manager	Terminated a 401(k) Manager
1994	28%	22%	19%
1995	21	18	16
1996	21	17	13
1997	19	15	11
1998	11	11	10
1999	14	11	na

In each of the past three years, we asked the several dozen companies that had terminated an investment manager to identify their main reasons (see Table 7.8). The pattern is clear: Companies have moved away from multiple service providers with disappointing investment performance and weak employee communications, weak systems, and slow reporting over to single-service providers with daily valuations. Use of single-service providers has increased substantially, rising from 40 percent in our 1994 research to over 60 percent.

Investment consultants are not nearly so dominant in the 401(k) market as in the traditional Defined Benefit market, but they are increasingly active.

TABLE 7.8 Reasons for Terminating 401(k) Service Provider

	1996	1997	1998
Moved from multiple to a single-service provider	42%	33%	40%
Lacks daily valuation capabilities	22	15	30
Disappointing investment performance	29	29	27
Weak employee communications program	14	13	24
Inadequate systems capability	19	22	24
Fees too high	23	33	24
Slow reports	18	13	19
Administrative or reporting errors	23	22	17
Weak client service staff	18	24	17
Too few investment options	4	11	14

The following shows the increase in the use of investment consultants from 1994 to 1999:

1994	37%
1995	48%
1996	57%
1997	46%
1998	49%
1999	51%
2000	53%

As shown in Table 7.9 the different investment options made available to plan participants has increased steadily, with the largest increase in usage being international equities and index funds. Stable value funds have displaced nearly one half of the demand for GICs, or Guaranteed Investment Contracts.

The largest investment managers, as measured by the number of 401(k) plans they serve, have, as indicated, changed substantially over the past 15 years, as shown in Table 7.10.

TABLE 7.9   Investment Options

	1994	1995	1996	1997	1998
Equity Investment Options					
Company stock	57%	59%	55%	57%	55%
Actively managed common stock	74	77	76	84	80
Common stock index fund	49	55	58	63	68
International equity fund	27	44	55	66	70
Real estate fund	2	2	1	1	1
Fixed-Income Options					
Guaranteed investment contracts	70%	63%	63%	43%	37%
Stable value fund	—	—	—	35	37
Money market fund	52	52	51	49	46
Intermediate bond fund	43	44	45	42	51
Long-term bond fund	14	12	13	16	15
Multiple Asset Class Options					
Balanced fund	62%	65%	66%	69%	67%
Life cycle fund	—	9	9	16	20
Self-Directed Account	3%	4%	3%	5%	6%

TABLE 7.10 Changes in 401(k) Investment Managers

1984	1999
The Equitable	Fidelity Investments
Metropolitan Life	Vanguard
Aetna Life & Casualty	Pacific Investment Management
The Travelers	T. Rowe Price
Fidelity Investments	Putnam Investments
Vanguard	State Street Global Advisors
John Hancock	Templeton Investment Counsel
CIGNA Investments	Capital Guardian Trust
State Street Bank	Janus
Prudential Insurance	Morgan Stanley Dean Witter
Citibank	Barclays Global Investors
Investors Diversified Services	INVESCO
Putnam Funds	J.P. Morgan Investment
First Interstate Bank	American Express
T. Rowe Price	Franklin Templeton

Seven of the ten largest providers in 1984 were insurance companies. No insurance companies are still among the market leaders today.

The 401(k) managers also compete for share of the business that can be won from each customer. Competition for share of assets, within the funds of each customer, is an increasingly important part of the 401(k) business; so each manager is encouraged to offer a full range of investment products. (Providing postretirement investment services that will keep assets under management for a longer period of years is another way to add to the profit potential of each account.)

For employee communications, employers emphasize, as shown in Table 7.11, three major types of communication to plan participants:

- On-site plan enrollment.
- Preretirement investment counseling.
- Continuous information and education.

However, as important as is voice-response telephone systems in selecting a new service provider, only 5 percent of the 401(k) plans now use them (see Table 7.12).

Getting "behind the curve" on communications innovations is highly visible and competitively very dangerous.

TABLE 7.11   Communications Provider Selection Criteria—
Total Corporations

	2000
Usefulness of reports to participants	71
Voice-response telephone system	71
Plan and participant account information over the phone	71
Capable account manager	67
Ongoing investment education and plan information	66
On-site plan enrollment capabilities	51
Regular newsletters to employees	49
Availability of services via the Internet	49

In participant record keeping, corporations have high expectations, based on their favorable experiences with present service providers. Corporate executives rate six selection criteria in Table 7.13 between "important" and "most important."

The important consequence is that hiring new participant record keepers has declined to a low level over the past five years, as documented in our research (see Table 7.14).

In the past 15 years, mutual funds have virtually overwhelmed banks and insurance companies as providers of record-keeping services. Back in 1984, our research documented that mutual fund organizations were, as a group, far behind the leading providers of record-keeping services. With nearly one third of the corporations—and 46 percent of the 100 largest—providing their own record keeping in-house or using actuaries, the three principal generic types of competitors were as shown in Table 7.15. Today, mutual funds clearly dominate.

TABLE 7.12   Communications Services Currently Offered

	1998
On-site enrollment capabilities	48%
Employee counseling available upon retirement	37
Ongoing investment education and plan information	23
Regular newsletters to employees	21
Custom-tailored reports to participants	9
Plan and participant account information over the phone	8
Voice-response telephone system	5

TABLE 7.13　Record-Keeper Selection Criteria

1998	
Low error rates on transactions	84
Prompt and accurate reports to participants	82
Prompt and accurate reports to plan sponsors	80
Quick correction of errors	79
Prompt and accurate calculation of loans or withdrawals	70
Capable administrative manager	69

Here are the leading participant record keepers. Note that the leading actuaries have experienced substantial losses in competitive position.

Fidelity Investments	Putnam Investments
Vanguard	State Street Global Advisors
Hewitt Associates	American Express
T. Rowe Price	PricewaterhouseCoopers
Merrill Lynch	Northern Trust

During the past 15 years, the mantle of market leadership has shifted substantially, away from the banks and insurance companies that then had the preeminent position and over to the mutual fund managers who dominate today.

The 401(k) revolution has revolutionized the Defined Contribution business—converting that market into a service-intensive business centered on daily reporting to beneficiaries[4] with participant direction of investments and numerous investment options or alternatives, and shifting most

TABLE 7.14　Hiring of Record Keepers

	Total Funds	Funds over $5 Billion
1994	15%	21%
1995	13	6
1996	9	8
1997	6	4
1998	3	2
1999	5	13

TABLE 7.15   Record-Keeping Providers

	1984	1999	Change
Mutual funds	13%	53%	40
Banks	48	7	−41
Internal/Actuaries	31	21	−10
Insurance companies	19	5	−14

of the assets away from insurance companies and banks over to mutual funds. Also, the 401(k) revolution is moving DC retirement plans ahead of DB retirement plans in total assets and causing an important consolidation of retirement asset management toward those investment managers who are systems and service proficient. And this part of the 401(k) revolution is by no means over.

CHAPTER 8

Institutional Investment Management in the Rest of the World

Rodger F. Smith, Berndt Perl, Lea B. Hansen, Peter Lee,
Glenn Wealands, Devereaux A. Clifford, and Charles D. Ellis

The Pension Market in the United Kingdom

Pension funds are one of the crown jewels in Britain. The mighty growth that has taken place in funded pension schemes over the past half century has created a treasure chest of capital that is not found in many countries across the globe.

In the upscale pension market covered by Greenwich Associates, total pension assets have quadrupled over the past dozen years to £600 billion currently. The British pension market has benefited greatly from balanced managers who moved aggressively to equities in the early 1980s, which fueled significant asset growth and created a fully funded pension system with a solvency ratio of 112 percent currently. But the market is changing in fundamental structural ways that promise to have a profound impact on the management of these growth assets.

Rodger F. Smith wrote "The Pension Market in the United Kingdom," Berndt Perl wrote "Institutional Investing in Europe," Lea B. Hansen wrote "Institutional Investmeant Management in Canada," Peter Lee and Glenn Wealands wrote "Australian Superannuation Funds," and Deveraux A. Clifford and Charles D. Ellis wrote "Japanese Institutional Investing."

TABLE 8.1 Client Share

1988	2000
Mercury Warburg	Merrill Lynch Investment Managers
Phillips & Drew	Schroder Investment Management
Robert Fleming	Legal & General
Schroder Investment Management	Deutsche Asset Management
Henderson	Phillips & Drew
County NatWest	Barclays Global Investors
Baring Investment Management	Capital International
Barclays de Zoete Wedd	Fidelity
Morgan Grenfell	Henderson Investors (AMP)
MIM	Gartmore
Legal & General	Baring Asset Management
Gartmore Pension Fund Managers	J.P. Morgan
Prudential Portfolio Managers	PPM Worldwide (Prudential)

A dramatic shift has taken place in the share of clients of the leading investment managers in Britain over the past dozen years, as shown in Table 8.1.

Asset allocation decisions benefited the growth of pension assets, as balanced funds adopted an above-average commitment to equities relative to other pension markets. When most other markets were below 50 percent in equities, British pension funds were already 70 percent invested in equities in 1989. Over a 10-year period, asset mix shifted to overseas equities and fixed income and away from property and U.K. equities, as shown in Table 8.2.

TABLE 8.2 Asset Allocation

Asset Class	1989	1999	Change
U.K. equity	55%	49%	−6
Overseas equity	16	24	8
Total Equity	71%	73%	2
Fixed income	13%	19%	6
Property	11	4	−7
Cash and other	5	4	−1
Total	100%	100%	—

FORCES DRIVING CHANGE

Many different forces have—and are—driving change dynamics in the pension market in Britain. These changes run to the very soul of the business and are causing investment managers to change their structures and their strategies significantly. We have been advising clients all along to listen to the "voice of the market" and build strategies around this market information and competitive intelligence.

Poor Performance

The poor performance by the leading balanced managers, particularly four of the "Big 5" over the past several years, has led to significant erosion in the dominance of the former "Big 5." Performance is the ultimate bottom line arbiter of an investment manager's success. Without good performance over a 3- to 5-year period, clients will leave. During the decade of the 1990s, firms like Robert Fleming suffered greatly and fell from the Top 10. In the mid-1990s, Gartmore suffered a bout of poor results, which cut short their brief tenure among the Big 5. More recently, Phillips & Drew, Schroder, and even Merrill Lynch Investment Managers (formerly Mercury) have lost client share. Only Deutsche Asset Management (formerly Morgan Grenfell) has gone against the tide, sustained good performance, and captured more balanced business.

Availability of Data

Greater availability of performance data—and the attribution of sources of value added—has raised standards. Coupled with poor performance of the leading balanced managers was an explosion in the availability of performance data and methods to dissect the results by portfolio characteristic, by style, and by the attribution of performance to a manager's sources of value added. These new tools gave consultants and their clients new and powerful insights into their managers. Not only could they see how their money was being managed, but also how effectively the strategy used was adding value.

We recommend embracing these new tools and using them to better understand the results before the clients and their consultants get too far out in front. Interestingly, managers find these new tools often lead to introspection about their current philosophy and process which, in turn, leads to enhancements that bring both greater value added and greater consistency. This produces the classic win-win for managers and clients alike.

New Client Criteria

Clients increasingly seek managers with greater integrity of their products and an emphasis on philosophy and performance. We advise our clients in Britain to move from the traditional second-generation investment platform over to the best-of-class model developed by most U.S. managers over a journey that has taken 15 or more years to achieve in the highly competitive U.S. market. This best-of-class model has three parts.

First, there is a clear and concise statement of *what* the manager will do with the clients' money. This begins with the manager stating the firm's fundamental beliefs about how value can be added and following this with the specific aspects of the philosophy used to take advantage of these value-adding opportunities. Second, a well-defined and transparent decision-making process describes *how* client portfolios are managed to implement the philosophy. And third, the model specifies a team of talented and dedicated investment professionals who will manage the money.

In the best-of-class model, a relatively small number of experienced and talented people make the key decisions. This is in sharp contrast to the old model where a growing number of junior fund managers select individual securities for clients. This structure failed because the best fund managers were often promoted to management. The multiplicity of managers also created dispersion of performance that clients did not want.

The Shift from Results to Process

A shift in manager selection decisions from a dominant focus on performance results and fund managers to greater relative emphasis on investment philosophy and decision-making process has taken place (see Table 8.3).

TABLE 8.3   Selection Criteria

Factor	1990	2000	Two-Year Change
Performance results	66	75	9
Capability of fund manager	64	70	6
Clear and consistent investment philosophy	44	69	25
Clearly defined decision-making process	42	66	24
Understand each client's goals and objectives	46	46	—
Low fees	19	30	11

Note: Average of scale ratings, "Most Important" or $5 = 100$, $4 = 50$, $3 = 25$, $2 = 12.5$, "Least Important" or $1 = 0$.

The shift in the criteria pension schemes use to select managers is in harmony with what has taken place in the U.S. market where what is called the "four Ps" dominate selection decisions (investment philosophy, decision-making process, portfolio managers, and performance results). We recommend that managers listen to the voice of the market when designing their structures and their sales presentations.

A Shift in the Selection Process

A subtle, but important shift has taken place in the dominant role consultants traditionally played in selecting new managers over to the plan of sponsors taking a more active role and showing willingness to meet with prospective managers to broaden their horizon and their knowledge. Traditionally, consultants dominated the selection process as trustees had little knowledge and not much interest in the often subtle aspects of investment management. But the need for change grew as assets expanded, legislation changed the governing rules, and current managers failed to meet performance targets.

At the same time, American managers began coming to Britain. Not finding the welcome mat out from consultants, some managers began calling directly on pension schemes as they did in the United States and found a receptiveness by some but not by all schemes. The combination of a need spawned by poor performance and greater availability of information to manage investments has led to a subtle but important shift in how plan sponsors use consultants and the role they play in manager searches and monitoring decisions. We recommend to clients that they acknowledge this shift and plan resource allocation decisions accordingly.

The Move toward Specialty Managers

Over a two-year period, there has been a rapid and important move away from balanced managers and toward specialty managers in the implementation of investment decisions (see Table 8.4).

TABLE 8.4 Change in Managers Used

Type of Manager	1998	1999	2000	Two-Year Change
Balanced manager	72%	70%	62%	−10
Specialty manager	40	59	64	24

The use of specialty managers jumped more than 50 percent between 1998 and 2000—from 40 percent to 64 percent—while the use of balanced managers has eroded. This is a seismic change of a magnitude that is unprecedented without a legislated driver in the nearly 30 years Greenwich Associates has conducted research on the upscale pension market.

The new style specialty model is focused initially on the core asset classes (U.K. equities, overseas equities, and fixed interest). As clients and consultants become more comfortable with these strategies, the market will likely evolve into even more specialized asset classes. We advise our clients to capitalize on core specialty product demand near term, but develop specialized capabilities now along geographic (Pan-Europe, United States, and the Far East), market cap (large cap or small cap), and style-specific (growth and value) dimensions. In the classic military model, managers need to shoot ahead of the plane so they will be there when the market arrives.

Indexation

One result has been significant growth in indexation. With more clients moving to the specialty model and seeking higher and more consistent returns, a growing number of funds have chosen to anchor their portfolios using passive or index funds. Our research shows the proportion of large pension schemes that index a portion of their domestic equity portfolios has increased from 27 percent in 1990 to 33 percent in 1999. At the same time, the share of assets indexed has expanded more rapidly—from 16 percent in 1990 to 28 percent in 1999.

Indexation is also catching on in fixed-interest investing, where the dearth of credit-related securities leaves managers with only "duration" and "yield-curve" strategies to add value. At present, 23 percent of the largest funds index their domestic fixed interest portfolio and, on average, invest 30 percent of their domestic fixed interest securities in a passive manner, as shown in Table 8.5.

TABLE 8.5   Passive Investments

	1990	1999
Domestic Equities		
Percentage of users	27%	33%
Share of assets	16	28
Domestic Fixed Interest		
Percentage of users	na	23%
Share of assets	na	30

Active managers should see passive as a viable alternative and focus on providing active products that will add value over and above passive alternatives.

The emergence of passive investing has brought highly concentrated competition for this business. Two local competitors currently dominate the business. Barclays de Zoete Wedd has transformed itself, first by moving into the passive business in Britain and then by acquiring the largest U.S. competitor and rebranding the firm as Barclays Global Investors. The resulting global firm has a strong franchise in the U.S. market, where the passive business was born and global standards are set.

Legal & General moved into the passive business primarily on a defensive basis in response to poor active performance. While primarily a domestic firm at present, they have grown rapidly and have challenged Barclays Global Investors for leadership in Britain. Both of these firms compete aggressively on the key success factors of low tracking error, flexibility to add or withdraw from the portfolio, a broad line of passive products, and low fees.

State Street Global Advisors leads the second tier of competitors, with an emphasis on international products, along with Gartmore and Phillips & Drew. Gartmore inherited the NatWest business when they were acquired by NatWest (Gartmore was recently acquired by Nationwide Insurance Company in the United States), while Phillips & Drew developed this business first to meet client needs and more recently to defend against client losses. Deutsche Asset Management and Merrill Lynch Investment Managers are standing in the wings; they have passive businesses of meaningful size in the United States but little in Britain at present.

We recommend to clients that they listen to the market as they build this scale business and develop client-centric strategies to broaden "share of wallet" using other products once passive clients are bedded down.

The Effect of Low Fees

Low fees have been harmful to the domestic industry. Management fees in Britain have traditionally been low. This was fine in an oligopoly situation, but even then the revenues generated were inadequate for use in the investment and business "factories."

The investment factory typically attracted greater support, but even here the emphasis was on quantity of fund managers more than on their quality and with little interest in building an internal research group to identify companies directly for investment.

On the business front, client service resources were undernourished and sales resources virtually nonexistent. We recommend that clients charge a fee that is consistent with expected value added and will provide the revenue stream needed to invest sufficient resources so they can make both the investment and business factories stronger, and equal in stature and importance.

Management fees have also changed structurally in Britain over from the broker approach in the 1980s of "we charge no fee" (but realize significant hidden brokerage commission revenues) over to a "clean fee" structure, as shown in Table 8.6. At the same time, fees are beginning to rise as specialty managers emphasize "less is more" and traditional managers raise fees under the umbrella of American competitors to provide needed service, sales, and infrastructure to meet client needs.

The Shifting Business Model

The business model is shifting, as managers respond to the need to bolster staff and add client service and marketing professionals. Without adequate fees, managers made too modest investments in such business aspects of investment management as client service platforms and new business-gathering resources. British managers were vulnerable on two accounts. First, client retention rates were lower because clients often came in when performance was unusually high and left after relatively short periods of underperformance. We advise clients to develop a strong team of client service professionals who can "walk the talk" of fund managers to keep clients happy and keep fund managers doing what they do best: manage money.

Second, new business "close ratios" were more volatile because prospects had their heads turned by managers with the hottest numbers and the best presentations. When performance tailed off relative to the manager with the current "hot hand," the close ratio at beauty parades typically dropped like a rock.

We recommend developing a team of sales professionals to develop relationships with pension schemes well before the transaction. This investment not only ensures that pension funds know more about the managers up front, but also increases the win ratio when performance is second

TABLE 8.6   Average Clean Fees Paid

Fees	1990	1996	2000	Ten-Year Change
All managers	19.5	21.2	23.3	3.8
Balanced managers	17.9	20.6	23.9	6.0

quartile and brings with it longer retention rates by the client. This is a win-win on both fronts.

The American managers have understood this and are beginning to change the British managers, but changes are coming slowly.

A Structural Shift toward Defined Contribution Plans

An early stage structural shift toward defined contribution plans and away from traditional final salary schemes is gaining momentum. Defined Contribution plans are catching a wave globally. In the U.S. market, nearly all of the largest companies now have a DC plan. In contrast, use of defined benefit (DB) plans has fallen to under 90 percent.

In Britain, DC plans are a relatively recent phenomenon. But our research shows the proportion of funds that use DC plans jumped 30 percent in 1999 (from 26% to 34%) and is expected to rise another 25 percent over the next several years, when 45 percent of the companies are expected to have a DC plan (see Table 8.7).

Technological Communications

A significant jump in technological communications is expected over the next several years as use of the Internet spreads.

The Internet promises to revolutionize many businesses, including the investment management business. The first step is getting connected to the Internet. In Britain, the number of large pension schemes that now have access has doubled in the past two years, from 38 percent to 77 percent, as shown in Table 8.8. More than 90 percent of pension schemes expect to have access to the Internet in the next year or two.

TABLE 8.7 Use of Defined Contribution Plans

Factor	1998	1999	2000	Two-Year Change
Now use DC plan	24%	26%	34%	10
Expect to add DC plan	12	14	15	3
Total demand	34	36	45	11

Note: Totals do not add as some funds expect to add a different type of DC plan.

TABLE 5.8 Use of Internet

Factor	1998	1999	2000	Two-Year Change
Now have access	38%	58%	77%	39
Expect to have access	36	30	14	−22
Total access	74	88	91	17

Note: Total access is based on current and expected Internet access.

We advise clients to move quickly to incorporate technology into their client service paradigm and stay ahead of their clients—and the competition—on this new and potentially powerful change factor.

CONCLUSION

Pension funds are one of Britain's crown jewels. Pension assets have mushroomed in recent decades and provide a substantial capital base to pay future retirement benefits and fuel continued economic growth. But the business of investment management is changing structurally in all areas of investment management and business management. The best-of-class firms of the future will be different. They will model some aspects of their business to reflect the learning by American firms in the highly competitive United States and engineer others to meet the changing and evolving market in Britain on its own terms. An important key to success will be to listen to the voice of the market.

Institutional Investing in Europe

The business of managing institutional assets on the European continent has both intriguing opportunities and considerable challenges for investment managers. Start with the obvious good news/bad news reality about institutional assets: The good news is that institutional assets are large and growing; the bad news is that the great majority are not available to managers because they are being managed *internally*. More than three quarters of the assets of large institutional funds in continental Europe are managed internally. Among very large funds (over 2.5 billion), the proportion managed internally is 80 percent. While internal management is expected to decline, the pace is expected to be quite gradual, going from 80 percent today to 74 percent over the next two years.

TABLE 8.9   Share of Assets Managed Internally

	1998	1999
Type of Institution		
Pension Funds	73%	70%
Corporate	60	57
Public/Industry	78	75
Corporate Treasury Funds	63	55
Foundations	81	55
Insurance	86	85
Other	72	91
Institutional Assets		
Over 2.5 billion	79%	80%
501–2,500 million	53	48
251–500 million	38	36
125–250 million	24	22
Under 125 million	31	13
Geographic Area		
The Netherlands	80%	76%
Switzerland	59	63
France	75	74
Germany	73	64
Belgium	12	4
Denmark	82	82
Norway	73	83
Finland	90	91
Sweden	74	76
Spain	85	79
Italy	73	96
Total Institutions	76%	76%

As shown in Table 8.9, internal management increases strongly with asset size. But with the clear exceptions of Belgium on the low side and Italy and Finland on the high side, internal management does not differ substantially from country to country.

In Germany, where spezialfonds account for nearly 90 percent of the institutional asset management business, funds *tripled* in four years.

The leading investment managers—when all of continental Europe is taken as a whole and when domestic clients in each country are not included—are primarily "non-Continental" firms, as shown in the following list, which is ordered by number of large institutional clients served:

J.P. Morgan Investment	ABN AMRO Asset Management
Schroders	Fortis Investments
Barclays Global Investors	UBS Asset Management
Fidelity	Morgan Stanley Dean Witter
State Street Global Advisors	Credit Suisse Asset Management
Capital International	Deutsche Asset Management
INVESCO	Alfred Berg Asset Management
Merrill Lynch Mercury	

The striking overall reality that the pan-European market leaders are not Continentals reflects several important underlying factors:

- Most Continental nations have few, if any, world-class investment organizations, and most large funds are managed *internally*. External investment management services are in limited supply—and limited demand.
- Most external managers are chosen only as "specialists" in specific types of investing, which tends to favor large international organizations with a wide range of specific skills that national organizations are less likely to have developed.
- Most Continental investment management organizations concentrate their business development efforts within their home countries where they have language, cultural, regulatory, and proximity advantages.
- British and American investment managers are accustomed to building their business with funds in other countries and are practiced in new business development. They are committed activists.

These lists show the primacy of home-country managers. The leading investment managers in six countries are listed in order of the number of clients served:

Germany	**Nordic Countries**
Commerzinvest	Alfred Berg Asset Management
dbi	Unibank Portfolio Management
Allfonds-BKG	Carnegie Asset Management
Deutsche Asset Management	SE Banken
DIM	Schroders
INKA HSBC/TCM	Indocam Asset Management
WestKA	Danske Capital Management
Oppenheim KAG	
Frankfurt Trust	
Metzler Investment	

Spain

BBV Asset Management
BSCH Gestion
Merrill Lynch
Argentaria Asset Management
BNP Paribas

France

BNP Paribas
Indocam Asset Management
SG Asset Management
CDC Asset Management
Credit Lyonnais Asset Management
CCF Capital Management
Lazard Asset Management
Fortis Investments

Natexis Banque Populaires
Robeco

Switzerland

Pictet Asset Management
UBS Asset Management
Credit Suisse Asset Management
Julius Baer Asset Management
Lombard Odier & Cie

Belgium

Fortis Investments
Banque Degroof SCS
State Street Global Advisors
Barclays Global Investors
Fidelity Investments

The typical large Continental fund has 13 investment managers soliciting its business. Funds in Finland average over 21 managers soliciting; funds in Italy, only 8, as shown in Table 8.10. Solicitations also vary with fund size.

New managers are hired each year by more than 40 percent of the funds, as shown in Table 8.11. Our research also shows that hiring activity is highest in the Netherlands and Switzerland, and lowest in Italy.

TABLE 8.10 Number of Investment Managers Soliciting

	1999	2000
The Netherlands	6.0	11.3
Switzerland	10.3	10.8
France	13.5	15.6
Germany	10.4	10.3
Belgium	9.4	16.8
Denmark	15.6	13.5
Norway	11.7	10.4
Finland	21.9	21.1
Sweden	18.1	17.6
Spain	7.0	9.9
Italy	8.5	8.3
Total Institutions	11.5	13.0

TABLE 8.11   Demand for New Managers

	Hired New Manager	
	1999	2000
The Netherlands	49%	55%
Switzerland	60	55
France	50	40
Germany	51	49
Belgium	31	40
Denmark	50	47
Norway	50	36
Finland	53	31
Sweden	53	42
Spain	22	35
Italy	21	8
Total Institutions	47%	42%

Specialty investment management is rapidly displacing balanced investment management: 55 percent of total assets are currently being managed by specialists, but 88 percent of new manager hiring is of specialty managers. We recommend to our clients that they focus on specific aspects of investment management—or products—in their business development strategies, because that is the way the market is moving.

The countries most strongly committed to using specialists are Germany, France, Belgium, and Switzerland, as shown in Table 8.12.

The most important criteria for choosing new investment managers are "globally familiar," particularly these first four:

1. Clear and consistent investment philosophy.
2. Capabilities of the professional manager.
3. Ability to achieve superior investment performance.
4. Clear decision-making process.

Low fees are given more importance in European countries than elsewhere. (In Germany, visible "fees" are very low, because managers are paid through such indirect means as custody fees and commissions on securities transactions. Fees in Germany are rising and becoming "cleaner.") We recommend to our clients that this means they have yet another reason for centering their business development strategies in those specialized investment products the Continental institutions will want *and* will be prepared to pay for, as shown in Table 8.13.

TABLE 8.12 Percentage of Externally Managed Assets Invested with Specialty Managers

	Proportion of Funds with Assets Managed by External Managers**	Proportion of "External" Assets Now Managed by Specialty Managers*	Proportion Expected to Be Managed by Specialty Managers in Three Years*
The Netherlands	17%	53%	58%
Switzerland	34	97	98
France	56	82	81
Germany	66	86	87
Belgium	46	75	77
Denmark	15	87	87
Norway	3	100	100
Finland	6	76	76
Sweden	9	61	54
Spain	11	70	70
Italy	2	100	84
Total Institutions	20%	80%	80%

* Based on funds using specialty managers.
** Euro weighted.

TABLE 8.13 Investment Manager Selection Criteria

Selection Criteria	Importance
Clarity and consistency of investment philosophy or concept of investing	72
Clarity of investment decision-making process	61
Capabilities of the professional managing your investments	66
Ability to achieve superior future performance over the next 3–5 years	63
Commitment to client service	49
Credibility with your investment committee or trustees	44
Investment performance over the past 2–3 years	46
Understanding of your organization's particular goals and objectives	47
Low fees	35
Ability to advise on overall investment strategy and policy	31

Note: Average of scale ratings, "Most Important" or 5 = 100, 4 = 50, 3 = 25, 2 = 12.5, "Least Important" or 1 = 0.

Our research documents that Continental institutions are less likely to use investment consultants than are comparably sizable institutions in other major markets. Investment consultants—firms that advise on the selection of investment managers and monitor their performance—are used by only 32 percent of the large institutions on the Continent. In Germany, use of investment consultants has increased from 4 percent of the funds in 1996 to 21 percent today. This means it would be difficult to build a major business with a dependence on the "consultant channel" for gaining access to investment manager "selection finals."

The use of investment consultants—which, unlike our experience in other markets, does not increase with asset size—differs substantially from country to country. Consultants are used most widely in Belgium, Sweden, and Switzerland, and are least used in France and Italy. Here is the use of consultants by country:

The Netherlands	38%
Switzerland	50%
France	7%
Germany	31%
Belgium	67%
Denmark	12%
Norway	21%
Finland	31%
Sweden	58%
Spain	39%
Italy	8%
Total Institutions	32%

Here are the leading investment consultants on the Continent as documented in our research:

William M. Mercer	KPMG (Actuarissen/Brans)
Towers Perrin	PPG Metrics AG
Watson Wyatt	Ortec Consultants
Frank Russell	Pragma Consulting
Wassum Investment Network	Consultores de Pensiones BBV
Arthur Anderson	

Looking ahead, there is a good reason to expect a transformation in European retirement plans toward a Defined Contribution structure, because the people of Europe will need funding for the retirement benefits they have come to expect as part of their "social contract." But this retirement funding will be difficult for governments to fund, because the taxation required to finance the system on a national basis would likely be politically unacceptable.

If so, it will probably be privatized, as in Australia and Peru, where to make privatization politically acceptable, retirement funds are accumulated in the names of, or for the benefit of, specific individuals.

Finding the right structural arrangement for European retirement funding will be important for employees, employers—and investment managers.

Institutional Investment Management in Canada

The Canadian institutional investment management business has many familiar characteristics such as the key selection criteria for managers:

- Consistent investment philosophy.
- Clear decision-making process.
- Confidence in the firm's ability to achieve superior future investment performance.
- Capable investment professionals.

Key changes in Canada are changing the competitive landscape. In determining long-term strategic objectives, our clients need to anticipate or "lead" these market trends:

- Funds have turned to international assets (primarily U.S. and EAFE [Europe, Australia, Far East] equities) for diversification and for higher returns. While foreign property limitations have been relaxed slowly from 20 percent to 25 percent and 30 percent by 2001, institutions have used derivatives to increase their exposures to international investments. Therefore, building strong international investment capabilities is increasingly a priority for Canadian domestic investment managers—through internal development, an acquisition, being acquired, or a joint venture with a global investment manager.
- Foreign firms, which historically have offered only international investments, are now entering the domestic investment management business, a natural extension of their international offerings. This trend presents even greater competition for the Canadian managers in their home market.
- International investment managers have been servicing their clients in Canada with the level of service and resources offered in their home

market. With well-honed skills from the intense competition in their home market, these foreign managers present formidable competition to the Canada-based managers.

■ Passive investing has proven to be a highly successful alternative in equities and bonds for Canadian plan sponsors. Currently, 22 percent of domestic equity assets are passively managed, up from 15 percent five years ago, and 17 percent of domestic bonds are currently passively managed, up from 2 percent five years ago.

■ Plan sponsors in Canada are shifting from balanced mandates toward specialty mandates—led in part by the increase in international equity exposure: 85 percent of plan sponsors use specialty mandates versus 62 percent five years ago (while 53 percent use balanced mandates versus 68 percent five years ago). The move to specialty mandates provides the potential for large multiproduct firms to develop strong specialty investing skills and offer strong investment counseling skills that integrate their specialty products into a strong overall proposition.

■ The growth in the use of Defined Contribution plans has been rapid, with 50 percent of the plan sponsors now using DC plans—up from 35 percent just five years ago. While DC assets are currently only 4 percent of total pension assets, they are expected to surpass 50 percent of assets in 10 years for those plan sponsors that use DC plans.

In addition to these market forces, individual fund executives are actively seeking to develop the optimal portfolio structures for their funds and to solicit investment managers.

Investment consultants are used in 70 percent of the investment management searches in Canada. Based on number of clients, the leading investment consultants are:

William M. Mercer	James P. Marshall
Towers Perrin	Brockhouse & Cooper
SEI Financial Services	Watson Wyatt Worldwide
Frank Russell Canada	COMSTAT Capital Sciences
Aon Consulting	Buck Consultants

We recommend developing a "two channel" strategy in new business development, coordinating direct selling with work with investment consultants—so both channels are complementary and mutually reinforcing.

Over the past 10 years, the leaders in domestic Canadian investment management have changed significantly, as shown in Table 8.14.

For international investing—including U.S. and EAFE mandates—most of the managers are foreign. However, there has been a major shift from

TABLE 8.14 Domestic Investment Managers

1991	2000
Jarislowsky, Fraser	RT Capital Management
Beutel Goodman	Phillips, Hager & North
TAL Investment Counsel	Barclays Global Investors
Knight, Bain, Seath & Holbrook	TD Quantitative
Gryphon Investment Counsel	Connor, Clark & Lunn
Phillips, Hager & North	TAL Investment Counsel
Sceptre Investment Counsel	Knight, Bain, Seath & Holbrook
Confederation Investment Counseling	Jarislowsky, Fraser
Canada Life	Sceptre Investment Counsel
Great-West Life Assurance	Perigee Investment Counsel
Mu-cana Investment Counsel	Beutel, Goodman
Barclays McConnell	Newcastle Capital Management
Sun Life of Canada	Guardian Capital
Corporate Investment Associates	McLean Budden
Baring	State Street Global Advisors

Note: Perigee is the combination of Mucana and MT Associates. Sun Life now has a major shareholding in McLean Budden. Corporate Investment Associates became RT Capital Management.

TABLE 8.15 International Investment Managers

1991	2000
Fleming Canada Partners	Templeton Management
Baring International	Sprucegrove*
Globe Finlay (MT Associates)	Brinson Partners
State Street Bank & Trust	Capital Guardian Trust
Confederation Investment Counselling*	Putnam Investments
Wells Fargo Investment Advisors	Brandes Investment Partners
Barclays McConnell	Morgan Stanley Dean Witter
HD International	Scudder Kemper
Templeton Investment	State Street Global Advisors
Alliance Capital	Baring Asset Management
Gartmore (McLean Budden)	J.P. Morgan
J.P. Morgan Investment	Sanford C. Bernstein
Batterymarch	Schroder Investment Management
BT Investment Management	Fleming Asset Management
Lazard Freres Asset Management	Jarislowsky, Fraser

* Confederation Investment Counselling became Sprucegrove.

British to American managers. Whereas U.K.-based managers dominated 10 years ago, now U.S.-based managers dominate, as shown in Table 8.15 on page 287.

Australian Superannuation Funds

Growth is the dominating characteristic of retirement fund assets in Australia. With an expected 1999 to 2002 increase in assets from A$145 billion to A$220 billion, fund executives expect assets to increase by over 50 percent for the period, or at an annual rate of nearly 15 percent.

While 35 percent of the superannuation funds—and 61 percent of the funds with assets greater than A$500 million—manage at least part of their fund assets internally, the opportunities for investment managers—both Australian managers and international managers—are attractive.[1]

The mandates for which investment managers are now most frequently used are:

- Domestic equities.
- Domestic bonds.
- Foreign equities.
- Real estate.

The mandates for which new managers are most frequently being hired are:

- Domestic equities.
- Real estate.
- Foreign equities.
- Domestic bonds.
- International bonds.

The distribution of investments—dollar weighted—for Australia's superannuation funds is shown in Table 8.16.

If present expectations are fulfilled, three types of investments will be increased:

1. International equities.
2. Domestic equities.
3. Passive equities.

TABLE 8.16   Asset Mix of Funds

	Percentage of Assets
Domestic equities—active	25%
Domestic equities—passive	7
Domestic bonds	15
Indexed/infrastructure bonds	4
International bonds	4
Private equity/development capital	2
International equities—active	14
International equities—passive	6
Emerging markets	1
Direct property	7
Listed property trusts	4
Cash/short-term investments	10
TAA overlay	2
Currency overlay	4

Australia's leading investment managers for superannuation schemes—in order of the number of clients served among the 300 largest funds—are as follows:

AMP Asset Management
Bankers Trust
Maple-Brown Abbott
Credit Suisse Asset Management
Lend Lease Investment Management
County Investment Management
SSB Citi Asset Management
Lazard Asset Management
Macquarie Investment Management
Portfolio Partners

First State Fund Managers
State Street Global Advisors
Mercantile Mutual
Merrill Lynch Mercury
Schroders Investment Management
UBS Brinson
HSBC Asset Management
National Mutual (AXA Australia)
Barclays Global Investors
Rothschild Asset Management

Note that behind the totals, different managers lead in different types of mandates:

■ Maple-Brown Abbott is the leader in *domestic* equities.
■ Lazard Asset Management leads in *international* equities.

TABLE 8.17   Hiring and Firing Patterns

Year	Hired	Fired
1996	60%	51%
1997	54	40
1998	68	55
1999	61	54

- State Street Global Advisors leads in *passive management.*
- Bankers Trust (now Deutsche Bank) and Lend Lease Investment Management lead as *balanced* managers.
- AMP Asset Management and Bankers Trust (now Deutsche Bank) lead in *fixed income.*

Australian superannuation schemes are very active in hiring—and in firing—investment managers. Our research documents that, in a typical year, more than 60 percent of the funds hire one or more investment managers, and 50 percent fire a manager. Nearly three out of four times when a manager is terminated, another manager is substituted. Table 8.17 shows the pattern.

When selecting new investment managers, four criteria are most important to Australian fund executives:

1. Clear and consistent investment concept or philosophy.
2. Ability to achieve superior future investment performance.
3. Clearly defined investment decision-making process.
4. Capable fund manager.

Table 8.18 shows the importance given to 10 criteria.

Investment consultants are used by three out of four of the 300 largest superannuation funds in selecting investment managers. The investment consultants used most in Australia—with considerable concentration among the largest firms—are:

Mercer	Quentin Ayers
Towers Perrin	PricewaterhouseCoopers
John Nolan and Associates	Buck Consultants
Industry Fund Services	InTech
Frank Russell	Van Eyk Research
Watson Wyatt	

TABLE 8.18   Selection of Investment Managers

Criteria	Importance
Clear and consistent investment philosophy or concept of investing	76
Ability to achieve superior future performance over the next 3–5 years	74
Clearly defined investment decision-making process	71
Capabilities of fund manager managing your account	71
Credibility with investment committee or trustees	55
Commitment to client service	51
Understanding of client's objectives and risk tolerance	45
Investment performance over the past 2–3 years	41
Low fees	40
Ability to advise on overall investment strategy and policy	32

In addition to advising on new manager selection, investment consultants are also used for monitoring current managers' investment performance, developing investment policies and objectives, designing investment manager structures, and conducting asset-liability studies.

Good working relationships are important to fund executives, and to investment managers determined to keep the business they have. Fund executives emphasize the importance of three client service practices:

1. Contact when making important changes in the portfolio.
2. Quarterly reports discussing the management of the portfolios.
3. Contact when major events take place in the market.

As shown in Table 8.19, smaller funds do not expect personal contact by telephone calls or visits, unless there is a specific purpose to the call.

Fund executives are in frequent communication with their managers, their consultants, and their fund trustees. The typical fund executive:

- Meets personally with investment managers almost four times each year.
- Meets with consultants monthly.
- Meets with trustees on investment matters eight times a year.
- Reports on investment matters in writing to the trustees at least quarterly.

The superannuation market for investment management services in Australia, while geographically remote from other centers of investment

TABLE 8.19 Importance of Client Service Practices

Service Practices	Total Funds	Plan Assets Over $500 Million	$251–$500 Million	$100–$250 Million	Under $100 Million
Contact when making important changes in portfolio	66	67	76	64	61
Quarterly letter discussing management of the portfolio	60	58	62	59	63
Contact when major events take place in the market	54	66	52	48	52
Personal access to portfolio manager	48	65	38	41	47
Personal meetings at fund offices	39	52	39	33	33
Regular telephone contact	37	45	34	33	36
Personal meetings at managers' offices	29	48	23	22	23
Seminars or conferences	20	19	16	22	22

Note: Average point score, with 100 for "Essential," 50 for "Very Important," 12.5 for "Somewhat Important," and 0 for "Unimportant."

professionalism, is committed to achieving Global Standard "best practices" in relationship management and in investment management.

Japanese Institutional Investing

The Japanese market for institutional investment management has for many years been characterized as being very large in assets and low on fees, dominated by a complex web of tightly woven reciprocal relationships, controlled by a cartel of large domestic institutional managers, and quite effectively closed to outside competitors.

This rigid structure—and the pension world it once controlled—are in a turbulent period of rapid change, as deregulation opens the Japanese market up to investment managers from other nations and to the Global Standard for investment management.

The Japanese market for institutional investment management services is going through two profound transformations at the same time—one on the supply side and one on the demand side. On the demand side, fund executives and their organizations are becoming more and more sophisticated, which means they are expecting and demanding more and more of their investment managers. So the pressure is increasing for all investment managers from both their clients and their competitors. And these pressures are virtually certain to increase in the years ahead.

The basis for competitive strength has been shifting and will continue to shift toward high value-added services in both investment management and relationship management—and away from historical relationships and low fees. For those investment managers who are most able to compete on *value,* this change in client priorities will be quite favorable.

The change forces at work in Japan are powerful, and they will gain strength and force over the next several years, as modern investment managers make contact with the large, increasingly sophisticated institutions of Japan and the process of interactive, mutual education accelerates.

The 15 largest investment managers are all traditional Japanese organizations, as shown in the following list, which is ordered by number of large clients served.

Nippon Life Insurance	Sumitomo Life Insurance
Dai-ichi Life Insurance	DLIBJ Asset Management
Mitsubishi Trust & Banking	Meiji Mutual Life Insurance
Chuo-Mitsui Trust & Banking	Tokio Marine Asset Management
Daiwa Bank	Nissay Asset Management
Dai-ichi Kangyo Fuji Trust	Daiwa SB Investments
Sumitomo Trust	Meiji Dresdner Asset Management
Nomura Asset Management	Sanwa Asset Management
Toyo Trust & Banking	

However, the next 15 managers—and the next 15 after them—are *not* all Japanese. Some are European and some are North American.

Even more important, of the 10 large investment organizations that are most favorably evaluated by these clients in our annual research, only half are Japanese. The other half are international firms. While not always fully recognized, the Global Standard is clearly coming to Japan.

We urge our clients to evaluate and benchmark the effectiveness of their own organizations, both in investment management and in relationship management, against these best-practices competitors—not just the organizations that now have the most clients—because these will be challenging competitors in the future, too. (We remind initially skeptical clients of Peter Drucker's dictum: "You don't choose your competitors, they choose *you*!")

As shown in Table 8.20, Japanese pension funds have, quite consistently across different types and sizes of funds, an asset mix of:

- Equities—55%.
- Bonds—32%.
- General account of an insurance company—11%.

The recent deregulation of asset mix has only begun to filter through the Japanese pension market. However, it's important to recognize the importance of deregulation and "unfreezing" of institutional investments when estimating the way the market will change.

The client expectations in Japan are remarkably similar to the client expectations our research documents in each of the other major markets of the world. Here's how Japanese fund executives would evaluate prospective new investment managers.

The two most important criteria are:

1. Consistent investment philosophy.
2. Clear decision-making process.

Four additional selection criteria are also important:

3. Capabilities of the portfolio manager.
4. Understanding of each fund's goals and objectives.
5. Investment performance in recent years.
6. Credibility with the investment committee.

TABLE 8.20   Yen-Weighted Asset Mix

Type of Investment	Kosei Total Institutions	Kosei Nenkin (Rengo)	Kosei Nenkin (Sogo)	Nenkin (Tandoku)	TQPP
Bonds—Total	32%	32%	37%	28%	39%
Domestic bonds	22	20	30	20	31
International bonds	10	11	7	9	8
Equities—Total	55	55	57	53	50
Domestic equities	34	35	37	34	29
International equities	20	20	21	20	20
Insurance company general accounts	11	10	3	18	9
Cash and short term	2	2	2	1	1
Total	100%	100%	100%	100%	100%

Larger funds put more weight on the clarity of a manager's decision-making process, while small funds emphasize a manager's ability to advise on overall investment policy and strategy and the manager's credibility with the investment committee, as shown in Table 8.21.

There is a trend in Japan toward hiring specialist managers rather than balanced managers. The mix of specialists versus current managers is 50/50, but virtually 100 percent of the new manager hiring is of specialist investment managers.

A majority of Japanese institutions use the services of investment consultants when hiring new managers. Half of the leading consultants in the market are Japanese firms, and the other half are Japanese branches of international firms. Here is a list of the leading investment consultants:

Japan R & I	BARRA RogersCasey
Frank Russell	Nikko Research Institute
Watson Wyatt	Nomura Research Institute
William Mercer	KPMG
Daiwa Research Institute	Towers Perrin
Fuji Research Institute	

The shift to Defined Contribution plan structures, when it comes, could be yet another change-force in the structure of the Japanese pension market, and in the nature of the demand for investment management services. And this would increase the challenges and the opportunities for institutional investment managers in Japan.

TABLE 8.21   Investment Manager Selection Criteria

Selection Criteria	Total Institutions
Clarity and consistency of investment philosophy or concept of investing	79
Clarity of investment decision-making process	68
Capabilities of the professional managing investments	59
Understanding of organization's particular goals and objectives	58
Investment performance over the past 2–3 years	53
Credibility with investment committee or trustees	50
Ability to advise on overall investment strategy and policy	45
Low fees	43
Commitment to client service	42
Ability to achieve superior future performance over the next 3–5 years	38

Note: Average of scale ratings, "most important" or 5 = 100, 4 = 50, 3 = 25, 2 = 12.5, "least important" or 1 = 0.

CHAPTER 9

Master Trust

Peter B. Garrison and Devereaux A. Clifford

Master Trust has gone through a complete industry life cycle—from conception to cautious early acceptance, to wide acceptance, to maturity, and then into substantial forced competitive consolidation—in just two decades.

The situation in the 1970s was ripe with opportunity and pressure for change in what had long been a stable, sleepy, low-margin business: custody of stock and bond certificates in vault.

In the early 1970s, large pension funds often comprised more than three or four dozen different retirement plans as a result of past acquisitions by the sponsoring corporation. These plans might jointly use 10 or 20 different investment managers, each managing varying parts of each plan's fund—with differing cash inflows and outflows keeping each manager's account in almost continuous flux.

The sponsoring corporations needed to maintain simultaneous, accurate records of numerous funds served by many investment managers, a complex task that was becoming more difficult through acquisitions and the addition of still more investment managers. In addition, investment managers, competing for superior performance, were vigorously increasing portfolio turnover. (Turnover *tripled* over the two decades from 1971 to 1990.)

All these forces for increasing the complexity of pension fund custody were multiplying each other, and record keeping was increasing in complexity geometrically. Finally, more accurate and timely information was needed to meet new and stringent government reporting and to meet the increasing internal demand for useful management information.

With pension funds seeking superior investment performance and more and more funds shifting from banks to specialist investment managers who did not and could not provide custody, the custodial divisions of several major banks were motivated to compete separately for custody business, which had historically been "bundled" with investment management, and provided by the leading banks at very low all-in-one fees.

CHANGE-FORCES

The burgeoning need to keep accurate and up-to-date records created an opportunity to use the custodian banks' computer power to deliver a valuable service in exchange for both fees and demand deposit balances. The familiar process of product innovation and adoption soon spread across the market:

- Initial experimental services were offered in the mid-1970s by a few pioneering custodian banks, that perceived the opportunity to serve the complex needs of pension funds and develop a better business for themselves.
- By the late 1970s, several dozen banks with strong organizational histories in the custody business were declaring themselves to be in the new Master Trust business.
- As pension fund executives found Master Trust services a real help, more and more funds signed up for the convenient new service.
- As demand increased, so did supply, and a "virtuous cycle of growth" developed. Large expenditures on computer systems generated greater service value delivered to customers and justified higher fees to Master Trustees.
- In addition, the ability of computers to keep accurate and contemporary records of cash balances made it possible for the Master Trustees to sweep all available cash into interest-earning money market investment accounts. The incremental interest earned by most pension funds more than paid for the new service. (If "cash" averaged 10% of pension assets—and it usually did that and more—at 5% interest, the pension fund would "save" 0.5%, which was less than the fee charged for the Master Trust service.)
- By 1980, competition—encouraged by increasingly aggressive and sophisticated comparison shopping by customers—was starting to squeeze the weakest and least committed competitors out of the business. Banks that had too little volume to support large incremental investments in computer systems were obliged to drop out of the business.

To understand the consequences of the competitive dynamics being unleashed, a comparison of the leading competitors, over time, is helpful. Table 9.1 shows the market leaders in 1980 and in 1999.

TABLE 9.1 Leading Master Trustees—
Domestic Custody

1988	1999
Northern Trust	Northern Trust
Bankers Trust	State Street Bank
Mellon Bank	Mellon Trust
State Street Bank	Deutsche Bank
Chase Manhattan Bank	Bank of New York
First Wachovia	Chase Manhattan Bank
Harris Bank	Norwest Bank
Boston Safe Deposit	Fidelity Trust
Bank of New York	Citibank
Manufacturers Hanover	
Security Pacific Bank	

■ Over two decades, the drop-out rate was nearly one bank every year. Among the banks to drop out were:

Bank of America	Hartford National Bank
Boatman's Bank	J.P. Morgan
C & S National Bank	Manufacturers Hanover Trust
Connecticut Bank & Trust	NationsBank
Continental Illinois	Republic National Bank
First Atlanta Bank	Seattle First National Bank
First Chicago	Security Pacific
First National Bank of Denver	St. Louis Union Trust
First Pennsylvania	U.S. Trust
Harris Bank	United Bank of Denver

■ Complex new types of securities such as Commercial Mortgate Obligators (CMOs), Medium Term Notes (MTNs), convertibles, American Depository Receipts (ADRs), options, and other derivatives increased the need for sophisticated computer systems requiring large investments to develop the requisite capabilities.

■ As international investing by pension funds mushroomed, a new change came to the business and global custody became a more significant business. It changed the terms of competition at least somewhat in favor of those banks with global custodial facilities. And foreign exchange became a significant add-on business.

■ Major bond dealers wanted to borrow huge amounts of bonds they could "sell short" in the market to hedge their "long" positions so they could maintain, large, well-hedged inventories for trading with institutional investors. Master Trustees found they could put huge amounts of bonds and stocks "out on loan" to the dealers. As a result, securities lending—particularly the lending of bonds (and most particularly of U.S. government bonds), as well as equities, including international equities—became an important add-on business and again tilted the terms of competition in favor of those who did the most of it.

Table 9.2 shows the leading *international* custodians for U.S. funds in 1989 and 1999.

Large pension and endowment funds with securities held by Master Trustees were in a particularly attractive position to compete for this incrementally lucrative business. While the premiums paid are not large in percentage terms, the total money that can be earned is large, particularly relative to the cost of Master Trust services. Moreover, the lending can be managed so it is nearly risk free when the borrower fully collateralizes the borrowing with cash. Profitability depends on low cost or high efficiency, and on the volume of securities kept out on loan. (The amount kept out on loan is driven primarily by the speed and accuracy of service given to the borrowing dealers.)

Lending is a "big fund activity" because only the big funds have a sufficient range and volume of assets to be competitive sources of supply. As our research documents, over half of the funds with assets over $1 billion engage in lending securities, but almost none of those with assets under $100 million do any lending. The Master Trustee and the pension fund would divide the income earned from securities lending. Soon another dimension of competition developed into two parts: How much of a fund's assets would

TABLE 9.2   Leading Master Trustees—Global Custody

1989	1999
State Street Bank	Northern Trust
Northern Trust	State Street Bank
Chase Manhattan Bank	Mellon Trust
Boston Safe Deposit	Deutsche Bank
Mellon Bank	Chase Manhattan Bank
Mitsubishi Bank of California	Bank of New York
Morgan Guaranty	Fidelity Trust
The Bank of New York	Citibank
Citibank	

be successfully put out on loan, and how would the income from securities lending be split between the Master Trustee and the pension fund?

CONSOLIDATION

The Master Trust industry has been—and is still going through—a grinding process of consolidation, forcing one after another competitor to relent and to leave the market. In fact, over the 20 years of its existence, the total Master Trust industry may have experienced no profit, even an overall net loss, if the accounting were done rigorously for both the competitive winners and losers.

Master Trust, like every other information management business dependent on major information technology systems, is fundamentally a *scale* business. The *capital* invested effectively determines the speed, variety, and flexibility (or customization) in the *services* that can be delivered to customers at competitive costs and prices. From the customer's perspective, Master Trust is a service business and the value received by customers is a function of such familiar measures of service value as speed, accuracy, reliability, and convenience. Delivering these services requires massive capital investments in computer systems. The more capital invested in the right way, the more effectively the Master Trustee can compete on service value delivered.

To afford the massive investments in necessary systems, Master Trustees need to build great scale into their business by adding more customers than competitors can add. The continually increasing capital costs will then be spread over a larger base of customers than competitors will have allowing the Master Trustee to produce more service value at a lower average cost and to deliver this greater service value at a lower price.

For the banks that "got it right," a virtuous cycle would develop more customers served at a lower cost and charged lower prices, reducing the cost-to-value ratio. And this increase in delivered value would lead to more customers. These new customers (and the continuing customers) could be charged lower prices, attracting more customers who could be served at still lower cost. Around and around the virtuous cycle goes, getting better and better for both producer and consumer.

The commercial "Continental divide" that separated the competitive winners from the competitive losers among Master Trustees started with the origin of their strategic thinking. Were they *producer*-oriented or *user*-oriented in the way they conceptualize their strategies? Those that began their strategic thinking with a producer orientation, we now know, were doomed from that starting point. Their decision leadership came from the data-processing department where major decisions on systems were understandably centralized. With many operating units competing for the major banks' limited computing capacity, the advocates for Master Trust were told to "be patient" and await their turn in the bankwide queue for time and attention for hardware or software and managerial time. They were later told to "be realistic" and accept the necessary compromises on various aspects of report formatting, processing speed, and accuracy. And some would be obliged to accept painfully serious delays in deliveries as other, "more important" departments jumped the queue and took up all the capacity of the centralized Computer Division.

The message that eventually got through to the Master Trust division—and to its customers—was clear: "In the overall strategy of this bank, Master Trust is *not* a priority business." These serious delays were not understood or accepted by corporate customers who wanted the information services they had, in fact, been promised. Besides, the aggressive competitor banks that specialized in Master Trust were insistently ready to deliver more services at lower fees, and the cost of switching was not large.

In the early years of Master Trust, many of the competitors with a strong cost advantage shared costs, as well as an organizational orientation to customer service in a processing business, with the bank's business in cash management. (Some banks attempted to share costs with their Personal Trust colleagues, but the apparent benefit was soon offset by real differences in customer needs and a consequent lack of emphasis on producing and delivering *institutional* service values to sophisticated corporate customers.)

Banks that thought of competing on the basis of low cost got caught in a trap: Their drive to keep costs low precluded them from investing in the technology that was soon driving committed competitors' costs to deliver service values even lower. Equally important, their cost structures were "frozen in time" while other competitors continued to advance by reducing their real costs with systems innovations. Competitive free markets are persistently dynamic, and the only defense is a strong offense,[1] including the capacity to continue competing more and more effectively over time.

Similarly, banks that had large custody businesses in other markets were subtly and decisively influenced by those other markets. For example, custodians for insurance companies felt little or no pressure to increase the convenience or attractiveness of reports to the standard of expectation that soon developed among corporate and public pension funds.

In contrast, custodians servicing mutual fund companies were constantly pressured to increase their user-friendliness and service value: This part of the market was continuously learning—and teaching—how to improve and how to deliver more service value.

As consultants, we could never fully understand why senior bank managements were often so reluctant to recognize the inevitably hopeless outcome of a producer-oriented strategy in a field with fast-changing technology. They could easily have executed a constructive and deliberate withdrawal instead of inflicting on their own banks (and their overall reputations) a desultory degradation to defeat. George Washington, when asked how he gained his best understanding of an army officer's military leadership capabilities, wisely answered: "In retreat." Orderly retreats are difficult to manage in war, and we found deliberate and timely withdrawals very difficult for bankers who were often driven by false pride or worse, caught up in parochial politics between divisions or caught up in the institutional imperative to hang in there and keep trying in the forlorn hope that something would turn up.

Meanwhile, Master Trustees that began their strategic thinking with a customer orientation, concentrated on delivering the service values the customers wanted and organized their strategies around achieving deliverable service objectives. Most of these banks were successful in creating enough volume to cover costs and build profitable businesses with real futures.

HIRING MASTER TRUSTEES

Master Trust hiring during the first decade was principally of two kinds:

1. Establishing a new Master Trust arrangement with an existing custodian bank.
2. Switching from a custodian bank to a bank providing Master Trust services.

During the period from 1975 to 1985, the 1,500 largest pension funds and endowments migrated from regional bank custodians to Master Trust banks at an annual rate of 7 to 8 percent, or more than 100 new accounts every year. Table 9.3 shows the remarkable consistency and persistence of the migratory movement.

The rate of hiring activity among large pension and endowment funds has continued at 7 to 8 percent each year, with hirings in recent years nearly equaled by terminations. But there has been an important change. In the past, most moves were *from* smaller, less committed competitors and *to* majors. Now, more and more of the current competition takes the form of a direct confrontation of "majors versus majors." New business success now depends on a pension fund switching from one large competitor to another large competitor because the smaller competitors have already been squeezed out of the market.

We continue to advise our clients to overinvest in developing relationships with prospective customers that have been carefully targeted because

TABLE 9.3   Plans to Hire Trustees and Custodians

	1994	1995	1996	1997	1998
Corporate Funds	8%	6%	8%	9%	8%
Over $5 billion	7	6	4	8	8
$1,001–$5,000 million	6	6	10	8	8
$501–$1,000 million	4	1	3	5	7
$251–$500 million	9	9	8	5	9
$100–$250 million	9	7	10	13	7
Public Funds	5%	6%	9%	11%	8%
State	8	5	7	11	5
Municipal	3	6	10	11	9
Over $5 billion	9	4	5	21	8
$1,001–$5,000 million	6	10	12	11	8
$251–$1,000 million	3	4	8	6	12
$100–$250 million	2	4	8	10	2
Endowments	2%	6%	10%	5%	5%
Over $1 billion	4	3	6	4	2
$251–$1,000 million	2	6	14	5	7
$100–$250 million	2	7	8	6	4
Total Funds	6%	6%	8%	9%	7%

of the advantageous matchup between the services our clients particularly want to sell and the services these well-chosen prospects will really want to buy.

In our consulting on business strategy, we emphasize the "one winner" reality of any Master Trust selection process and the multitiered challenges in winning the selection competitions. They include:

- The inherent uncertainty of the decision-makers regarding which Master Trustee's computer system is and will continue to be superior.
- The relatively low fee differentials between competitors, particularly compared with the career risks of getting it wrong on the selection decision.
- The relative unimportance—particularly compared with other decisions a major corporation will make each year—of the differences between the several demonstrably capable "finalists" in any Master Trust competition.

All these ingredients combine into a situation in which trust and confidence based on personal working relationships, familiarity, and institutional credibility can be decisive to decisions. Despite all the hardware and hard data involved in Master Trust, the soft aspects of service and people and organizational commitment can and often do dominate selection decisions.

The criteria considered most important by fund executives selecting new Master Trustees are dominated by *speed* and *accuracy,* as they have always been. The importance given to a dozen selection criteria are documented in Table 9.4. The importance of most factors has been continually rising. Across the array of selection criteria the rank order holds stable over time. The one criterion that has increased the most over the past 20 years is predictable: *advanced computer systems,* which is so fundamental to achieving speed and accuracy on reporting.

The main reason, by far, for terminating a trustee or custodian is the same every year: *inaccurate reports.* As the pace and complexity of pension fund investing have increased, producing accurate reports in a timely manner has become more difficult and simultaneously more important to fund executives—prompting the need for advanced computer systems and the major capital costs required.

TABLE 9.4 Importance of Trustee and Custodian Selection Factors

	Total Funds	Corporate Funds	Public Funds
Accurate reports	94	91	95
Low error rate on securities transactions	77	75	78
Quick correction of errors	75	76	73
Responsiveness to information requests	73	68	77
Quality of staff	72	71	69
Advanced computer system	71	70	71
Usefulness of reports	71	71	68
Prompt reports	69	71	64
Capable administrative manager	65	69	61
Global custody capabilities	64	63	63
Senior management commitment	62	69	57
Reasonable fees	53	56	49
High yield on short-term investments	39	38	39
Effectiveness of RFPs	37	31	42

Note: Average of scale ratings, "Most Important" or $5 = 100$, $4 = 50$, $3 = 25$, $2 = 12.5$, "Least Important" or $1 = 0$.

When we aggregate all the evaluations given all Master Trustees by their current customers, two key "people" factors move to the top, even ahead of the three factors of accuracy:

1. Senior management's commitment to Master Trust as a specific line of business for their bank.
2. Capable administrative managers working on each customer's account.

Because of the importance of the individual service representative in the Master Trust organization, you must define this role carefully. Superior customer service that fosters customer satisfaction and loyalty depends on the capabilities and continuous commitment of the particular professionals actually delivering that service. It is essential to act on this recognized importance in recruiting, training, and compensating—and retaining—key service professionals.

As always in a service business, "All excellence is local." Having superior service *capability* is a prerequisite, but the crucial evaluation of service is in the way each customer actually receives and experiences that service. And superior customer experience depends on the sincere commitment to consistent good service by each and every person who has contact with *each* customer—*every* time. As we cheerfully admonish during our consulting with our clients, customers do know, and do care.

INTERNATIONAL INVESTING AND CUSTODY

As international investing has become increasingly prevalent among pension funds and endowments, the terms of competition in Master Trust have shifted somewhat in favor of those with strong global custodial capabilities,[2] either through their own branch network or through correspondent custodians. While the former gives the Master Trustee a strong base for competition, the latter has been acceptable in the market.

PRICE COMPETITION

Price competition has been and continues to be virulent among Master Trustees, with five times as many fund executives reporting reduced fees as report increased fees. And these reductions are coming even as services proliferate and assets rise in price in the securities markets. Price competition involves such adjacent services as foreign exchange, short-term cash management, and securities lending. Among funds with over $1 billion in assets, the ratio of lowered versus increased fees is a forceful 25:1. As shown in Table 9.5, four times as many funds report fee reductions as report fee increases, year after year.

As competitive pressures increase, fee-based competition results in more and more reasonable fees. The pricing structure in the market collapsed as service-buyers played service-sellers off against each other almost remorselessly.

Aggressive bidding—particularly for relationships that have been long established with a competitor and may not have enjoyed the benefits of continuous "voluntary" repricing to stay abreast of the current market for Master Trust services—has frequently resulted in lost business or at least a rush-rush scramble to rebid at fees low enough to keep an account. The right strategy on pricing takes a long-term perspective. Charging above market rates may seem a clever way to meet a current budget, but this sharp practice risks seriously harming an important customer relationship and losing the business.

TABLE 9.5   Fees Paid to Trustees and Custodians

	Raised Fees				Lowered Fees			
	1995	1996	1997	1998	1995	1996	1997	1998
Corporate Funds	3%	2%	2%	3%	18%	14%	17%	13%
Over $5 billion	7	2	4	2	37	34	24	20
$1,001–$5,000 million	3	1	2	4	27	29	26	18
$501–$1,000 million	0	5	0	2	17	11	19	9
$251–$500 million	2	0	2	4	18	8	10	9
$100–$250 million	6	4	3	2	8	5	9	11
Public Funds	2%	2%	4%	6%	23%	12%	15%	12%
State	5	1	6	5	25	12	15	10
Municipal	1	2	3	5	21	11	14	13
Over $5 billion	5	2	10	10	30	16	22	18
$1,001–$5,000 million	5	4	3	6	29	16	26	10
$251–$1,000 million	0	1	3	5	23	12	11	10
$100–$250 million	2	2	1	2	12	6	4	12
Endowments	5%	5%	3%	6%	18%	15%	14%	9%
Over $1 billion	0	0	3	2	31	30	21	7
$250–$1,000 million	5	6	4	6	20	15	15	10
$100–$250 million	8	5	2	9	13	10	10	8
Total Funds	3%	3%	3%	4%	19%	14%	16%	12%

GLOBAL MARKETS

As U.S. funds have internationalized the investment of their assets, another major dimension of "internationalization" is being felt by Master Trustees with increasing force. The market for Master Trust services has been opening up in more and more overseas national markets, as large funds (including overseas subsidiaries of U.S. multinationals) in those other countries recognize the value of the sophisticated services available at low cost in the United States and Canada.

Fund executives in other countries often are not able to obtain these service values from their own countries' local custodians because these custodians do not have the overall volume of demand, over which huge fixed costs can be spread, to justify or force them to modernize aggressively. So, North American Master Trustees are finding opportunities for business, and further scale advantages in their total business, in markets abroad. The massive Japanese market has been largely closed through regulation so far, but may well open up as that nation's pension assets get more active and contemporary investment management develops. In the United Kingdom and Australia, North American Master Trustees are expanding their business by competing for business with a global strategy.

As Harvard Business School's professor Michael Porter astutely observes:

> National prosperity is created, not inherited. It does not grow out of a country's natural endowments, its labor pool, its interest rates, or its currency's value—as classical economics insists. A nation's competitiveness depends on the capacity of its industry to innovate and upgrade. Companies gain advantage against the world's best competitors because of pressure and challenge. They benefit from having strong domestic rivals, aggressive home-based suppliers, and demanding local customers. Ultimately, nations succeed in particular industries because their home environment is the most forward-looking, dynamic, and challenging.
>
> With few exceptions, innovation is the result of unusual effort. Once a company achieves competitive advantage through an innovation, it can sustain it only through relentless improvement. Competitors will eventually and inevitably overtake any company that stops improving and innovating. Ultimately, the only way to sustain a competitive advantage is to upgrade it and adopt a global approach to strategy.[3]

Four broad attributes of nations that foster globally competitive industries are, as Porter advises, identifiable:

1. *Availability of relevant factors of production.* In the case of Master Trust, advanced computer systems from competitive manufacturers and skilled computer technicians are good examples.
2. *The nature of the home market.* Demanding, sophisticated buyers are important motivators. Again, for Master Trust, the American market is huge in assets and in number of funds; and the willingness to pay for service value is unusually active. Since U.S. funds have unusually complex manager structures, complex securities, and complex pension plan structures, they are much more likely to want and need the sophisticated services the most advanced Master Trustees provide.
3. *The presence of "supplier" industries that are themselves internationally competitive.* Investment managers and securities firms in the United States are highly advanced because of the intensity of their own species' competition. So, too, are U.S. computer manufacturers.
4. *Domestic rivalry and a dynamic structure of the domestic industry.* The U.S. banking industry—regulated into having many competitive entities, each striving for competitive advantage—has been widely and correctly criticized for overinvesting in computer systems. But one benefit may be seen in Master Trust, where the ultimate result of overinvesting in adding capacity—and the consequent race for competitive advantage—has driven Master Trustees to innovate and upgrade their services because they truly felt they had to.

Large as it is, the domestic U.S. market is only one part of the global market for Master Trust services. In developing an effective *global* strategy, the U.S. market has, in effect, become "too small" for the leaders in Master Trust. So in our consulting, we urge our clients to adopt a global strategy with coordinated local country strategies in such open markets as Australia, Canada, and the United Kingdom—as well as in insurance and mutual funds—and to position themselves for the eventual opening of such potential markets as Japan, Southeast Asia, Switzerland, and Germany.

Not only will global competitors obtain a potentially decisive advantage in scale by being actively engaged in each of several different markets, they may also learn more about possible innovations from one or more of these markets, each of which can prove to be a center of innovation and a source of learning.

THREATENING OUTSIDERS

Another round of competition may be threatening, driven by innovative competitors from outside the industry, which is where so many examples of "blindsiding" are to be found in business. Securities firms invest massively in information technology: $1 billion every year is not uncommon for individual firms. Their main businesses require remarkable capabilities in processing securities: transactions in all stock, bond, commodity, currency, and derivatives markets around the world, plus immediate and accurate pricing in numerous currencies. If two or three of these giants chose to compete in Master Trust services, they could be formidable competitors. Ironically, the low level of profits in the Master Trust industry may be a modest blessing. Securities firms may be dissuaded from entering a business in which—even on a marginal costing basis—they cannot earn the high returns on capital they typically require.

Competitive forces continue to drive the Master Trust industry's life cycle, now in a period of global competitive consolidation. The history of this industry is certainly not over. The competitive grind we have documented in the United States is spreading around the world. As all participants know, if and when the shakeout—on a global scale—is over, the leading survivors will have a very large, very good business.

CHAPTER 10

How to Manage Investor Relations

Charles D. Ellis and Rodger F. Smith

Investors have changed profoundly over the past 25 years as active, informed institutions have become the dominant "investor" in the market, vastly outweighing individual investors in market activity. Consider these measures of change:

- Twenty-five years ago, professional or institutional investors represented 10 percent of New York Stock Exchange trading volume. Now, professionals do nearly 90 percent of NYSE trading.
- The number of CFAs has ballooned from a few thousand to 30,000, with an equal number "in the queue," taking exams to qualify.
- Institutional brokers that had 20 to 25 analysts now have research departments of 200 to 250—and more.
- With First Call and "Blast Faxes" and the Internet, analysts that used to call one account at a time can virtually instantly contact hundreds.
- Analysts contact portfolio managers directly, and the fund managers take action.
- Portfolio turnover continues to increase. Block trading has become routine and dominant. Block trading has increased from 10 percent of NYSE trading to nearly 60 percent, outstripping the overall increases in trading volume by increasing 15 *times* in just 15 years. The pace of action continues to accelerate.

At more and more major corporations, senior management is taking a serious new look at investor relations *management*—the overall process by which the corporation communicates with investors, discussing present

311

strategy and past performance, explaining the company's future challenges and opportunities, and developing a constituency of informed and interested investors. While, strictly speaking, managing a corporation's investor relations differs from marketing professional financial services, success depends on developing strong relationships, based on information and trust, with sophisticated buyers who have plenty of alternatives. As with other financial services, developing good relationships takes careful planning, real discipline—and time.

WHY BOTHER?

An effective investor relations program can help a well managed company gain appropriate recognition and credibility within the business community for its true capabilities and its long-term prospects. Recognition and credibility can in turn improve the morale and loyalty of employees and their families, make it easier to recruit new employees and executives, help sales (particularly to new customers), and contribute to good relations with government officials, regulators, and the press.

Effective investor relations can also help corporate executives to fulfill their implicit fiduciary responsibility to ensure that investors who are selling (for all the various reasons investors do sell) *or* are buying know they are able to do so at prices that fairly and reasonably reflect true value.

A well-informed constituency of professional investors will understand the long-term significance, or insignificance, of current developments and reduce possible distortions of the company's share price. It's important that incentive stock options fairly reflect the long-term investment value of the corporation. And an informed investor group's valuation may help the company avoid hostile takeover bids that might be attracted by an apparent bargain price in the market.

Managements that do not actively and consistently communicate with the investor community may inadvertently create an opportunity for an aggressive few to capture a competitive advantage by ferreting out significant information not known to others, enabling them to buy shares from present shareholders at advantageous prices. In the extreme form of this problem, a hostile takeover can result in managers losing their jobs.

Conversely, acquisitions will be easier if the company is well known and respected by employees and by shareholders, particularly institutional shareholders, in the company that is to be acquired.

A widely known and respected company will find it easier and less costly to raise new capital—debt or equity.

Although different corporations place different emphases on these various factors, most would agree on one basic proposition: In building an informed and interested constituency, the vital ingredient is time. It takes a long time to build the knowledge and understanding of a large and complex company. When recruiting senior executives, or proposing an acquisition, or striving to block a hostile takeover, you can be sure your prospect or opponent will "check with the experts." If you wait until you *need* a constructive constituency or a favorable reputation, you will surely be too late.

CHOOSE YOUR AUDIENCE

An investor relations program must inform and communicate. But to whom? Two quite different concepts of the investor—and consequently two quite different concepts of an effective investor relations program—compete for management's attention and endorsement. One concept focuses on *individual* investors, the other on *institutional* investors.

The focus on individual investors may be more popular; but the focus on institutional investors works.

WHO NOT TO TARGET—AND WHY

If individual investors were defined as the target constituency (which would be an error), then the right marketing strategy would be a *consumer* strategy. Broad reach would be wanted to get to the largest number of actual and potential investors, and media advertising would be brought into play. The selling proposition would be kept simple and easy to recognize and accept. Retail brokers would be courted as centers of influence. Marketing objectives would be set in terms of recognition and acceptance among the more than 50 million individual investors.[1]

Many corporate executives' idealized, but quite inaccurate, picture of the typical individual investor would be an individual who owns 6 to 10 stocks in a portfolio worth $200,000 to $500,000; invests primarily for long-term gain; buys a little more on price weakness; and is knowledgeable about the companies he owns because he reads annual reports carefully and "does his homework" on a regular basis. In truth, this idealized investor is very rare. Some may exist, but only a few.

As Table 10.1 indicates, the average individual investor has total stock holdings of less than $95,000 and owns 1.5 stocks; only 15 percent of all individual investors buy or sell shares in a typical year; less than 30 percent

TABLE 10.1 Characteristics of Adult Shareowners

	Total Number (millions)			Percent of Shareowners			Percent of Shares Owned		
	1989	1992	1995	1989	1992	1995	1989	1992	1995
Age:									
21–34	9.3	11.1	17	21.7%	21.7%	25.6%	5.4%	5.1%	5.0%
35–44	12.6	13.8	19.6	29.3	27.0	28.2	18.2	17.8	15.6
45–64	14.4	18.9	22.9	33.7	36.9	33.1	47.8	47.3	49.4
Over 65	6.6	7.4	9.8	15.3	14.4	14.1	28.6	29.8	30.0
Total	42.9	51.3	69.3	100.0%	100.0%		100.0%	100.0%	
Education:									
Less than 4 years of high school	3.6	2.8	4.6	8.3%	5.4%	6.6%	3.3%	3.0%	1.9%
4 years of high school	12.9	12.7	19.3	30.1	24.8	27.9	16.5	15.6	15.4
0–3 years of college	10.2	12.7	17.7	23.7	24.8	25.6	22.3	24.1	22.3
4 years of college	8.2	12.9	16.5	19.1	25.2	23.8	27.7	27.6	30.5
Postgraduate work	8.0	10.2	11.2	18.8	19.9	16.1	31.0	29.7	29.9
Total	42.9	51.3	69.3	100.0%	100.0%		100.0%	100.0%	
Family income:									
Under $15,000	2.3	2.7	2.4	5.4%	5.3%	3.5%	1.9%	2.9%	1.6%
$15,000–$25,000	5.2	4.9	7.6	12.1	9.5	10.9	3.0	2.6	4.5
$25,000–$50,000	15.5	15.2	24.6	36.2	29.6	35.4	15.6	15.6	13.0
$50,000–$75,000	10.5	13.2	16.5	24.4	25.6	23.7	16.0	18.2	15.2
$75,000–$100,000	4.5	6.1	8.4	10.5	11.9	12.1	9.2	12.0	11.9
$100,000 & over	4.9	9.3	9.9	11.5	18.1	14.3	54.3	48.7	53.9
Total	42.9	51.3	69.3	100.0%	100.0%		100.0%	100.0%	
Stock Portfolio:									
Under $5,000	16.7	16.5	18.4	39.1%	32.2%	26.6	1.3%	0.6%	0.5%
$5,000–$10,000	6.5	5.7	9.0	15.1	11.2	12.9	2.1	0.8	1.0
$10,000–$25,000	8.2	8.0	13.5	19.1	15.7	19.5	5.9	2.8	3.4
$25,000–$50,000	4.2	6.3	10.0	9.9	12.3	14.4	6.9	4.7	5.5
$50,000–$100,000	3.4	6.0	7.3	7.9	11.7	10.6	11.5	9.3	7.7
$100,000 & over	3.8	8.7	11.1	9.0	17.0	16.0	72.3	81.7	82
Total	42.9	51.3	69.3	100.0%	100.0%		100.0%	100.0%	

Source: Tabulations are based on the 1989 and 1992, 1995 Triennial Surveys of Consumer Finances, carried out by the Federal Reserve Board.

of all individual share owners have an account with a stockbroker; the median investor's annual family income is $50,000; the number of substantial individual investors active in the market (including hyperactive traders) is remarkably small. Using $50,000 of total purchases and sales as a threshold (which might involve no more than, say, selling 100 shares and buying 100 of a typical $40 stock every other month), a few years ago the New York

Stock Exchange estimated there were less than 500,000 active, substantial investors.

If reaching desirable individual investors on a direct basis would be too expensive to be cost-effective, a possible alternative might be to work through established channels of distribution to reach target investors with an indirect approach[2] through stockbrokers.

The preliminary data look appealing: There are 120,000 registered representatives—a manageable number for an effective direct mail campaign at substantially lower cost than either print or broadcast media. But will it work? Here are some of the realities of the situation:

- A majority of individual investors have *never* purchased a share of stock through a stockbroker. Instead, they received their shares as gifts from relatives or through their employer's stock purchase program.
- Of the shareholders with brokerage accounts, only half look to their brokers for investment advice and recommendations. The other half make all their own decisions, expecting their brokers only to execute the trade.
- Most "stockbrokers" are not really stockbrokers. A majority of brokers make a majority of their income selling insurance, mutual funds, tax shelters, and new stock and bond issues—not buying and selling listed stocks.
- The typical stockbroker does not have any large individual investors as customers. In the Wall Street vernacular, the typical broker "talks to less than $10 million": The total invested assets of all the 250 to 350 customers of a typical broker amount to less than $10,000,000. This means his or her typical customer has less than $25,000 "in the market." Even for the most enthusiastic advocates of an individual investor relations program, these small investors are not the target market.
- Because the aggregate assets of their customers are relatively modest, brokers who want to earn an income of $100,000 must gross $300,000 in annual commissions. This amounts to about 3 percent of their customers' invested assets, annually. For most stockbrokers, the business is not built on long-term "buy and hold" investors; it depends on turnover by active "traders." For investor relations purposes, the in-and-out "trader" on whom stockbrokers depend is not the target market. If most of the stockbrokers' customers are either too small or too active, then reaching out to individual investors through brokers—the indirect approach—holds little promise. The data in Table 10.1 documents these propositions.

If both the direct (to individual investors) and indirect (through stockbrokers) consumer marketing concepts are not practical, what should management do?

THE RIGHT TARGET

In impressive contrast to the virtually insurmountable costs and difficulties facing the consumer marketing approach is a straightforward, effective, and low-cost alternative. This alternative is an approach based on *industrial* marketing, addressed to the now predominant *institutional* investors.

The stock market is not dominated by individual investors; in fact, individual investors account for less than 10 percent of investment activity. The stock market is dominated today by institutional investors. Large in assets but relatively few in number, these easily identified professional investors are full-time, active, and well informed. The effective strategy for reaching them focuses on direct contact and is conceptually based on industrial marketing.

In little more than three decades, institutional investing has gone from less than 20 percent of public trading on the New York Stock Exchange to more than 90 percent, and it is still growing in relative importance. In addition to their preeminence in sheer size, as measured by trading volume, institutional investors are even more powerful because they are well staffed with full-time, well-informed professionals who know a lot about a wide variety of alternative investments, and are constantly examining alternatives and deciding what to buy and what to sell. These professionals are in continuous contact with market developments, and are both ready and able to make prompt large-scale decisions to buy or sell. Their decisions dominate the market, so they set share prices.

Investing institutions are in some ways concentrated and in other ways quite diverse. Depending on the definition used, there are between 750 and 2,500 institutional investors in the United States. They are located in over 100 different cities and follow a variety of approaches to investing. Some manage less than $25 million while others manage over $250 billion—a ten-thousand-to-one ratio.

Concentration characteristics are even more impressive. Where the familiar 80-20 rule applies to many industrial markets, the concentration in this market is even greater. The 75 most active investing institutions do an impressive 75 percent of all institutional buying and selling of securities. And the 50 largest institutions do more than 50 percent of all transactions on the New York Stock Exchange every trading day.

Despite this concentration, corporate executives have no reason to fear that institutions will act (i.e., trade) together. They don't and they won't. Institutional investors not only differ in size and type, they also differ considerably in their approach to markets, their time horizons for decisions, their methods of operation, and their attitudes toward price and earnings changes. They are as diverse as the equity markets in which they operate. Even more important, they are earnest and persistent *competitors,* always seeking opportunities to profit from the buying and selling decisions of their competitors—by going the other way.

They can act very quickly in response to significant new information—competing to act first on startling news—but they do not follow one another like sheep. In fact, it would be difficult to find any market as vigorously and relentlessly competitive as the institutional stock market.

THE CENTRAL MARKET

The volume of information gathered by and distributed to institutional investors is enormous by any standard. The speed, breadth, and precision of communication is also impressive. Many institutions have direct access to this information most of the time. A small bank in Tulsa or Boise will have access to 80 percent of the information available at any time to the largest bank in New York City. This is truly the concentrated "village" of shared telecommunications that Marshall McLuhan described. Or as one participant has observed, the "central market is not a geographical concept, it is a communications concept."

The central market communications system can be divided into four main communication networks:

1. *Company-generated written information.* Each public company must publish an annual report, proxy statements, and quarterly reports; and must file with the SEC and offer for distribution to investors detailed 10-K reports and 8-Ks. It must hold annual meetings and distribute prospectuses on all public offerings. Most companies go well beyond these requirements: They strive to give investors extensive and relevant information and interpretation. Most companies distribute press releases on all significant events, and many produce historical "fact books" on the company and its business and financial record.

2. *Service- and media-generated information.* Few industries have as many newspapers and magazines specializing in serving information needs as does the investment community. In addition, continuous ticker

tapes, video display devices, and instant recall monitors provide real-time information on all transactions and the current bid and offer prices on thousands of securities. The media provides wide-ranging financial and economic news, reports on companies and industries, and so on.

3. *Brokerage-firm-generated information.* Investing institutions each year pay over $5,000,000,000 in commissions to brokerage firms for their research and execution services. (This figure exceeds the combined budgets of the CIA, MI-6, and the KGB—and is four times the R&D expenditure of Bell Labs.) Approximately 150 stockbrokerage firms, with up to 300 analysts, provide institutional research services.

These static measures do not give a full sense of the dynamic intensity of the service provided by brokers. The typical broker analyst will produce between 4 and 10 major reports (10–30 pages apiece) on specific companies—and twice that many follow-up reports. Telephone calls and personal visits by analysts are frequent, and most brokerage firms have at least as many people engaged full-time in research "sales" as in developing research. The typical institutional sales representative will have 10 to 15 institutional accounts, so sales coverage can be intensive. With annual compensation for effective research salespeople easily reaching $250,000 and often over $500,000, the motivation to service accounts is strong.

4. *Company generated person-to-person communication.* More and more companies are developing planned programs for direct contact with institutional investors. These include the following main elements:
   - Annual or biannual one- or two-day meetings provide anywhere from 50 to 350 institutional analysts and portfolio managers with in-depth briefings by senior management and divisional executives on the corporation's long-term strategy, past performance, and future prospects.
   - Numerous stockbrokerage firms hold frequent, well attended industry conferences, usually featuring presentations by several interesting corporations.
   - Luncheons and other meetings are held with groups of analysts who specialize in the company's industry or follow the company closely.
   - The Association for Investment Management and Research and its more than 50 regional analyst societies and two dozen industry specialist groups hold frequent meetings to which they invite company managements to make detailed presentations and answer analysts' questions.

- Similar meetings are frequently sponsored by brokers, while others are organized by the companies themselves. Such meetings are sometimes directed toward analysts, sometimes toward portfolio managers, and are sometimes mixed.
- At quarterly meetings, the quarter's earnings are released and the CFO provides background perspective and answers analysts' questions to help ensure that the raw accounting data are not misunderstood.
- Meetings at corporate headquarters with the CFO, CEO, and key operating executives allow analysts with particular expertise on the company and its industry to develop a more substantial understanding of how top management thinks through its major strategic challenges and opportunities—and how effectively the corporation is performing.
- More and more corporations are not only responding to requests for information from institutional analysts, but are also actively initiating such contacts by having their investor relations managers go out and call on institutions to encourage their interest in the company.
- Companies are increasingly utilizing telephone conference calls and close circuit TV to communicate with investors.
- Telephone contact between analysts and investor relations managers for a single company can easily exceed 5,000 calls each year.

In all this activity, corporations recognize they are in competition for institutional investors' "share of funds" and "share of mind." It takes time to develop professional expertise on a company, its management, its products, its competitive position in its industry or industries, its accounting policies and practices, its long-range strategy, its current problems and opportunities, its culture, and its way of communicating—candid or guarded, conservative or optimistic—with investors.

Most analysts are "fully booked" keeping current with companies they already know well. To win time on their busy calendars often requires displacing another company in which the analyst already has expertise—and a reputation with customers for having that expertise. And a company has to win that time commitment in competition with all the other companies that want the same analysts to follow their company more closely.

INSTITUTIONAL DECISION MAKING

An effective investor relations program must work with all three tiers, or constituencies, in the institutional investor market—portfolio managers, institutional analysts, and broker analysts. Portfolio managers are the ultimate decision-makers at most institutions, and corporate executives are naturally particularly interested in developing a strong constituency or franchise among them. Given the structure of the institutional decision-making process, however, this is the group with which to *end,* not to start.

Broker Analysts

Broker analysts are the *first tier* in the institutional market for these reasons:

- Broker analysts make their living by doing original or primary research. To be successful, they need to be fast to perceive and understand change. They are always striving.
- Their research output is widely disseminated. Broker analysts' written reports are distributed to thousands of institutional analysts and portfolio managers. In addition, their firms' salespeople spend most of their time calling and visiting institutional investors, stressing the key points in the analysts' written recommendations. And broker analysts themselves merchandise and communicate their own research through visits and phone calls to institutions, talks to groups of institutional investors, letters, and follow-up reports—and answers to questions put to them by institutional analysts and portfolio managers.
- Broker analysts are recognized experts, and they command a hearing.
- Once committed to following a company or industry, broker analysts will usually stay with it for many years, whereas institutional analysts and portfolio managers will shift their attention as they change their portfolio. The time invested in developing a constituency among broker analysts can prove rewarding for many years.

Even though there are usually some two dozen broker analysts covering each major industry, most companies will find it sufficient to have just six or eight important broker analysts covering their own company closely—generating regular in-depth written reports and carefully developed earnings estimates on the company. These analysts should have considerable detailed knowledge about the company and its industry that they will share with—even broadcast actively to—institutional investors.

In fact, except for the very largest and most widely held companies, it would be difficult to have more than half a dozen top analysts covering the same company. There is an understandable "crowding out" phenomenon; after several capable competitors have established themselves as experts on a company, the opportunity to add incremental value will not be sufficiently attractive for another analyst to become fully competitive—or well compensated—as yet another research source on that same company. Most broker analysts concentrate their research coverage on less than a dozen companies, and their coverage is intensive.

Broker analysts are particularly important to an assertive investor relations program, and more and more corporations actively court the attention of these analysts—particularly the most favorably regarded senior analysts working at the largest and most widely influential brokerage firms. Of course, the major brokerage firms are usually "majors" in all investment areas: institutional research, equity trading, bond dealing, investment banking, and retail brokerage. (There are exceptions that can be important to an individual company developing its own investor relations program. In some industries, such as insurance, firms that specialize intensively in that one industry do the most influential research, and they may not be well known outside that industry.)

INSTITUTIONAL ANALYSTS

The *second tier* in the institutional decision-making structure comprises the analysts working at the investing institutions. Typically, these analysts will cover three or four major industries, and will follow 40 to 60 companies.

Institutional analysts often do a considerable amount of original or independent research on present or prospective investments. But, because they have such a large resource available to them in the form of research from broker analysts, they naturally spend a substantial majority of their time studying reports of and talking with analysts at research brokerage firms.

The typical institutional analyst spends one to three days preparing for a company visit. He or she will complete the following tasks:

- Call two or three senior analysts at major stockbrokerage firms.
- Read the past two or three years' Annual Reports.
- Study three to five research reports from leading broker analysts.
- Analyze 5 to 10 years of financial data.

During the institutional analysts' meeting with corporate management—for which so much preparation will have been done—our research documents that the three most important factors in an effective group meeting will be:

1. Discussion and analysis of current problems and opportunities.
2. Explanation of the corporation's long-range business strategy.
3. Candid answers to analysts' questions after management's formal presentation.

The next most important factors are discussion of current company strengths; discussion of near-term projected results; and presentations by the CEO and/or CFO.

And, after the meeting, analysts like to have copies of all formal presentations made available for their convenience.

When institutional analysts meet individually with corporate executives, they tell us that these are their two main objectives:

1. Gain better understanding of the company's long-term business strategy.
2. Get specific facts and details about important aspects of the company's business.

Other important objectives include getting a better "feel" for the capabilities and motivations of key people in management; getting more perspective and understanding of important industry trends; and testing the analyst's own understanding of important issues.

Our research of nearly 20 years documents that analysts consistently consider these to be the most important characteristics of a company for investment:

- Rapid growth in earnings over next several years.
- Effective cost control in operations.
- Clearly defined long-range business strategy.
- Unusually capable chief executive.

Other characteristics that are important include rapidly growing markets; strong balance sheet; consistent year-to-year earnings; new products; and a dominant share of markets served.

Our research also documents the reasons institutional analysts would stop following a company. The most compelling reason is *senior management lacks credibility.* Other important reasons are the company is not cooperative with analysts; too little liquidity in stock; and analysts' inability to get enough information.

Institutional analysts have strong views on how management can best communicate with them and their colleagues. Two factors are most important: informative annual reports and availability of senior management for private meetings with analysts.

Two additional factors are also important, informative quarterly reports and quarterly meetings conducted by management on the days that earnings are released, to brief analysts on details behind EPS.

Given the importance of informative annual reports, in our research we naturally go on to document just what the analysts want in these reports. Four kinds of information are most important:

1. Explicit statement of future business strategy.
2. Candid discussion of business problems and uncertainties.
3. Line of business reporting of profits.
4. Line of business reporting of sales.

Six other factors are also important: detailed flow of funds statement; discussion of past year's results; discussion of new products and markets; candid forecast of upcoming financial needs; disclosure of capital expenditure plans; and income statements for the past 10 years.

Whether working as original analysts or as interpreters and endorsers of research from broker analysts—or both, as is usually the case—institutional analysts are a powerful group. At most large institutions with in-house research departments, little if any investing will be done in companies that are not being actively followed by the analysts at that institution.

Because institutional analysts usually are not able to spend as much time developing their understanding of each company as broker analysts can and do spend, they need more assistance from corporations. Developing a constituency among institutional analysts will be facilitated considerably by a company's investor relations manager having established a strong prior constituency among the broker analysts who supply institutional analysts with written reports and a regular flow of written reports and updates.

The investor relations manager should conscientiously develop a large and strong constituency of institutional analysts—adding names to the standard mailing lists, inviting interested and informed analysts to meetings with management, visiting with analysts in their offices—in a continuing program to establish a reliable flow of communication to the analysts and to build their understanding and confidence in the company's strategies and policies.

Portfolio Managers

The *third tier* in the institutional decision-making process is populated by the portfolio managers—as many as 10,000 of them at the various institutions—who make the final buy and sell decisions on specific stocks. At the 100 largest institutions, portfolio managers will typically concentrate their investing on those companies that are covered by their staff analysts. At other institutions, portfolio managers will be more directly dependent on broker analysts and on their own direct contacts with companies.

Again, the investor relations manager should conscientiously develop a constituency of portfolio managers—both those at smaller institutions who are doing their own research on the company and those at larger institutions who have staff analysts doing research on the company, but should concentrate on those working at larger institutions.

BREAKDOWN TO BUILD UP

Concentrating on that segment of the overall institutional market that is most likely to want to buy what you are offering makes just as much sense in institutional investor relations as it does in any other industrial market. Particular emphasis should be placed, naturally, on those who already own the company's stock.

Institutions typically concentrate their investments in a particular type of stock such as high dividend yield stocks, emerging growth stocks, or established growth stocks. The investor relations manager should concentrate on that segment of the overall institutional market that will see his or her company's shares fitting into the kind of portfolio they are now managing.

Smaller companies might concentrate on smaller and medium-size institutions, realizing that their limited "float" may be too small for the liquidity needs of larger institutions. Companies that have been through difficult times and are engaged in a turnaround might concentrate on *contrarian investors* who may be intrigued with a changing situation.

Another way of segmenting the overall institutional market is in accordance with the present and prospective investment position different institutions might have or take in your company. Here are some examples:

- Large shareowners with positions over 500,000 shares—to *maintain* positions.
- Present shareholders with positions over 100,000 shares—to *maintain* or *increase* positions.
- Large institutions with small- to medium-size investment positions—to *increase* positions.
- Large institutions with capable industry analysts and positions in stocks of other companies in the industry—to *initiate* positions.
- Large institutions that sold the company's stock, but might repurchase—to *recover* position.
- Medium-size institutions with relatively large positions—to *maintain* holdings.
- Medium-size institutions experiencing rapid growth in assets under management—to *grow* with them.

Having defined the targets—listed name by name—conduct the systematic, direct sales process so familiar to industrial marketing. Steadily build the desired constituency among institutional investors, and (guarding against getting spread too thin by trying to contact too many institutions) concentrate on achieving substantial success with the priority target groups.

CONSISTENT INFORMATION DISCLOSURE

Consistency is the hallmark of all good communications programs, and investor relations is no exception. Each company's policy on information disclosure should be worked out carefully and explicitly—and in advance. Analysts always want more information; the corporation has to set limits and then stick to these limits, not saying more and not saying less. There is a simple, clear test on how far to go in disclosing information: Say no more in good times about good news than you will say in bad times about bad news. And then be consistent—forever. In particular, "when bad things happen to good companies," the rules are simple: Tell the truth, the whole truth, and promptly. After all, the shareholders *are* the owners.

In addition to making an explicit commitment to consistent factual disclosure, decide *who* will disclose *what* kind of information to *whom*— and *when* and *how*. While executives will care considerably about fairness, this usually does not mean that all analysts get exactly the same information. Some analysts are so well informed and careful in their preparation for meetings that they can skillfully and comfortably discuss subjects that would be well beyond the competence and interest of other investors. On the other hand, the company spokesperson must be careful not to play favorites or to give one analyst an unfair advantage over competitors.

ROLE OF THE INVESTOR RELATIONS MANAGER

Our research documents that institutional analysts have very high expectations on numerous criteria when evaluating a corporate investor relations program.

Two criteria are considered "essential" by over three quarters of the analysts when defining the best practice role of an investor relations manager:

1. Understand your company's business strategy.
2. Know your company's future plans.

A majority of the institutional analysts categorize three additional criteria as "essential":

3. Know your company's past record.
4. Know the details of current developments.
5. Maintain access to senior management.

Three other criteria are "very important" to analysts: Understand major industry trends; know your major competitors; and understand analysts' needs.

When evaluating the job performance of investor relations managers, the characteristics the institutional analysts tell us they look for are direct access to senior executives and commitment to keeping analysts informed, fully and promptly.

Finally, the analysts believe the following *mistakes* by investor relations managers are most serious: not answering questions candidly; not being readily accessible to analysts; and not being sufficiently informed.

The most *frequent* mistakes made by investor relations managers are not answering questions candidly; not returning telephone calls quickly; and not initiating contact when new or important information is available.

One of the happy advantages of the industrial marketing approach to investor relations management is this: This most effective strategy also incurs the lowest cost.

For most companies, if the CEO and CFO are prepared to lend moderate support by making themselves available once or twice a week as needed, one talented executive—often rotating through one of a series of assignments in financial management with a modest travel and entertainment budget—can do all that is needed for an effective institutional investor relations program over and above the costs already incurred for annual reports, quarterly 10-Ks, and shareholders' meetings.

Good investor relations is a real bargain. There are not very many corporate activities that are so limited in cost and can have so much impact as a well designed and sensibly executed institutional investor relations program.

INDIVIDUAL INVESTORS: A REPRISE

With all the attention directed at *institutional* investors, one might wonder whether adequate concern is being given to *individual* investors. Serendipitously, a strong program of institutional investor relations will also serve the interests of individual investors. Here's why.

First, most institutions are the representatives of individual investors. Overall, institutions function as the investment intermediaries for nearly 50 million individuals who invest in or through mutual funds, pension funds, life insurance companies, property insurance companies, life and property, bank trust departments, and investment advisory firms.

Second, the same commitment to providing more and more information to the institutional portion of the market results in an increase in information to individual investors. Written communications such as annual and quarterly reports, are sent out to individual investors. More important, the major retail brokerage firms serving individual investors are typically the same major brokers that serve the institutions. The biggest retail brokerage firms are among the biggest institutional firms: Merrill Lynch, Dean Witter, Morgan Stanley, Smith Barney, Prudential, and so on. These firms use the same central research capabilities to serve both institutional and individual investors. Consequently, efforts to inform the major broker analysts will develop parallel conduits of information to both individuals and institutions.

Corporations will find that two important groups of individual investors are both cost-effective to serve and likely to respond favorably. These two groups are the company's present shareholders and the company's employees.

Present shareholders are far more likely to pay attention to the messages communicated by a corporation about its future investment attraction. They are far more likely to want investments of the kind represented by the shares of companies they already own. They are far less costly to serve: The typical cost is about $15 per year per shareholder,[3] and is unaffected by size of holding.

Employees are another group far more likely to pay attention to the corporation's messages, and many corporations offer incentive plans to encourage employee share purchases.

CONCLUSION

Good investor relations is good communications. As always, communication is in the control of the receiving party. And in modern investor relations, the right receiving party is made up of the institutional investors who dominate the stock market and set share prices. Superior communications in an effective program of investor relations can go a long way toward preventing inaccurate or uncertain—volatile—pricing and assuring informed, fair pricing. In a world that is alert to shareholder value, sound valuation is the objective reason senior managements at more and more corporations are interested in effective investor relations.

notes

Chapter 1   Foreign Exchange: One Certainty in an Ever-Changing Business

1. Douglas Bowman, a PhD at the Wharton School of the University of Pennsylvania, worked with thesis advisers John U. Farley, then a Partner of Greenwich Associates, and David C. Schmittlein on his dissertation in marketing, "The Role of Buyer-Seller Relationships and Service Quality in Business-to-Business Services Marketing." Analysis was conducted on data on foreign exchange buyer-seller relationships in the United States, United Kingdom, Canada, and Germany between 1989 and 1991.

Chapter 4   Corporate Banking

1. The banks discussed in this chapter are:
   - Fully committed to all financings of the business.
   - Providing a full range of products.
   - Using the relationship manager as the key contact and adviser.
2. Of course, many corporations disappeared individually, but the total of 1,600 to 1,700 firms Greenwich Associates classifies as "large corporates" has been carefully and consistently maintained, even though the makeup of this classification has changed markedly over the past 25 years. Every major bank has participated in the Greenwich Associates Large Corporate Banking program, many of them on an annual basis. In fact, confidence in the program is so high that the interview participation rate is now above 70 percent.
3. Based on research findings, Greenwich Associates has carefully adjusted the criteria used to measure relationship manager performance as corporate executives changed their priorities. This is the reason for deleting and adding performance characteristics over time.
4. Greenwich Associates defines "midsize companies" as those with sales between $5 million and $50 million that are headquartered companies (not subsidiaries and affiliates) and that represent business services, healthcare, manufacturing, retail trade, wholesale durables, and

wholesale nondurables. These industries represent 96 percent of the 195,000 companies in this sales range. Note: 195,000 is based on an estimate by Dun & Bradstreet for companies in the domestic United States. This universe excludes the U.S. Postal Service, auto dealers, banking, security, brokers/dealers, holding companies, medical offices, educational services, museums, and so on.

5. Greenwich Associates defines second- and third-tier banks as the top 20 banks in California based on customer penetration, excluding Bank of America, Wells Fargo, and Union Bank of California.

6. Defined as having customer penetration of 9 percent or more of the commercial banking market.

7. Dun & Bradstreet has the broadest and largest database of companies, but it is not the only resource.

8. Greenwich Associates defines the full middle market as those companies with sales of $5 million to $500 million.

Chapter 5   Investment Banking

1. For this chapter, Greenwich Associates defines a typical U.S. company as one with $500 million in sales or a $1 billion market capitalization.

2. In his recent book, *The Death of the Banker,* author Ron Chernow describes "blue-ribbon" companies as becoming increasingly skeptical of their Wall Street bankers. After all, the upper ranks of these companies tend to be peopled with their own set of lawyers, accountants, and MBAs—many of them smart, ambitious, experienced, *and* convinced that they can do for their company precisely what an investment banker does and do it for a lot less money. As Chernow writes: "A conspicuous trend of late has been the tendency of companies to conduct their own takeovers, dispensing with investment bankers. By the mid-1990s, more than a quarter of merger deals around the globe were being handled without the assistance of high-priced financial advisors. . . . It's another sign that corporations which once slavishly genuflected before their Wall Street bankers no longer feel the need to bother with them."

Chapter 6   Stockbrokerage

1. For firms that "stayed retail," the secret to success would be to minimize the *costs* of delivering their service, not to maximize the perceived *value* of their delivered services.

2. Compensation for large bank demand deposits and other "less-charming" purposes.

3. Government negotiators found an ally in Gus Levy of Goldman Sachs, the leading block trader on The Street. Levy's firm was paying out huge amounts of give-up to other brokers. He was glad to see it stopped. As chairman of the NYSE, he could help arrange it. That left fixed rates visible—and assured their end.

4. Napoleon, during the dreadful retreat from Moscow, during which 95 percent of the soldiers died, slept each night on clean silk sheets; not because he wanted to, but because his generals insisted. They knew their lives depended on his genius, and his genius depended on his health and his rest.

5. Actually very few major stockbrokerage firms are located on or even near Wall Street or the New York Stock Exchange. With the elimination of paper certificates (and the once ubiquitous messengers with their wheeled trunks), most firms have moved uptown.

6. Strunk and White's *Elements of Style* is short, direct, and a first-rate manual for writers. So is William Zinsser's *On Writing Well.*

7. Bill Fisher, one of Donaldson, Lufkin & Jennette's all-time "All Star" analysts invented and marketed this process He began each call with this announcement: "I'm going into a meeting, but wanted to get this important information to you first," which made the client see the call as important and also made the client comfortable that this call would be brief. As soon as the call was complete, Bill would ring off and immediately go to the next name on his list. Who cared that the meeting he was going into wouldn't start for two hours? Bill's brevity and relevance and commitment to service were what really mattered to everyone on his list.

8. Fairfield county in Connecticut and the adjoining New York county, Westchester.

9. Or shorting.

10. As Prime Minister of the United Kingdom, Margaret Thatcher emphasized the need to open this particular market by beginning each and every conversation with a Japanese by asking, "When will Barclays get its seat?" The Barclays Group, one of Britain's largest banking and financial institutions, had applied for membership on the Tokyo Stock Exchange but had received no indication of when it would be judged "acceptable." Today, many non-Japanese brokers hold seats on the TSE.

11. The classic text on this conflict is Alfred Chandler's *Strategy and Structure: The History of American Enterprise.*

12. One happy "footnote to history": In the traditional Japanese stockbrokerage firms, women had long found it difficult to advance professionally. In the Western firms, they received substantial encouragement and so

were often "first over the ramparts" in joining the Western firms, particularly in research. Many gifted Japanese women are enjoying great professional success in Tokyo—in Western firms.

Chapter 7   Institutional Investment Management in the United States

1. Defined Contribution assets have been dominant in multiemployer Taft-Hartley plans since the 1940s, and most retailers have primarily used Defined Contribution plans. (Sears Roebuck's profit-sharing plan has been one of the largest.) Self-employed workers have used Keogh Plans, and individuals have been tax-encouraged to establish and fund IRAs (Individual Retirement Accounts). Both Keogh Plans and IRAs have historically been invested in mutual funds for convenience.
2. Our research shows only 8 percent of large corporations are using alliances, and openness to exploring alliances has declined.
3. Fifteen years ago, the favorable prospects for mutual fund managers were shown clearly in our 1984 results: On all three of the most important selection criteria—and on perceived commitment to the 401(k) business—mutual funds were recognized by their customers as much stronger than insurance companies or banks.
4. Insurance companies with accounting systems and procedures focused on meeting the requirements of state insurance regulators had grown accustomed to reporting, literally, months later.

Chapter 8   Institutional Investment Management in the Rest of the World

1. Also, while Australia is far away from most overseas investment centers, the great majority of schemes are conveniently headquartered in either Sydney or Melbourne, and both are delightful "destination cities" to visit regularly.

Chapter 9   Master Trust

1. David Fox, a Partner of Greenwich Associates and a graduate of the U.S. Naval Academy, reminds us that since you cannot dig foxholes or build walls on the open sea, navies are necessarily *offensive* arms: There *is* no "defense" in the navy.
2. Less than one in five funds uses a different bank for global custody than it uses for domestic custody.

3. "The Competitive Advantage of Nations," Michael E. Porter, *Harvard Business Review.*

Chapter 10   How to Manage Investor Relations

1. As defined by the NYSE. But note the NYSE's definition of shareowners includes all who invest only in equity mutual funds and all who participate in a 401(k) or other defined contribution retirement fund. This is a very generous definition.

2. We urge our clients never to advertise for investor relations reasons because when media advertising is lined up with the figures on the number of potential realistic targets, it is clearly not cost-effective. By contrast, specialized advertising in carefully chosen trade and professional magazines can be an extremely cost-effective way to communicate with the community of institutional investors.

3. An increasing number of corporations now offer automatic dividend reinvestment programs as an easy way for investors to accumulate more shares and as a way for the company to raise equity capital.

index